COUNTY
FOREST

Supported by

GEDLING
BOROUGH COUNCIL
LEISURE SERVICES

Helping to create the
GREENWOOD
COMMUNITY
FOREST

COUNTR/SIDE
COMMISSION

Nottingham Health Authority

NOTTINGHAM
GREEN
PARTNERSHIP

CARING FOR THE ENVIRONMENT
Nottinghamshire County Council
Green Grants

CITY COUNTY FOREST

Forty bike rides to suit all abilities in Nottingham and Nottinghamshire

Compiled by members of Pedals and Nottinghamshire District Association, Cyclists' Touring Club

Cyclographic Publications

First published in 1997 by
Cyclographic Publications,
Nottingham NG15 7RS/22
on behalf of Pedals and the
Nottinghamshire District
Association of the Cyclists'
Touring Club

Sketch maps © Gillian Moss 1996

Line drawings © Stephen Wallwork 1995

Photographs © Tim Hughes 1996
    (except p99 – © Johanna Cleary 1996)

Routes compilation by Johanna Cleary and Tim Hughes

Design and layout by Tim Hughes

*Front cover: Crossing the River Meden, near
Bothamsall.*

*Back cover, top to bottom: City – crossing the River
Leen at Bulwell; County – preserved pithead gear in
Bestwood Country Park; Forest – in Foxcovert
Plantation, near Calverton*

ISBN   0 907191 02 9

Typeset by Express Typesetters, 11 Riverside Park,
Farnham, Surrey GU9 7UG

Printed and bound by Warwick Printing Co Ltd, Theatre
Street, Warwick CV34 4DR

Contents

Acknowledgments

Pedals and the Nottinghamshire District Association of the Cyclists' Touring Club gratefully acknowledge the generous support of the following in producing *City County Forest*:

Countryside Commission

Cycle Touring and Countryside Trust

Gedling Borough Council

Nottingham City Leisure and Community Services Department

Nottingham Health Authority

Nottinghamshire County Council Green Grant

Nottingham Green Partnership

RJB Mining PLC

The compilers wish to acknowledge the help of members of Pedals and the CTC upon whose suggestions many of the routes are based and who also supplied entries for the listings. They also gratefully acknowledge the considerable work of Gillian Moss, who drew the sketch maps, and Stephen Wallwork, who made the line drawings.

Publisher's notice   All the practice recommendations and route directions in this book are given in good faith and are believed to be correct at the time of going to press but neither the publishers, compilers nor supporting bodies can accept liability for any errors or omissions. The information is supplied on the understanding that users of the book are responsible for their own road conduct and safety, acting with appropriate caution where necessary. The listing of any café, public house, restaurant or cycle shop does not imply recommendation or endorsement. Although we mention inns and public houses as suitable sources of food and refreshment, it should be noted that it is an offence to cycle under the influence of alcohol. However, no legal blood alcohol limit is specified, nor is there any obligation to submit to a breath or blood test.

Welcome to cycling!

Cycling has made a remarkable comeback. After years of being ignored, bikes are fashionable in a way they haven't been since the end of the last century. Part of it's due to the popularity of the mountain bike of course, but a lot is because people are quite simply looking for a  way to travel that's healthy, inexpensive and fun. What's more, riding a bike is open to almost everybody. You may be too young, even much too young, to hold a driving licence – but you can ride a bike. If you think your joints are getting too old for jogging, then riding a bike is gentle by comparison. If you don't want to lavish a lot of money on a car, then buying a bike is far less painful. And in any case, many people have bikes already. There are at least 14 million of them in Britain. They may be leaning at the back of the garage, dusty, a bit old and not very fashionable-looking; they may not have dozens of gears and look rather drab by comparison with the latest mountain-bike. But even the oldest and simplest of bikes can take you the few miles to follow most of our routes.

A bike isn't just for weekend fun, though – it's a great form of everyday transport, too. Surveys by motoring organisations – of all people! – have shown that almost a third of people's car journeys are less than a mile. You could bike that in a very few minutes – probably in less time than it would take you to find a parking space! Another third of all car journeys are less than three miles – less than twenty minutes even at a very modest biking speed. Not only is cycling much cheaper, but by riding a bike for even a few of those trips you are helping to cut noise, pollution and the exhaustion of precious fossil fuel – and helping your own health as well as the planet's. Only swimming comes higher than cycling as a way of toning up the body's heart, lungs, circulation and muscles – and not many of us are in a position to swim to work or down to the shops. Twenty minutes of steady exercise – that 3 or 4-mile bike ride – three times a week can work wonders for your vitality.

The forty routes in this book, ranging from 4 to 45 miles, on- and off-road, have been specially selected, surveyed and described, with beginners and the not-so-fit in mind, by experienced cyclists from the Nottingham cycle campaign group Pedals and Nottinghamshire members of the national body, the Cyclists' Touring Club (usually known as the CTC). If you'd like to join either, there's more information at the back of the book.

Welcome to Nottinghamshire

Nottinghamshire is one of England's finest counties to begin cycling in. For a start, there's a surprising range of scenery. Everyone has heard of Sherwood Forest, of course, but there are many other superb forests and woodlands. The Trent, one of England's great rivers, flows gently through the southern part of the county, largely through a tranquil landscape. The city of Nottingham dominates the south but throughout the county's 50-mile length and 25-mile breadth there are historic market towns, villages and secret, hidden hamlets. The county is steeped in history and literary associations. There are cycling associations, too: Beeston and Nottingham were important cycle manufacturing centres as early as the 1880s, while for most people Raleigh is still the first cycle maker's name that springs to mind. The great Nottinghamshire coalfield, source of much of Britain's prosperity at the beginning of the century, has now faded to a handful of pits but enough is left to show that the county was at the centre of England's industrial heartland. With the passing of the coalfield the great spoil heaps that dominated the mining villages are being landscaped, planted with trees and opened as public recreation areas: as country parks, several of which feature on our routes. But above all Nottinghamshire is gentle country at a human scale, rolling enough that you can find broad sweeping views from its modest summits – yet even if you're new to cycling or making a long-delayed comeback, you won't have to walk up many hills!

The county boasts 3000 miles of minor roads, most of them carrying very little traffic – ideal for cycling – and many miles of bridleway, on which you are legally entitled to cycle, canal towpaths where you can ride with a permit (free from British Waterways), firm-based forestry tracks and several special cycle tracks and paths. This book shows you how to get the best out of them.

Going for a bike ride

You can ride *any* kind of bike for most of the routes in this book (though we wouldn't advise an out-and-out specialised road-racing one with flimsy tyres). But there are differences which make some bikes easier to ride than others. Provided your bike is in good mechanical condition – and we'll give you a checklist later – there are really only three fundamental factors which make a real difference between easy-going bikes and those that aren't. These are your *riding position* (which really means having a bike the right size correctly set up), the *gearing* and your own *fitness* (which determine how easily you'll go up hills). Everything else is secondary, even the weight of the bike – and your fitness will develop fast once you start biking.

Riding position and the right size of bike

Your body contacts the bike at three points (or five, if you like) – hands, feet and seat. Comfort depends on getting the right balance between these, and making sure that your saddle is at the right height for effective pedalling.

For a general riding or touring bike, the **correct size of frame** is usually defined as about two-thirds your full inside leg measurement, from crutch to ground, measured without shoes. So, somebody with an inside leg measurement of 33 inches (84cm) would need a 22in (56cm) frame. This frame size is usually measured from the centre of the 'bottom bracket axle' (the axle onto which the pedal cranks are fixed) to the centre line of the 'top tube' ('crossbar'), following the line of the 'seat tube' (the frame tube that leads from the bottom bracket towards the saddle). This is really a maximum: what *is* essential is that you should able to stand on the ground astride the bike's top tube in front of the saddle without difficulty or discomfort. If you can't, the bike really is too big for you. Sizes for mountain-bikes are usually specified at least a couple of inches shorter than this, partly because the bottom bracket is further off the ground. If you're buying a new bike, a good specialist cycle dealer will make sure that you buy the right size.

To achieve a **riding position** which lets you pedal comfortably and effectively the saddle has to be adjusted, by moving the 'seat pillar' (the tube to which the saddle is fixed and which fits into the seat tube of the frame) up or down, by undoing the frame bolt or clamp. The right height is where your leg is not uncomfortably stretched at the lowest point when pedalling, nor too bent at the highest. You can get close to this by raising the saddle until the top

9

One of the simplest ways to make a bike run more easily is to pump the tyres up. There are three types of tyre valve: car-type Schraeder (left), fitted to most mountain bikes; Woods, as found on many older bikes, especially roadsters, and Presta, fitted to most sporty road bikes. Each one needs a different pump fitting or connector. Before you can pump up a Presta valve, you have to undo the small top knurled nut (right). Correct pressures are marked on the tyre wall (see p16).

is about 90% of your inside leg measurement above the bottom bracket, still measured along the angle of the seat tube. The top of the saddle should be horizontal. You can test the height by sitting on the saddle and pedalling slowly backwards with your heels on the pedals, using shoes with at the most thin heels. Your leg should be just about straight at the longest reach, but not so straight that you can feel the tendons behind the knee pulling.

When you are sitting on the saddle in the normal riding position, with the ball of your foot, *not* the instep, on the pedal, your knee joint should be over or a little behind the centre of the front pedal when the pedal cranks are horizontal – the quarter-to-three position. You may have to move the saddle forwards or backwards by loosening the clamp on the saddle wires underneath. If you're buying a new or secondhand bike from a good bike shop, the dealer should sort all this out for you before you leave the shop.

For small children who may not have learned the necessary control skill yet, you may have to set the saddle rather lower than this so that they can touch the ground with both feet while still sitting on the saddle. As their confidence grows to the point where they're happy to start off with only one foot touching the ground you can move the saddle up a little at a time until they are in the best position to pedal efficiently.

Experienced cyclists find the most comfortable height for the handlebars (the whole handlebar for flat or mountain-bike bars, the straight top portion for dropped ones) is a little below level with the saddle. You may well find that you want them rather higher, at least to begin with, although you will still be leaning forward. Women often prefer a rather more upright position. In any case, for leisure riding you are unlikely to be using the 'drop' part of the bars very much.

You may find that the forward reach is not comfortable, quite possibly too long; it depends partly on how the upper half of your body relates to your arm length. To change this you need a different length of handlebar stem, which is really a job for the bike shop unless you are sure you are competent to do it – it will involve removing brake levers and any handlebar covering and replacing them afterwards. (Diameters of handlebars where they fit into the stem are one of the few things on bikes not to be standardised yet, while mountain bikes have different fittings, too. Whenever you go to a bike shop for *any* new or replacement component it is always worth taking the original one with you if you're in the slightest unsure about sizing.)

Gears

Most modern bikes have variable gears: you can change how far the bike travels for each turn of the pedals. A 'high' gear travels further for each pedal turn, but you have to put more force on the pedals, while a 'low gear' travels a shorter distance per turn but with less force. The object is to change the gears so that you can keep up a comfortable pedalling speed, and load on the pedals, no matter how fast or slow you're travelling. In general, comfortable pedalling rates are between 70 and 90 pedal revs per minute: you may find this seems quite fast to begin with but as you get more experienced you'll find that the brisker rate becomes more natural.

Gear change mechanisms are of two types: **hub gears** (which have a miniature gearbox inside the rear wheel hub) and **derailleur gears** which shift the chain between a series of different-sized sprockets on the rear wheel hub (from five to eight, with seven as the commonest on new bikes nowadays) and between two or three different-sized chainwheels at the front. Remember: bigger rear sprockets and smaller front chainwheels (both are the *inside* ones) give *lower* gears – and conversely bigger front chainwheels and smaller rear sprockets (the outside ones) give *higher* gears. The advantage of hub gears has always been simplicity of use: there are separate click positions on the gear control for each gear. Their disadvantage was that the range of gears was restricted and often the jumps between gears were too big. The advantage of derailleur gears has always been the wide gear range available, while modern ones are

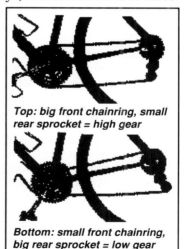

Top: big front chainring, small rear sprocket = high gear

Bottom: small front chainring, big rear sprocket = low gear

now 'indexed' so that they, too, have definite click-positions on the gear lever for each gear. Hub gears are fighting back with new five- and seven-speed versions.

The large number of rear sprockets, multiplied by the number of front chainrings means that modern bikes with derailleurs have enormous numbers of different gears: the three on the front and seven at the back on current mountain- and touring bikes gives a total of 21! You do *not* go through the lot in sequence – and, *definitely* unlike a car, you certainly *don't* work your way up to top and stay there. We think the best way to use a bike equipped like this is to use the big, outer chainwheel for very easy conditions, the middle one for moderate conditions, and the tiny inside one for when it's hard – which usually means uphill, or perhaps off-road. Then you can make your 'fine-tuning' changes to a comfortable gear using the rear gear alone. The aim, as we said, is to be able to turn the pedals at a comfortable rate ('cadence' is the trendy term) in all conditions, though it is natural to pedal a little slower uphill (say 50 to 60rpm) and faster when it's very easy. The chain has to be moving – that is, you have to be pedalling – to change a derailleur gear, and it's better to change down earlier rather than later on a hill, while you're still pedalling at a reasonable speed. With a hub gear you freewheel momentarily to take the load off the gear while you're changing.

If you do find riding hard, or that it's impossible to keep up a reasonably brisk pedalling rate, then your whole gear range could be too high – this is most likely on sports 'racer'-style bikes of a few years back. Discuss it with the bike shop.

Comfort

The type of **saddle** for comfort is a very personal choice. It has to be wide enough to support your ischial bones (the small bony bumps you can feel by sitting on your hands) at the back, while not so wide that it chafes your legs further forward. The distance between the ischial bones varies enormously between individuals and is on average greater for women than for men. A saddle should be firm enough to give good support while at the same time not being so hard that it bruises. A very wide soft saddle may seem the most comfortable when you sit on a bike in the shop but may well not be after a few miles on the road. The real answer is to try other saddles – your friends', ones on other bikes in the shop – until you find one that suits. Then stick to it – even if you swap the bike for another one. Saddles often get blamed for causing soreness – because that's where you feel it – but the cause can be wrong clothing or a too stretched-out or forward-leaning riding position.

Once your riding position and saddle are right, what affects comfort most are riding within your natural personal limits and suitable clothing.

Taking it steady Many people seem to think that once you get on a bike you have to go as fast as you can. You don't – after all, most people out on a ramble don't expect to break into a trot. Everybody has a natural cycling rhythm and effort of riding, which is likely to change with experience and fitness. Go at your own speed, especially uphill. If you're with other people who want to go faster or slower, arrange to meet up with them at intervals. Don't struggle to keep up – and it's not much more comfortable having to hang back to ride at a slower speed.

In the same way, everyone has a natural length of time that they can keep up their comfortable level of effort. To begin with this may be, say, only an hour at a time, followed by a longish rest. At least to start with be prepared to underestimate your strength. You might surprise yourself – after all, four hours' riding at only 7 or 8mph, spread over the whole day, will still take you around 30 miles.

Clothing For comfortable cycling you need clothing that allows free movement, protects from heat and cold and doesn't chafe where you sit on it. You can wear virtually what you like for the sort of routes in this book (perhaps not overcoats and wellies!) but they should still follow the same principles as special cycle clothing. Shirts, sweaters and jackets need to be quite long at the back, otherwise the leaning-forward position leaves a chilly gap, and shorts or trousers must be flexible enough to allow full movement. Jeans usually don't, while tracksuit bottoms or shellsuits are often baggy enough to rub on the chain. 'Proper' nylon-Lycra cycling 'skin shorts' or tights may look strange or rather revealing but they are really comfortable to wear. Unlike conventional trousers and underwear, they have no hard seams across the saddle area, and a special lining which is meant to be worn next to the skin. Wearing seamed underwear inside them completely defeats the object. Obviously, they have to be washed as often as you'd wash underwear. These skin shorts also make a good undergarment under trousers or tracksuit bottoms designed for cycling in cooler weather.

The other thing which makes cycling different from walking, and has an effect on clothing, is the windchill as a result of the higher speed of cycling. On a gentle open downhill – even on Notting-hamshire's modest slopes – you can easily freewheel at 25mph or more. If you've been riding uphill and sweating a bit just before, you'll feel the wind chill all the more. Going uphill, cycling clothes – tops, in particular – have to be porous enough for sweat to evaporate. Going downhill, they have to be windproof enough to prevent chilling. The best compromise is to have several thin layers so that you can adjust what you are wearing as necessary. You will soon learn what your best combination is. This windchill from your own movement also means that bits of the body that aren't keeping warm by working, particularly hands and, in winter, feet – can get much cooler than you'd expect. Gloves can be a great comfort even on only moderately cool days.

Shoes for cycling need to have a fairly stiff sole to spread the pedalling load. Special cycling shoes have almost rigid soles but this makes them not so comfortable for walking in, the ones with a built-in cleat to fit the fancy 'step-in' ski-binding style of pedal even more so. Mountain-bike pedals, except the 'step-in' versions, are designed to be used with anything up to walking boots.

Whatever anybody tells you, **if it rains**, there is no way of keeping completely dry on a bike. All that you can hope for is to keep out the worst and keep warm – but not so hot that you get even wetter by sweating. Some people find tops made out of one of

Helmets

Cycle helmets have received a lot of publicity – a great deal of it from non-cyclists – over recent years. A helmet can help to protect your head from certain types of impact but it doesn't make you invulnerable. The current tests for compliance with the published standard only require it to protect in an impact at about 12mph – comparable with falling off a bike – and not in more violent collisions with motor vehicles. The view of both Pedals and the CTC is that the choice of whether or not (and when) to wear a helmet must remain a personal decision by the user, or parent or guardian. If you do choose to wear one, then:

● Choose one that conforms at least to the current British Standard (BS6863), or to the more stringent requirements of the American Snell Institute.

● Make sure that it is the right size and properly secured. This is just as important for children's helmets as for adults'.

● Be prepared for it to affect the way in which you move your head and hear other traffic at first and take extra care.

● Replace it if it suffers any hard blow or shows surface damage.

● Remember that it is not some sort of magic talisman rendering you immune from injury: you still need to be just as careful and wary of other traffic when riding.

the 'breathable' fabrics that are supposed to let moisture out effective (Gore-Tex is the best-known), others find them too clammy. It is cold from chilling that is the main discomfort of being damp. If you can stay warm until you can get a change of clothing you will have won the battle.

Clothing, tools, food, and anything else you want to take with you, have to be carried. The best place for any load is on the bike, not on your back. Some mountain-bikers prefer a small securely-held backpack, but for on-road use bike-mounted loads, with bags on a proper carrier rack or even a front basket or bag, are more comfortable.

Servicing your bike

Bikes don't have a regular servicing schedule like cars. Perhaps they should – so we suggest the following:

Before using a bike, particularly if it hasn't been used for some time, and also at intervals of a couple of months:

● Check that tyres, brake cables, transmission (front chainwheel, chain, gears, rear sprockets) and wheels are in a good state of repair. Tyres should be checked for holes, bulges and twists; if in any doubt, buy new ones. Brake cables should operate smoothly with no stiffness or grating. Again, if in doubt lubricate or if necessary replace them. Brake blocks or pads (on brakes that act on the wheel rim) should have at least $\frac{1}{4}$in of thickness left. Wheels should be true (that is to say, the rim shouldn't wobble from side to side when you spin the wheel), with their full number of spokes evenly tensioned, and wheel hubs should run smoothly with no crackling or grating. The chain and gearing should not be so worn that you feel unevenness or grinding when you ride. With any of these, if you don't feel competent to carry out the work yourself get a good bike shop to give the machine the once-over.

● Check that bolted-on components, such as brake mechanisms where they attach to the frame, brake levers where they are fitted onto the handlebars, mudguards, the saddle where it fits onto the seat pillar, the seat pillar where it fits into the frame, lights, carriers or baskets, are all tightly fixed. Check that wheel hubs are tightly bolted to the frame, or firmly clamped by 'quick-release' mechanisms. Check also that the handlebar stem cannot rotate easily in the frame. Check that the handlebar stem is exactly lined up with the front wheel and that the saddle is exactly lined up with the top tube of the frame.

● On a bike with a single gear or a hub gear, check that the back wheel is far enough back for the chain to be reasonably tight. You have to undo the wheelnuts with a spanner to do this. The correct adjustment is when you can move the chain up or down about half an inch midway between the front chainwheel and the rear hub. After this, you may have to readjust a hub gear: if you don't know how, ask your bike shop.

● Check that bearings – wheel hub, bottom bracket, pedals, steering head – are correctly adjusted. They should rotate freely and smoothly but at the same time not be loose.

● Check that brakes are correctly adjusted and working. The levers should pull the brakes firmly onto the rim within about the first half of their possible movement, long before they pull up against the handlebar. The law – and common sense – requires that you should have an efficient brake operating on each wheel. (There are slightly different regulations for very small children's bikes, tricycles and 'fixed-wheel' bikes that don't have a freewheel.)

Every few times you go out:

● Lubricate, with a medium oil, the chain and exposed bearings or sliding surfaces: where bare cable wires go through stops or guides or over pulleys, bearing pivots of derailleur gear mechanisms, front or rear. Don't overdo it: each, even a chain, needs no more than a drop or two. Too much oil can run down spokes or spatter onto the tyres and rims. The need for lubrication varies with the weather, particularly rain.

Every time you go out:

● Check that tyres are pumped up correctly. The correct pressure is moulded on the side of the tyre, but you need a pump with a gauge, or a separate pressure gauge, to check these. If in doubt, get the shop to pump them up with a 'track pump' which has a gauge and then get used to how hard that feels between finger and thumb.

● Quickly check the tyres for bulges or misshapen sections, major cuts in the tread or sidewall, and for glass or thorns .

● Spin the wheels to make sure that they're not touching the brakes or mudguards.

● Check that there is no stiffness or jerkiness in the steering (lift the front wheel off the ground and try turning the handlebars).

● Check that the chain is lightly lubricated (but not too much).

● Check that the brakes work.

Where you can cycle

By right

● On any **public roads** that are not motorways (in Nottinghamshire, that's the M1, west and north-west of Nottingham, and the A1(M) Doncaster bypass north of Blyth), nor on which there is a valid no cycling order. These latter are marked by the standard 'no cycling' sign: a red circular sign with a black bicycle symbol on a white background. They are usually either short sections of heavily-trafficked road, such as the section of the A52 from the Dunkirk flyover to the Derby Road roundabout in Nottingham, or pedestrianised streets. For the major part of our routes we have chosen quiet minor roads.

● On designated **cycle tracks**. These are marked by a blue circular sign with a white bicycle symbol, if for cyclists only, and with pedestrian figures in addition if the path is for the use of both cyclists and pedestrians. Rectangular blue signs with a white cycle symbol are recommended cycle routes on roads used by other traffic, generally quiet residential roads. We have incorporated quite a number of both urban and rural cycle tracks into our routes where we can.

● On **bridleways** – but you must give way to walkers and horse-riders if necessary. Bridleways are usually marked at either end and at most road crossings by finger posts reading 'Public bridleway' or 'Bridleway'. In addition, they may be waymarked by small blue arrows. Sometimes a bridleway follows the line of a private road, and sometimes the 'Private Road' sign is – presumably deliberately – a lot more prominent than the bridleway sign; you are nevertheless entitled to cycle on the bridleway.

Although you are legally entitled to cycle on any bridleway the surface may not always be very comfortable for riding on – it may be muddy, or badly rutted or even rocky. If it is only really suitable for mountain bikes, we say so. Bridleway surfaces can vary with the weather and season, too. They may be muddy in winter and after wet weather, or with hoof-marks baked into concrete-like ridges in a drought, while vegetation, such as nettles, can encroach in summer. As far as possible, where we use bridleways as parts of our routes they are ridable using conventional bikes at most seasons, though you might have to walk short sandy stretches.

There is another classification, 'road used as public path' (often shortened to RUPP). These are gradually being reclassified as footpaths, bridleways or 'byways open to all traffic' (which naturally get shortened to BOATs). (A byway is defined as a road which the

17

highway authority has no obligation to keep surfaced.) You may take it that you can cycle on any remaining RUPPs, and of course on any which have been reclassified as bridleways or byways. These vary in surface quality as much as any other path or track. The position on cycling on country public footpaths is ill-defined. You certainly have no legal right, as with a bridleway, but equally riding on one is not a criminal offence, though you leave yourself open in theory to proceedings for trespass. Probably more important is the damage you may cause to goodwill between cyclists as a whole and landowners and walkers. In addition, while a bridleway must not have stiles, you are very likely to meet them on footpaths. You may not ride legally on a footway beside a road (what most of us call the 'pavement') except to cross it or if it has been designated and signed for shared pedestrian and cycle use.

As a privilege

● On certain designated **canal towpaths**, with a permit from British Waterways. These permits are free and last a year. They are obtainable from British Waterways, Trent Lock, Lock Lane, Long Eaton, NG10 2FF; tel (0115) 946 1017. The permit has a 'cycle code' of advice printed on the back. The whole 66km (42-mile) length of the Grantham Canal towpath is a permitted route, although the surface varies greatly from section to section; most is grassy and in exploring the routes we met some parts where you would have to lift bikes over locked stock gates. We have avoided putting these sections in the routes! Also permitted is the 7.5km (5-mile) stretch of the Nottingham and Beeston Canal from Turnover Bridge to Meadow Lane lock, and on the Erewash Canal the 4.9km (3 miles) from Hallam Fields Lock to Dock Holme Lock. Most of this is in Derbyshire. Where a section of canal towpath is incorporated into a designated cycle route you may use it without a permit.

● On firm-surfaced **tracks** (that is to say, not on soft horse tracks or routes designated for walkers only) **in Forestry Commission forests** – subject to restrictions when the tracks are being used for forestry operations. Some of these firm tracks have been waymarked by Forest Enterprise (the FC's commercial arm) as cycle routes, notably in Sherwood Pines Forest Park in Clipstone Forest.

● On certain **paths and roads** in **Country Parks** and some **National Trust** properties, such as Clumber Park – where cars have to pay to enter but bikes go in free!

On payment

● On the road through the grounds of Newstead Abbey.

CYCLE CODES OF CONDUCT

Riding on the road

● Make sure that your bike is safe to ride – read the servicing advice on pp15-16.

● Ride on the left of the road – but don't cringe in the gutter. If you ride about 18 inches out from the kerb you won't have to swerve round drains or debris that has accumulated there.

● Remember that you are part of the traffic. Ride in a straight line as far as possible, don't weave in and out of lanes or round parked cars. If there are many parked cars, follow the overtaking line unless traffic density makes it essential to pull in between them. When passing parked cars look out for the possibility of a door opening unexpectedly (it's an offence but it happens).

● Act predictably by obeying traffic lights, no entry signs etc, and being in the right part of the road for any manoeuvre you may want to make. Don't block a left-turn-only lane at traffic lights or other junctions if you're going straight ahead. Get into the proper right-turn lane for a right turn if you're confident enough; if you're not, it may be better to get off your bike and walk across to where you want to be.

● Signal if you're going to change direction – but look behind in good time first or use a mirror to make sure it's safe. If you can, look directly at and catch the eye of whoever you're signalling to.

● Be conspicuous in your positioning on the road. All vehicles have blind spots behind door and window pillars and so on. Don't creep into a place where a van, lorry or bus driver can't see you.

● Don't go to the left of a vehicle, moving or stopped, that's signalling a left turn. Don't go to the left of a bus near a bus stop and keep an eye out for people hailing taxis from the kerb.

● In slowly-moving traffic don't ride into a gap between long vehicles which could close before you get to the front.

● Expect drivers to do daft things. They shouldn't, of course, and you may well feel that they ought to be boiled in oil as a penalty – but they do. Don't get angry!

● Use your ears as well as your eyes, and make use of every scrap of available evidence as to what's going on around you – reflections in shop windows, feet moving between parked cars and so on. Don't muffle your ears with a personal stereo.

● Use lights after sunset.

● Don't try to compete with other traffic – including other cyclists.

Riding off-road

Several bodies have issued codes of practice for cycling off-road in both town and country. The points below are condensed from these. The main point to remember is that you have to share with walkers on urban shared-use paths, and with walkers and horse-riders on bridleways and byways.

● Give way as appropriate and when necessary to pedestrians and horse-riders – be prepared to slow down when approaching them.

● Let pedestrians and riders know that you are there, say with the gentle tinkle of a bell. Don't surprise them – many pedestrians may be hard of hearing, while horses often shy at the mere sight of a bicycle. If a rider is obviously having difficulty in controlling a horse or pony, stop and wait until they have passed or pulled off the path to let you by.

● When passing other path users give them as much room as possible.

● Be particularly cautious at blind spots such as junctions, bends, entrances and near obstructions, such as trees.

● On urban shared-use paths where the pedestrian and cycle sections are divided by a white line or kerb, keep to the cycle section, marked by the bike signs painted on the path.

● Ride carefully and under control downhill.

● Take particular care on unstable or wet surfaces.

Out in the country:

● Enjoy the countryside and respect its life and work

● Guard against all risk of fire

● Re-fasten all gates that you find closed

● Keep to rights of way across farmland

● Cross fences, hedges and walls only at gates (or stiles on footpaths)

● Leave livestock, crops and machinery alone

● Take your litter home

● Help to keep all water sources clean

● Protect wildlife, plants and trees

● Make no unnecessary noise

In the forest:

● Except in designated areas, ride only on firm-based tracks and paths.

● Do not obstruct gates (for example, by leaving bikes locked to them) and keep clear of forestry operations.

● Don't pass any vehicle loading timber until you are told it is safe to do so.

Beside the canal:

● Ride with care on slippery or rough bits – by definition a canal towpath has a canal on one side of it! Ride at a moderate pace, and don't make slippery sections worse by skidding.

● You may need to get off and walk when passing under a low bridge and you must when going by a lock.

● Don't bunch up along the towpath.

● Watch out for anglers, and spikes and mooring ropes from moored boats.

Maps

Although we intend that you should be able to follow any of the routes in this book without one, a map can add to your enjoyment by showing you what features of interest lie just off the route and also by allowing you to make up your own routes and links. The most useful map for general cycling is the Ordnance Survey Landranger series, in deep pink covers at a scale of 1:50 000 – 2cm on the map represent 1km on the ground, or about 1¹/₄ inches represent one mile. Unfortunately they're quite expensive (currently – 1996 – £4.75 a sheet), and to cover the whole of Nottinghamshire you'd need *six* sheets: 111 *Sheffield and Doncaster area*; 112 *Scunthorpe*; 120 *Mansfield, Worksop*; 121 *Lincoln*; 129 *Nottingham*; and 130 *Grantham*. Each sheet covers an area 40km (about 25 miles) square. Most of the routes in this book lie on the Mansfield/ Worksop and Nottingham sheets, 120 and 129.

These maps are detailed enough to show all roads and most paths and tracks. They also show which of the latter are rights of way by marking them in red: public bridleways are shown by a line of long red dashes (— — — —), RUPPs as a succession of alter-nating short and long red dashes (— - — - —), and BOATs as a succession of small red crosses and short dashes (+-+-+-+-).

For off-road riding, the Pathfinder series in green covers at a scale of 1:25 000 can be useful. These are double the scale of the Landrangers (and need correspondingly more sheets, which are of smaller size anyway, to cover an area completely). They do show more detail which is helpful to off-road riders, particularly field boundaries, and on which side of them bridleways etc lie. Rights of way are marked in green, sometimes printed so heavily that you have to look carefully to distinguish any other detail they might be covering up.

Grid references Both types of Ordnance Survey map allow positions of features etc to be defined to the nearest 100 metres by means of a 'grid reference'. The maps are divided into 1km squares by a grid of lines (blue on the Landranger maps, black on the Pathfinder maps) which are numbered on the edges of the map, and at 10km intervals on the actual map page of the Landranger.

The position of a point is defined by estimating the number of tenths of a square it is *east* of the nearest *vertical* line to its *left*: this forms the first part of the grid reference (GR in our route descriptions) made up of the number of the line e.g. 58 and the number of estimated tenths of a square, say 3, to give 583. Then the second part of the reference is obtained similarly by estimating the

21

number of tenths of a square *up* from the nearest *horizontal* line *below* it, e.g. 52 for the line, and 2 for the estimated tenths, to give 522. The complete six-figure grid reference, which only repeats every 100km and is accurate to about 100m, is 583 522. The two groups of numbers are *always* given in this order. For ease of reading, we separate the groups by a space; not everybody does. (If you check on sheet 120, Mansfield and Worksop, you will find that our example, 583 522, is the grid reference of Papplewick Pumping Station, a prominent local landmark that features on route 14. The Victorian pumping engine is open to the public, and 'under steam' on certain weekends.)

The key panel printed down the right-hand side of the Landranger maps incorporates a section on 'How to give a grid reference'. You don't *have* to be familiar with grid references to follow our routes but if you are using an Ordnance Survey map it's a very useful system for defining and finding the positions of such places as starting points of routes and, naturally, teashops.

Other routes

There are several other sources of published routes in Nottinghamshire.

The Rights of Way Section of **Nottinghamshire County Council** has devised three packs, each comprising five circular cycle routes. The **Trent Valley Pack** routes cover the *Wolds* (26 miles, south from Nottingham), the *Dumbles* (28 miles, south-west from Southwell), *Newark and the Vale* (37 miles, south-west from Newark-on-Trent), *Sherwood Forest and Laxton* (43 miles, east from Edwinstowe), and the *Great North Circuit* (49 miles, north from Newark-on-Trent or south-east from Retford). The **North West Pack** extends beyond the boundaries of the county to include the *Pilgrim Fathers* (28 miles, north from Worksop), *Three Shires* – Notts, Yorks and Derbyshire (30 miles), *Pleasley and the Five Pits Trail* (22 miles, north west from Mansfield), *Sherwood Forest and the Maun Valley* (15 miles) and a *D H Lawrence Ride* (20 miles, based on Eastwood). Finally, the **Southern Pack**'s five routes also stray out of Nottinghamshire in places. They are the *Almost no Hills* ride (37 miles, from Newark-on-Trent), *Soar Valley* (35 miles, south from Nottingham), *Vale of Belvoir* (33 miles, from Bingham), *Byron Country* (15 miles, from Hucknall), and *Park to Park* (20 miles, from Wollaton Park to Shipley Country Park in Derbyshire). The routes are mainly on minor roads with some relatively short sections of bridleway or cycle track. Each route has a descriptive leaflet with a sketch map, route directions and indications of places of interest. Each pack of five leaflets costs £1.50 plus 50p postage, or you can have the lot for £5, including postage, from the Rights of Way Section, Nottinghamshire County Council, Trent Bridge House, West Bridgford, Nottingham NG2 6BJ. Packs are also available from the visitor centres at Edwinstowe and Rufford, and from local libraries.

Bassetlaw District Council and the County Council have joined forces to devise two *Dukeries Cycle Trails* in the north of Nottinghamshire. The first links Clumber Park with Welbeck and Worksop and is 22 miles in length, which may be reduced to a minimum $13^1/2$ miles by a series of short cuts. The second route links Clumber Park with Sherwood Forest and Thoresby, and can be varied in distance from $17^1/2$ to $25^1/2$ miles, or covered as four separate short loops. Each route has a descriptive leaflet with sketch maps, and other information such as cycle hire, picnic sites and sources of refreshment. The leaflets are available from the visitor centres at Clumber Park and Sherwood Forest, from the Tourist Information Centres in Worksop and Retford and from other local sources.

The waymarked cycle route in the **Sherwood Pines Forest Park** – Clipstone Forest – is described in a leaflet *Cycling in the Forest* produced by Forest Enterprise, Sherwood and Lincs Forest District, Edwinstowe, Mansfield, Notts NG21 9JL; tel (01623) 822447. The leaflet includes a sketch map and background information on the forest. It is available from Tourist Information Centres and visitor centres or from Forest Enterprise.

Cycle routes in the City of Nottingham are shown on a free map, *The Greater Nottingham Cycle Route Network*, produced by Nottinghamshire County Council in conjunction with Halfords. The map marks on- and off-road designated (and proposed) cycle routes in the city as well as showing the location of cycle parking stands and lockers in the city centre.

Cycling in Greater Nottingham – over an area extending north-to-south from Bulwell to Ruddington, and from west-to-east from Stapleford to Carlton – is dealt with in the **Pedals** publication *The Pedal Pusher's Guide to Nottingham* (editor: Lawrence Geary). The routes suggested are mainly on-road but include a few sections where walking may be necessary, and – with an appropriate warning – some sections of off-road which may not always have the best of cycling surfaces. The *Guide* is currently being revised and reprinted; details are available from Pedals (see p202).

Organised rides

Nottinghamshire County Council promotes each year a programme of leisurely cycle rides in all parts of the county under the label **Rural Rides**. Distances are generally modest and there is a mixture of on- and off-road rides. All are led by volunteer leaders, mainly from Pedals, the CTC and the Women's Off-Road Racing Club. Rural Rides leaflets are available from: Planning and Economic Development, Countryside Group, Nottinghamshire County Council, Trent Bridge House, Fox Road, West Bridgford, Nottingham NG2 6BJ. They may also be found in local libraries, Tourist Information Centres, visitor centres and some bike shops.

The Nottinghamshire District Association of the **CTC** organises regular led cycle rides with a range of paces and distances. **Pedals** has some evening rides in the summer. There are more details and contact addresses on pp202-204.

Taking a bike with you

Bikes on trains

The position on taking bikes on trains is liable to change with the onset of privatisation. At present you can take bicycles free of charge and unbooked on the **Robin Hood Line** which runs from Nottingham to Mansfield Woodhouse and several of our routes start from or finish at stations on this line. These are Bulwell, Hucknall, Newstead, Kirkby-in-Ashfield, Sutton Parkway, Mansfield and Mansfield Woodhouse. It is planned eventually to extend services to Worksop. Monday-to-Friday services are hourly, with five extra trains on Saturdays. Unfortunately, at present there is no service on Sundays. The service is operated with two- or three-car diesel units and there is an area of convertible tip-up seating to give bike space near the end of one coach (marked with a wheelchair symbol). You load and unload your bike yourself; it may not be possible to get a bike on board during rush hours.

On other services, booking is necessary and you have to pay a fee – £3 per journey at the time of writing. On **Midland Main Line** services, from Nottingham to Loughborough and Leicester, and on **East Coast Main Line** services, from Newark Northgate to Retford and Doncaster, several bikes can be carried. There is a luggage van at one end of the train, the opposite end to the first-class accommodation on 125s, the same end as first class on the East Coast line. If you can, ask station staff where the van will be– these trains are *very* long if you have to leg it from one end to the other! On local **Regional Railways** services from Nottingham to Newark Castle and beyond, from Nottingham to Grantham, from Nottingham to Beeston and Attenborough (and on to Derby, Leicester or beyond), and from Nottingham to Langley Mill, Alfreton and Chesterfield (and beyond) only one or two bikes are carried per train, with a ban on weekday peak-hour services – and you still have to pay your £3, as well as having to book on some trains. Bookings are accepted up to a few minutes before the train leaves. In some other areas of the country restrictions have been eased or lifted, so there is hope. Tandems, tricycles and bikes with trailers are not carried. A folding bike that folds away completely or is carried in a bag can be taken on any train as hand baggage free of charge. As far as we know, as yet no **bus** service in Nottinghamshire carries bikes.

Bikes on cars

Frankly, we'd rather you didn't use a car to get to the start of a ride – but as you will have seen from the last section, getting farther afield may not be easy by other means. We also appreciate that families with young children might like to start them off first on some of the traffic-free routes in parks and forests. Please try to fill your car if it's appropriate: if two couples, say, are going to go on a ride together, use one car if you can rather than two. And if you're parking a car out in the country, make sure it is not obstructing the road or any entrance to a field, track or path.

Apart from using a trailer, there are three ways to carry bikes on a car: inside, if there's room; on a roof rack; and on a rear-mounted rack. The back of an estate car or hatchback, possibly with one or more of the seats folded down is the best – the bikes are out of the weather, not liable to come adrift and reasonably secure when the car is parked. When you're carrying more than one bike it is a good idea to put an old blanket or thick plastic sheet between the bikes so that pedals, chains and gear mechanisms don't get tangled or damaged. If you are carrying bikes on any kind of rack you must make sure that the rack is securely mounted on the car (read the instructions!) and that the bikes are securely fixed to the rack. Special bike roof racks have bolt-on or clamp fittings that hold the bikes secure. If you are carrying them on an ordinary rack – whether upright or lying down – make sure that they are tightly strapped on. Elastic 'bungee' straps alone are not enough. The type of leather or nylon strap sold by bike shops as 'toestraps' is very good for this since they can be adjusted more closely than straps with buckles. When using a rear-mounted rack, remember that is a legal requirement that the number plate, indicators and brake and tail lights should not be obscured. You may need an accessory lighting board and number plate. Remove pumps, lights, cycle computers, bags and bike bottles – anything that can come adrift or be stolen – before mounting bikes on any rack, and remember that the bikes themselves may not be secure against theft if the car is parked. Check that you are not exceeding the rack's specified weight limit (to be on the safe side, consider each adult bike to weigh 30 lb or a child's one 20 lb). Any rack, and particularly a roof one, can affect the handling of the vehicle and its susceptibility to side-winds, as well as increasing petrol consumption. Drive a bit slower than usual if you are carrying bikes.

What to take on a bike ride

Always

- Pump – with a fitting to match the valve on your tyres
- Spare inner tube of the size to fit your bike
- Puncture repair outfit (in case you get two punctures!)
- Tyre levers (three is usual)
- Wheel spanners (usually 14mm for the front, 15mm for the back) if your bike hasn't got 'quick-release' hubs
- Lock and key if you're expecting to stop at a teashop or pub
- Money (or credit card, depending how far you expect to live it up)
- Some form of identification
- Spare sweater (depending on weather of course)
- Waterproofs

Could be useful

- Maps
- Picnic lunch (according to taste)
- Small first-aid kit
- Emergency nibble in case you get what cyclists call the 'bonk' (or used to before *The Sun* hijacked the term for something quite different): a weak-kneed quivering from lack of food.
- Gloves
- Lights if you expect to be out after dark, or near to lighting-up time (which is officially sunset)
- Water bottle, or vacuum flask in cooler weather
- And, of course, **City County Forest** – *Leisure bike routes in Nottingham and Nottinghamshire!*

THE ROUTES

How to follow our routes

All our routes start and finish in Nottinghamshire or the city of Nottingham – and various organisations in the city and county have generously supported the production of this guide. However, except where it follows the Rivers Trent, Idle, Erewash and Soar the county boundary is not a natural barrier and we have to admit to breaching it on a few occasions for a short distance – either to make a more pleasant or even possible route between two Nottinghamshire villages or, you might think much more importantly, to reach a tea-stop or place of interest lying just over the border.

The routes are listed in order of length, shortest first. The key map on page 29 shows roughly where in the city and county each one is situated. Each route description has a heading bar giving distance, whether it's on- or off-road, a rough idea of how hilly it is, and the name of the place where it starts. This is followed by a short introduction to the area, a sketch map, and a box giving the exact position of the starting point, more details on the surface quality, notes on possible refreshment stops, useful Ordnance Survey map sheets, public transport links and other possible linking routes. The main part of each route entry is a detailed route description that we intend you should be able to follow without having to use a map if you don't want to.

We have used one or two conventions in the route descriptions:

● We use *italic* type for information on signposts, while place names in **bold** type highlight the village or hamlet you have reached at that stage of the route – for example: 'In **Willaston**, turn left opposite the church into Main Street, signed *Nottingham*'.

● **Distances** (approximate) are given in yards up to half a mile, and in miles for longer ones. If you have a cycle computer or cyclometer in decimal miles, rough equivalents are: 0.1 miles = 200yds; 0.2 miles = 350yds; 0.3 miles = 500yds; 0.4 miles = 700yds; and 0.5 miles is of course half a mile. If you have one calibrated in kilometres, or prefer to work in metric measures, you can take the yards figures as metres for all practical purposes, while rough equivalents for longer distances are: 1 mile = 1.5km; 2 miles = 3km; 3 miles = 5km; 4 miles = 6.5km; 5 miles = 8 km; 10 miles = 16km.

● We use the road number – A- or B-road – where it is appropriate. Other **roads** we refer to as minor or unclassified road. You may take it that all these are hard-surfaced. If you are emerging from an off-road section (or if you're going onto one), we refer to a hard-surfaced, metalled road as a 'tarred road' (unless it's something noticeably different, such as concrete). We use the word 'track' to mean a well-defined but unsurfaced road or track at least wide enough for a tractor or cart, with further description as necessary – such as 'firm stone-surfaced' or 'grassy'. We use the word 'path' to mean something narrower, usually too narrow for two cyclists to ride along side by side, again with more details if needed.

● From time to time in the route description at a junction or crossroads we give the instruction 'Turn left (or right)' followed by the expression '(effectively straight on)'. In these cases, while the markings on the road indicate a left or right turn manoeuvre, you continue riding in roughly the same compass direction as before.

● Although one or two routes are described as starting from a public house or inn, please note that this is because they are prominent local landmarks. **We have not negotiated parking facilties for users of this book at these places.**

● There is no reason why you shouldn't follow only part of a route, even return by the same route. For example, the bridleways on farm and estate roads and tracks north-east of Worksop to the hamlets of Scofton and Bilby (routes **12** and **21**) would make a good out-and-home traffic-free outing for a young family – with a possible side trip to the river and canal at Scofton. There are also obvious short cuts on some of the longer circuits.

Our sketch maps

The starting point of the route on each sketch map is marked with a little cycle symbol and an arrow to show the direction in which the route is described. There are repeat direction arrows at other points where there might be some doubt. Obviously you can go round a route in either direction, but we think our direction is the better one – besides which it isn't always too easy to follow route directions in reverse. It's also possible to link up some routes to make longer ones, and in several cases we give link routes between them. All the maps are the conventional way up – with north at the top. There's also a scale bar showing – very approximately – how far a mile is on the map. Finally, if you need to be told what the little teacup symbol stands for, then we're sorry but you really have still got some way to go before you qualify as a *real* cyclist!

Where the routes are

The large key map on the right shows approximately the position of the centre of each route. **Circles** mark the main routes, numbered 1-40, described on pages 30-170; **diamonds** indicate the link routes L1-L12, described on pages 171-193. Near the start of each route

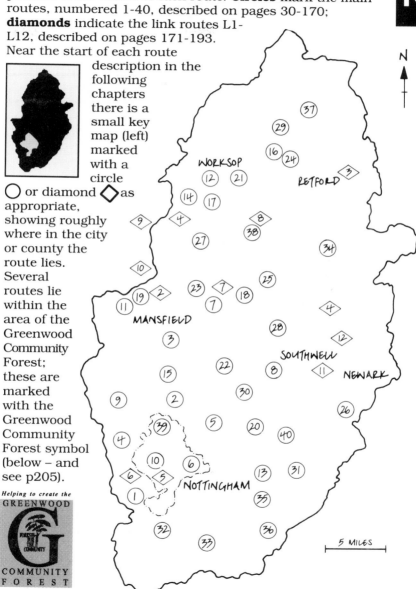

description in the following chapters there is a small key map (left) marked with a circle ○ or diamond ◇ as appropriate, showing roughly where in the city or county the route lies. Several routes lie within the area of the Greenwood Community Forest; these are marked with the Greenwood Community Forest symbol (below – and see p205).

Helping to create the
GREENWOOD

COMMUNITY FOREST

CIRCULAR ROUTES UP TO 10 MILES

1

4 miles • on- and off-road • flat • Beeston

Attenborough Nature Reserve

This very short route from Beeston visits the wetlands of the Attenborough Nature Reserve. Gravel extraction has for centuries been one of the activities along the flood-plain of the River Trent. Once extraction has finished in a particular spot, the gravel pits rapidly fill with water and become colonised by water-loving plants, with wildlife quickly following. The Reserve, which is managed by the Nottinghamshire Wildlife Trust, was opened some thirty years ago and covers over 350 acres of these former pits, now broad lakes fringed with reed beds and lush vegetation. The Reserve is noted particularly for its bird life – so it could be worth taking a bird book and binoculars.

From **Beeston Square** go south-west through the pedestrianised area, leaving the Midland Bank and Post Office to the right. Just before the Post Office, join Chilwell Road. This comes to a T-junction with the B6464, which continues to the right still as Chilwell Road (although not signed at this point). Turn right on Chilwell Road which becomes High Road, **Chilwell**. Opposite Chilwell College House Junior School on the right after about 3/4 mile, turn left into Meadow Lane. Cross Queens Road West, A6005, still on Meadow Lane. Where Meadow Lane bears round to the right after the golf course, becoming Long Lane, turn left by the *Attenborough* sign into an short unnamed no through road. Bear right on a gravel track and through a swing gate to cross the railway by the level crossing, then through a second white swing

30

gate. You next cross a little bridge over a stream to turn right on a bridleway through Attenborough Nature Reserve.

This unsigned but well-surfaced track follows the railway line on its right for a short way, then veers away to the left alongside a stream. After about 400yds there is a 'crossroads' of paths, with the entrance to gravel workings to the right. Continue straight on over a humpbacked wooden-slatted

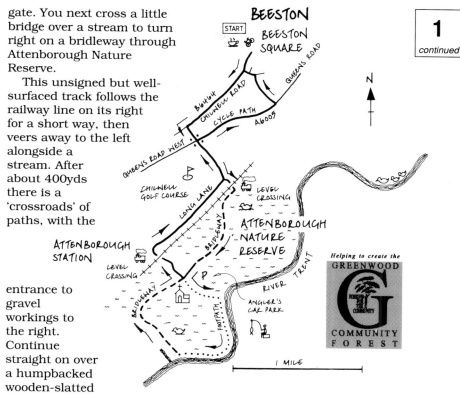

1 continued

bridge with green metal sides, along a spit of land between two lakes. After leaving the water the path passes between a stone wall to the right and a fence on the left, to join a tarred road (The Strand, but not named at this point). At the far end of the playing fields on the left, where The Strand bears round to the right, there is an anglers' car park on the left. Turn left into the car park. From this point the path is a *footpath* for a while: see p18.

For a short tour of the **Attenborough Nature Reserve**, go round the metal barrier at the end of the car park, then straight on to cross another wooden-slatted green humpbacked bridge and along the well-marked path with water both sides. There is then a choice of two routes: the *shorter* follows a path which bears off to the right along a spit of land between two lakes, while the *longer* goes straight on to meet the bank of the River Trent. Turn right to follow the river for about ³/₄ mile until a stream joins it from the right. Don't cross the stream but turn right, inland, along a fairly wide track which at some stables becomes a bridleway. (The shorter route rejoins at this point.) This wide but potholed track – although

1

continued

it is easy enough to avoid the holes – passes between two lakes with an attractive view across the water to Attenborough church on the right. Cross over a bridge which crosses a link between the two lakes; shortly after this there is a car park area. Just after this car park turn right on a marked bridleway towards **Attenborough** church. After about 300yds there is a fork in the paths; follow the right-hand path, signed *Registered horse-riders only*. This leads across a finger of land between waters, which takes you back to the anglers' car park where the Nature Reserve tour began.

Turn left to The Strand, then left on The Strand and follow this where it bears right and left to become Attenborough Lane to pass over a level crossing by Attenborough Station. Take the first right after the level crossing into Long Lane, and follow this until it becomes Meadow Lane and comes to a traffic-light-controlled junction with the A6005, Queen's Road West. Cross to the north side of the road and – provided it has been reopened after extensive works which were about to start at the time this route was prospected – follow the shared-use cycle track on the north side of the road for about a mile to its junction with Dovecote Lane, just before a pelican crossing. Turn left into Dovecote Lane to its T-junction with Middle Street. Turn left and then second right into Chilwell Road to **Beeston Square** to complete the circuit. (If the shared-use cycle track has not been re-opened, or if you don't wish to use it, go straight on at the Meadow Lane/A6005 junction to follow the outgoing route back to Beeston Square.) 🚲

Distance: 4 cycling miles; optional ½ to 1 mile of footpath

Terrain: **minor** suburban **roads** and **bridleway**, with some *footpath* involved if you wish to explore the Nature Reserve

Refreshment opportunities: various cafés etc in Beeston town centre (GR 528 369).

Ordnance Survey maps: Landranger sheet **129** Nottingham and Loughborough, or Pathfinder sheet **833**, Nottingham (South) and Long Eaton. The whole route is also on the *AZ Premier Street Map of Nottingham*

Public transport links: Regional Railways services (and a few Midland Main Line trains) call at Beeston station, about ½ mile south-east of Beeston town centre; a few Regional Railways services from Nottingham to Derby and vice versa call at Attenborough station (on the route).

Other routes: Route **L5** links the Beeston start of this route with Nottingham city centre and Midland Station, largely by the signed cycle route; this route also links with route **10**. Route **L6** links Beeston with Strelley village, where route **4** starts.

The Dover Beck at Lowdham Mill (see route 20)

Right: even close to a large town a few poplars and a clear stream soon make you feel right out in the country. This is the Vicar Water, alongside the bridleway between Mansfield and Clipstone (see route 23).

Below: a tranquil autumn day beside a much bigger river – the Trent, seen here from the bridleway between Hoveringham and Gunthorpe Lock (see route 20).

6 miles · off-road · hilly · Bestwood Lodge

2

Bestwood Country Park and Mill Lakes

Bestwood Country Park, like many of the country parks that have emerged to the north of Nottingham, owes its existence largely to the demise of coalmining. The old spoil heaps had become naturally colonised by vegetation, and careful landscaping has made for a seamless graft between the open and airy artificial hill and the extensive established woodland which is a remnant of an old deer park to the east. Bestwood's mining past is commemorated by the retention of the old pit-head gear and engine house as a feature. The park is easily accessible by bike from the northern areas of Nottingham, or by the Robin Hood Line to Bulwell or Hucknall. In the country park, cyclists and walkers share most of the paths that are not marked as 'horse trails'. Many of them are broad tracks or untarred roads, but some are narrower paths, so take care. This route also goes round the Mill Lakes, a nature reserve adjacent to Bestwood Country Park, to the west. Information leaflets on the wildlife to be seen around the lakes and woodland are obtainable from the Country Park Administration Office at Bestwood Country Park, tel (0115) 967 0042.

At the entrance of the **Bestwood Lodge Drive car park** turn right up the hill; the road bears quite sharply round to the left, then right, past **Bestwood Lodge Hotel**. You are on Main Drive, following signs to *Alexandra Lodges*, and a short distance after the hotel the tarred surface of this road gives way to crushed stone. About $1/2$ mile from the hotel Main Drive continues through a five-barred gate. Here, turn right along a narrower path (not signed). At the end of the wood, after about 600yds, turn left at the track crossroads into Colliers' Path and follow this down to **Alexandra Lodges**. Turn right onto the tarred minor road, past the field studies centre, and immediately left along Woodman's Path, signed to the *Adventure Playground*. Go up the hill, past toilets and the Adventure Playground.

2
continued

Helping to create the
GREENWOOD
G
COMMUNITY
FOREST

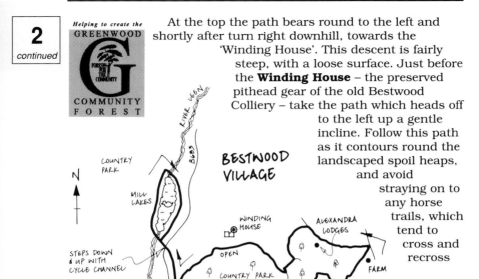

At the top the path bears round to the left and shortly after turn right downhill, towards the 'Winding House'. This descent is fairly steep, with a loose surface. Just before the **Winding House** – the preserved pithead gear of the old Bestwood Colliery – take the path which heads off to the left up a gentle incline. Follow this path as it contours round the landscaped spoil heaps, and avoid straying on to any horse trails, which tend to cross and recross

the firm-surfaced path on this stretch. After about ¹/₂ mile turn right on to the first path not signed as a horse trail, which heads downhill, across a small bridge and then bears round to the right. Continue on this path, ignoring any turnings, through a wooden kissing gate, and when it joins a disused rail line path turn very sharp right – almost doubling back. After about 400yds this track descends to a road, B683 (steps with a gully to wheel bicycles).

Cross over the B683 at the bottom, and up the other side, signed *Mill Lakes* (steps again, with the bike-wheeling gully on the wrong side if you're right-handed!). *(The Leen Valley Path, route **39**, from or to Bulwell Station joins/leaves here.)* Then follow the broad firm-surfaced path over a wooden bridge which crosses the River Leen at a small weir and then in a clockwise direction around the **Mill Lakes** – keeping the water on your right. At the far end of the lakes pass through one kissing gate onto a tarred path. *(The Leen Valley route from or to Hucknall Station joins/leaves here.)* Turn right across a wooden bridge over the River Leen and immediately right through another kissing gate, to rejoin the waterside path, here narrower but still firm crushed-stone-surfaced.

Having completed a tour of the lakes, you will need to retrace your route back into Bestwood Park, via the disused rail line. From the kissing gate leading into Bestwood Park, go straight on, ignoring any side turnings. This path soon passes through two wooden farm gates and climbs a fairly steep hill. At the summit follow the path as it bears round to the right and then curves to the left until you reach an entrance to Bestwood Park from a housing estate. Take the second left path, signed to *Big Wood*, which runs along the perimeter of the park. Stick to the main path through the woods, and when this veers away from the housing estate, bear right at a Y-junction, and right at the next T-junction, signed to *Lodge Gardens* and *Bestwood Lodge Drive*. At the next fork, just after a sign for *Wood-man's Path*, keep right. Through a wooden kissing gate you emerge onto Main Drive; turn right and fol-low this ¹/2 mile or so down to **Best-wood Lodge Drive car park**. 🚲

2
continued

Distance: 6 miles

Terrain: An entirely **off-road** route, undulating

Refreshment opportunities: Bestwood Lodge Hotel (en route) offers morning coffee, afternoon tea, lunches etc; as the route is situated on the urban fringe there are also some shops and pubs near to this route. If you're picnicking, there are several sets of wooden benches and tables dotted around the park.

Start: Bestwood Lodge Drive car park, Bestwood Park (GR 572 464)

Ordnance Survey maps: Landranger sheet **129** Nottingham and Loughborough, or Pathfinder sheet **812**, Nottingham (North) and Ilkeston.

Public transport links: Robin Hood Line to Bulwell or Hucknall stations, then follow the Leen Valley Path, route **39**; in either case you join the circuit part-way round.

Other routes: The Leen Valley Path, route **39**, follows part of this route, and also forms a link to route **15**, Hucknall and Newstead Abbey.

---

6 miles • off-road • undulating • Mansfield

3

Harlow Wood

This is a short, off-road route route, going round Harlow Wood and Thieves Wood, two woodlands divided by the A60, south of Mansfield. The forest tracks are not signed, but the route sticks

3
continued

to the main thoroughfares used by forestry vehicles, which are clearly differentiated from the numerous minor footpaths which crisscross the area. The woodland is a characteristic Nottinghamshire mix of conifers and broad-leaved trees, with attractive clearings, and some open views where the route skirts the edge of the wood.

Close to the edge of Harlow Wood and just off the route itself, on the east side of the A60, is a memorial stone marking the spot where a 17-year-old Papplewick girl, Elizabeth Sheppard, was murdered in 1817. The motive was apparently theft, since a man was later apprehended, tried and hanged after trying to sell her shoes and umbrella. The stone is marked on the Ordnance Survey Landranger map as 'Sheppard's Stone' (GR 551 563). It is rather hidden, a little down a bank from the road verge and about 50yds on the Nottingham side of the point where the route crosses the A60.

With Bellamy Road, **Mansfield**, behind you, start by travelling a short distance eastwards along Old Newark Road. Just after Shelton Road, but before Syerston Road on the left, turn right along an unsigned bridleway. Follow this for about ³/₄ mile up a slight hill, and on reaching some farm buildings turn right on a bridleway indicated by a *blue arrow* – ignore the narrower bridleway that goes straight ahead. This is a sandy track in places and progress many be fairly slow in very dry weather. After about ¹/₂ mile, soon after entering **Harlow Wood**, you come to a significant crossroads of woodland tracks; turn left passing a low wooden barrier and follow this track for a further mile. Soon after passing another low wooden barrier you emerge onto the A60, Nottingham Road; there is a coffee shop just off to the right.

Cross straight over the main road, onto a track leading into **Thieves Wood**; pass round a low wooden barrier and continue straight on for about ¹/₂ mile, ignoring any smaller paths leading off to left

Helping to create the
GREENWOOD

COMMUNITY
FOREST

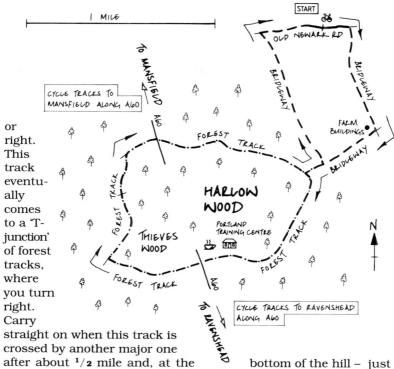

or right. This track eventually comes to a 'T-junction' of forest tracks, where you turn right. Carry straight on when this track is crossed by another major one after about ¹/₂ mile and, at the bottom of the hill – just beyond a further low wooden barrier – turn right to return to the A60. Cross back over the main road, bearing slightly right to re-enter **Harlow Wood**, again passing a low wooden

---

Distance: 6 miles

Terrain: An almost entirely **off-road** route on forest tracks and bridleways, which are loose-surfaced in places so sturdy tyres and low gears are advisable.

Refreshment opportunities: There is a coffee shop at Portland Training Centre – on the Nottingham Road (A60) – about half way round.

Start: Junction of Old Newark Road and Bellamy Road – these are fairly minor residential roads in south-east Mansfield – (GR 562 588)

Ordnance Survey maps: Landranger sheet **120** Mansfield and Worksop; Pathfinder sheet **795** Sutton in Ashfield

Public transport links: Robin Hood Line to Mansfield or Mansfield Woodhouse (no Sunday service)

Other routes: About 1¹/₂ miles of the A60, southwards, links this route to route **15**, Hucknall and Newstead, at The Hutt, Ravenshead. There is a narrow shared-use cycle-and-pedestrian path on the west side of the A60 for part of the way.

3
continued

barrier. This wide track winds through the trees for nearly a mile before you reach a distinctive crossroads of forest tracks – you should recognise this spot from earlier on the route. Turn left, then left again after a short way – just before leaving the woods – down a waymarked bridleway. Descend with care as the sandy surface can be quite unpredictable. When this bridleway ends at a T-junction with an unsurfaced minor road on the outskirts of Mansfield – Old Newark Road, in fact – turn right and after a further $^1/_2$ mile the route comes back to the junction where it started. 🚲

4

6 miles · mostly off-road · undulating · Strelley village

Strelley, Cossall and the Erewash Canal

This short route follows bridleways, towpath and a small proportion of minor road through rural agricultural land right on the fringes of the city.

The little village of Cossall, about halfway round, has several features of interest, including some attractive almshouses dating from 1685. Church Cottage in the village is notable as

the home of Louise Burrow, D H Lawrence's fiancee. Like most canals, the Erewash Canal which the route follows for a couple of miles has become the naturalised home of many water birds. The wrought-iron Bennerley Viaduct which you can see on the left just after you leave the canal towpath is now a listed 'building'. It was built in the 1870s for a branch of the Great Northern Railway using a patented lattice design to overcome possible unstable foundations as a result of mining activity. It was in use right up to 1968 when the line closed.

From **Strelley** church head south-east (towards Nottingham) for about 300yds, then at the sharp left bend in the road, turn onto a bridleway on the right (where the grass verge has a line of posts with red and white markers). Go through the gap at the side of the metal gate. The bridleway, between hedges, bears round to the left. Ignore the first wide track on the right after about 150yds. About

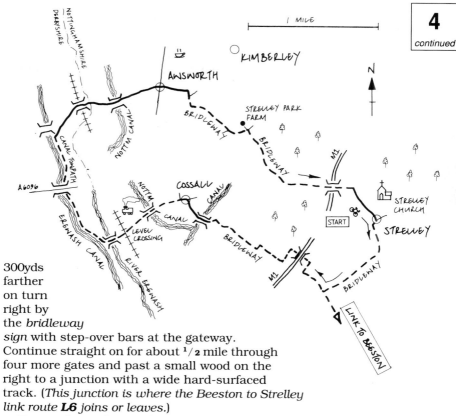

4
continued

300yds
farther
on turn
right by
the *bridleway*
sign with step-over bars at the gateway.
Continue straight on for about ¹/₂ mile through
four more gates and past a small wood on the
right to a junction with a wide hard-surfaced
track. (*This junction is where the Beeston to Strelley
link route L6 joins or leaves.*)

Turn right on this track as it winds under the M1 motorway.
Continue for about a mile through two large five-barred gates and
two bridleway gateways. (The path becomes narrow for a short
section so take care to avoid the ditch on the right.) The path
emerges onto a tarred road at a bend, by a bridge where it crosses
a short arm of disused canal. Turn right towards Cossall village for
about 300yds. At a T-junction on the outskirts of the village, where
the right-hand arm is signed *No through road*, turn left and, at the

Helping to create the
GREENWOOD

**COMMUNITY
FOREST**

right-hand bend about 150yds later, go straight on
onto a track signed *Bridleway to Ilkeston*. (If you
want to explore **Cossall** village itself, go right at this
last bend and then retrace your route to this corner,
where it will of course now be a *right* turn. Take care
turning right: visibility is limited at this corner.)

Follow the track down hill, over the disused
Nottingham Canal, for about ¹/₂ mile to the railway

4
continued

level crossing. Go through the swing gate and cross the railway with care: fast trains use this line and there are several tracks but visibility is good in both directions. After going through the gate on the far side keep on the main track, veering right to join the **Erewash Canal** towpath. Keep the canal on your left and follow the towpath which has a good hard surface. Continue on the towpath for about a mile to pass under one road bridge but leave the towpath immediately before the next road bridge (this avoids steps). Turn right – quite steeply uphill – on the road to the junction with the A6096. Cross this very new Awsworth bypass (not on map) by the shared pedestrian/cycle crossing to the right of the junction and join the road on the other side (effectively straight on). At the crossroads at the top of this road, Newton Lane, go straight across on Westby Lane, marked as a 'no through road' and signed *Babbington 1¹/₄*. Continue downhill for about 300yds to a sharp right-hand bend, followed by an even sharper left one.

At this left-hand corner, go straight ahead on a track signed *Bridleway Strelley, footpath Cossall*: keep to the bridleway This reasonably-surfaced track climbs steadily for about ¹/₂ mile and bears round to the left to a junction of tracks, with the left leading to Strelley Park Farm. Turn right onto a wide firm-surfaced track, signed *Bridleway*. Ignore two tracks on the right and the one on the left (to Turkey Fields Farm) which appears to be the main track. Instead go straight ahead on a narrower path – which is the official public bridleway – between a hedge on the left and a wire fence on the right. After about 350yds this path rejoins a wide stone-surfaced track from the left (the other entrance to Turkey Fields Farm). Go straight ahead on this track for about 500yds to cross over the M1 motorway and join the tarred road opposite the gateway to Strelley Hall. Turn right on this road; **Strelley** church is 200yds or so farther on.

Distance: just under 6 miles

Terrain: quite undulating but with the only steepish hill the climb up from the Erewash Canal towards Awsworth. Over two-thirds of the route is **off-road**, on easily ridable firm-surfaced **bridleway** and **canal towpath**

Refreshment opportunities: the route appears to pass only two pubs – the Gardeners Inn at the crossroads on the outskirts of Awsworth, and the Bridge Inn where the route leaves the Erewash Canal towpath. The Broad Oak, Strelley, just under ¹/₂ mile on the Nottingham side of the starting point, also serves food.

Start: Strelley church (GR 506 421)

Ordnance Survey maps: Landranger sheet **129** Nottingham and Loughborough; Pathfinder sheet **812** Nottingham (North) and Ilkeston

Public transport links:

Other routes: Route **L6** links this route with Beeston town centre via Bramcote

8 miles • on- and off-road • hilly • Woodborough

5

The Woodborough rounds: taking the rough with the smooth

These two short circuits – one an all-weather version, the other with some fine-weather off-road sections – have one main attraction: the views across the tumbling hills just to the north-east of the city. The intricate interlocking of the spurs of the hill and the changing light and colour make this a pleasant diversion well worth a visit at any season. This is by no means the highest part of the county but four of Nottinghamshire's very few steeper-than-1-in-7 hills, marked on the OS map by a black arrow, are on these roads. The on-road version of the route touches the large mining village of Calverton, which can boast a still-working pit. However, industry has been here even longer: at the foot of Bonner Hill is a run of restored frame-knitters' cottages, with their characteristic long windows to let in the light the workers needed in those pre-electricity days.

The rough – or fair-weather – version: Leave **Woodborough** westwards towards Calverton on Foxwood Lane, signed *Calverton*. This climbs away from the village and at the crest of the hill, just after Foxwood Lodge and just before the road drops steeply into Calverton, turn left onto a public bridleway signed to *George's Hill and Arnold*. Follow this rather variably-surfaced bridleway for about 1¹/₂ miles until you reach a tarred road at a bend in the road. Turn left on the road from the bridleway to climb gently to a crossroads junction with B684 at **Dorket Head**; turn left on B684, signed *Mapperley 3*. Continue for about 1¹/₂ miles, ignoring the first

turning on the left to Woodborough but taking the second, Catfoot Lane, just after the Traveller's Rest, signed *Lambley*. (About 200yds further along the B684 is a teashop at Brookfields Garden Centre, Mapperley Plains.) Follow Catfoot Lane for about 2 miles gently downhill through a pleasant valley, becoming steeper at the end into Lambley. At the T-junction by the Nags Head in **Lambley** turn left, signed *Lowdham*. After about 500yds, just after

41

5
continued

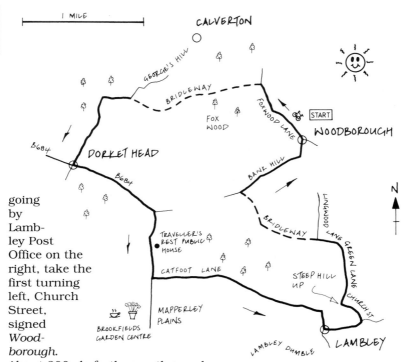

going
by
Lamb-
ley Post
Office on the
right, take the
first turning
left, Church
Street,
signed
*Wood-
borough.*

About 300yds farther on the road bears round to the right and begins to go steeply uphill, becoming Green Lane. After about $3/4$ mile, the road becomes Lingwood Lane and bears round to the right to go steeply downhill into Woodborough. ***Do not go down the hill*** but continue straight ahead on a wide unsurfaced track, a bridleway with a weathered and unreadable finger post. After about 100 yds go round a metal gate, then after about $3/4$ mile, just after the hedge on the right of the track stops, and just before a seemingly rather purposeless five-barred gate into an unhedged field, also on the right, there is a sign on the left reading 'Private road ahead: turn right for bridleway'. The bridleway runs between hedges and is signed with a blue bridleway arrow. After about 450yds it emerges onto a tarred road. This is Bank Hill (not signed at this point); turn right downhill into **Woodborough**.

Helping to create the
GREENWOOD

COMMUNITY
F O R E S T

The smooth all-road version: Leave **Woodborough** westwards towards Calverton on Foxwood Lane, signed *Calverton*. This climbs away from the village and then drops steeply down Bonner Hill to its T-junction with Bonner Lane, **Calverton.** Turn left along Bonner Lane, which becomes Main Street and after about ³/₄ mile, opposite Martin's Garage, turn left into George's Lane, signed *Arnold 3*, to

Morning mist at Dorket Head

go up George's Hill. This is quite a tough climb for the first part but with the reward of fine views to the left . The upper part of the climb is more gentle and brings you to a crossroads junction with B684 at **Dorket Head**; turn left on B684, signed *Mapperley 3*. Continue for about 1¹/₂ miles, ignoring the first turning on the left

to Woodborough but taking the second, Catfoot Lane,

just after the Traveller's Rest, signed *Lambley.* (About 200yds further along the B684 is a teashop at Brookfields Garden Centre,

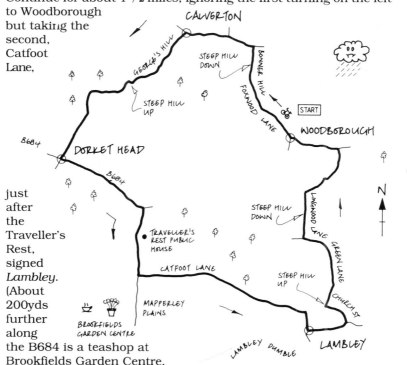

5

continued

Distance: 8 miles for the ***bridleway*** version; about a mile longer for the ***all-road alternative***

Terrain: decidedly hilly – but rewarded by fine views. The mix on the bridleway version is about 1½ miles of **B-road**, which can be quite busy at times on weekdays, 4 miles of **minor road** and 2½ miles of **bridleway**. The bridleway surfaces are reasonable for most of the time but with a definite tendency to muddiness in wet weather. They would be best tackled on a mountain-bike or by experienced riders on touring bikes – definitely not for smooth, narrow racing tyres. Despite the short distance, we wouldn't recommend the bridleway route for absolute beginners. However, we checked it when it was frozen hard and it was fine!

Refreshment opportunities: Brookfields Garden Centre, Mapperley Plains.

Start: At the western end of Woodborough (GR 624 478). You could also start from Lambley or Dorket Head.

Ordnance Survey maps: Landranger sheet **129** Nottingham and Loughborough.

Public transport links:

Other routes: Route **30**, Daybrook to Southwell uses some of the same roads near Dorket Head and between Woodborough and Arnold. The westernmost point of route **20**, Lambley and Lowdham, lies only about 200yds east of this route in Lambley village.

Mapperley Plains.) Follow Catfoot Lane for about 2 miles gently downhill through a pleasant valley, becoming steeper at the end into Lambley. At the T-junction by the Nags Head in **Lambley** turn left, signed *Lowdham*. After about 500yds, just after passing Lambley Post Office on the right, take the first turning left, Church Street, signed *Woodborough*. About 300yds farther on the road bears round the right and begins to go steeply uphill, becoming Green Lane. After about ³/₄ mile, the road becomes Lingwood Lane and bears round to the right to go steeply downhill into **Woodborough**. Turn left by the church on Main Street to complete the circuit.

6

9 miles • on- and off-road • almost flat • Nottingham Station

Colwick Country Park

This short route lies entirely within the boundaries of the City of Nottingham and uses sections of marked cycle route to reach out to one of the city's fine green spaces: Colwick Country Park, an area of lakes between the heights of Sneinton and the River Trent.

From **Nottingham Midland Station** turn left, signed as *cycle route to Trent Bridge and West Bridgford*, and keep in left-hand traffic lane. At traffic lights, go straight ahead on Arkwright Street, passing between Barclays Bank and the Queens Hotel, signed as *no through road except cycles*. After about 100yds at a crossroads with traffic lights, go straight ahead and bear almost immediately right on a pedestrian and cycle route underpass below a road and straight on

6
continued

up the other side. In about a further 100yds you reach the Bridgeway Shopping Centre, passing between houses. Turn left following *cycle route sign to Trent Bridge and West Bridgford* passing Bridgeway Hall Methodist Mission on the left. Turn right, still following *cycle route sign to Trent Bridge and West Bridgford*; there is also a red and blue metal fingerpost signed *Meadows Housing Centre and St Xavier's Church*. This is Arkwright Walk (not named at this point), a heavily traffic-calmed area. Continue to the end of Arkwright Walk, continue straight on on a 'normal' road and just before this road bears round to the left, where Radcliffe Street turns right, bear right at a shallower angle to follow a *cycle track sign* for *Trent Bridge Embankment*. At end of the short stretch of cycle tracks at a complex junction, use the double light-controlled pelican crossing to cross Bathley Street (named only on a wall behind you). Turn immediately left, using another pelican crossing to cross the dual-carriageway, and use short sections of cycle route and traffic lights to cross a second dual-carriageway into Meadow Lane, following blue *cycle route sign* to *Colwick*. Pass Notts County football ground to the left and at a T-junction go right, effectively straight on, still on Meadow Lane, following *brown tourist route signs* for *Colwick Park and Nottingham Racecourse*. After about 400yds, just before a light-controlled junction (part of a large roundabout), some more *cycle route signs* appear: follow them using a shared-use path. After about 20yds, blue *cycle route signs* marked *all routes* direct you to the central island of the roundabout. This manoeuvre allows you to cross to the far side of busy Manvers Street.

Turn left on the shared-use pedestrian and cycle path on the far, east, side to go over a railway bridge. Just before the light-controlled junction, bear right (unsigned), almost a U-turn, through a wooden entrance gateway to join a gravel path, the start of the Gedling Greenway. Follow this path which bears round to the left to follow the railway line. After about $^1/_2$ mile, the path goes down a gentle slope, and at the foot go right through a pair of swing gates to cross the railway line at a pedestrian-and-cyclist level crossing (again no signs). Immediately after crossing the railway, turn left on another path, this time keeping the railway on

6 continued

your left. After about ¹/₂ mile this path emerges onto Racecourse Road, by a roundabout junction with Daleside Road. On the right is the entrance to Colwick Park. Follow *cycle path markings* to cross Daleside Road into **Colwick Park**.

Pass the entrance to the racecourse and the park-and-ride site; do not turn into these but continue straight ahead. Follow this access road as it bears round to the left, following the curve of the racecourse; the River Trent appears to the right. Just before the road approaches a church tower, a distinct path, fenced on one side but unsigned at this point, bears off to the right, following the line of the river. After a short distance at a T-junction of paths just before a children's playground, bear right to continue to follow the river. Go through two wooden five-barred gates to approach a large lake. The path splits to go either side of the lake. Take the right-hand branch, keeping the lake to the left and the river to the right. The Holme Pierrepont water sports centre is on the opposite side of the river at this point.

At the far side of the lake the path splits again, and once again take the right-hand option to follow the river. This path shortly also bears round to the left, leaving the river and passing a marina on the right. About 50yds after the bend, the path joins a tarred road. Turn right on the road, still with the marina to the right. Another lake, Colwick Lake, appears to the left. Continue on this traffic-calmed road round the lake. Shortly after an information hut on the left, the tarred road bears sharp right to leave the park. Continue straight on past a five-barred gate along a cinder path round the lake, with the lake still on the left.

When you reach the head of the lake, the path you are on bears quite sharply off to the left and two cinder tracks go off to the right. Take the *first* of these cinder tracks to reach a second lake, which you keep to your left. At the head of this second lake, you join a section of path that you used earlier, this time with the River Trent on your left. At the children's playground, turn left to retrace your

6

continued

incoming route out of Colwick Park. At the roundabout junction on Daleside Road, go straight across into Racecourse Road.

From here it is possible *either* to retrace your outgoing route via the Greenway path, *or* take an alternative road route. To follow this alternative, continue on Racecourse Road, which soon bears round to the left to become Colwick Road, and go over a level crossing. At a light-controlled junction go straight on into Sneinton Hermitage and on to another light-controlled junction with Manvers Street. This junction has an advance stop-line for cyclists. Go straight on on an unnamed road marked *Site of Nottingham City Challenge Lenton Railway Land Development*. Pass either through the gate which is closed at 5.30pm, or beside it at other times, past a rather derelict warehouse marked Nottingham Antiques Centre, past beside another metal gate and continue straight on past more dilapidated buildings and a disused station. Opposite the entrance to the old station, bear right through an entrance and then left opposite Sam Fay's Barn Restaurant to cross the canal into Great Northern Close. At a light-controlled crossroads go straight on into Station Street. Follow Station Street to its T-junction with Carrington Street, then turn left to **Nottingham Midland Station**.

Distance: about 9 miles

Terrain: a mix of **minor roads**, shared-use **cycle**-and-pedestrian **path**, some tarred, some crushed stone and **park roads and tracks** – but all suitable for any type of bike. The route is virtually flat.

Refreshment opportunities: Cosy Teapot Café, Carrington Street (about 150yds north of Midland Station)

Start: Nottingham Midland Station (GR 574 393)

Ordnance Survey maps: Landranger sheet **129** Nottingham and Loughborough

Public transport links: Midland Main Line, Robin Hood Line and Regional Railways services go to Nottingham Midland Station

Other routes: Routes **10**, City Canals and Castles; **32**, Sutton Bonnington; **33**, Villages beginning with W; **36**, Grantham Canal; and **40**, Newark to Nottingham, all start or finish at Nottingham Midland Station. Link route **L5** joins this route to routes **4**, Attenborough Nature Reserve, and **L6**, Beeston to Strelley

7

6½ to 9 miles • off-road • gently rolling • Sherwood Pines

Sherwood Pines Forest Park

Sherwood Pines Forest Park – Clipstone Forest – is the largest single tract of woodland open to the public in the East Midlands and is very popular with visitors, particularly at weekends. There is a wide variety of trees, although much of the area is planted with conifers, and a range of wildlife. The main attraction for cycling, particularly for beginners, is that there are about 12 to 15 miles of firm-surfaced but untarred traffic-free tracks with mostly gentle gradients. Cycling in a forest gives a tremendously exhilarating feel of adventure, an impression of being in far wilder country that you actually are, even though you are only a few miles from the centres of Nottingham and Mansfield.

You may cycle on any of the firm-surfaced tracks in the Forest but not on waymarked walking paths. There is also a general mountain-bike play area at the south-west corner of the Forest. In any working forest, tracks may be closed temporarily for timber operations: see the noticeboards on the official cycle route and in the Sherwood Pines Forest Park 'Cycling in the Forest' leaflet available from Forest Enterprise, Edwinstowe, Mansfield, Notts NG21 9JL; tel (01623) 822447 and Tourist Information Centres. The route suggested here

incorporates part of the waymarked cycle route and there is no difficulty in following its red markers. Nevertheless, forest roads can look very similar and it is possible to get lost if you go off the waymarked route. However, remember that the the waymarked cycle route is a big irregular-shaped loop quite near to the edge of the forest, so that if you continue straight on in any direction you will eventually see the reassuring red waymarker posts of the official cycle route once more.

Turn left out of **Eakring Road car park** to the road and follow the red cycle waymarkers left and then right past a green and yellow barrier onto a forest track; follow this over a slight hill for about 1 mile to a cross-tracks. Turn right to follow the waymarked route for about 1 mile to another green metal barrier by a cross-tracks with an information board marked 'Start of cycle route'. Turn left on the forest road and follow red cycle route signs on red posts as far as

the **Sherwood Pines Forest Park visitor centre** area. Here, ignore cycle waymarking and follow car park *Exit* signs until you reach a tarred road, where *Exit* is signed to right. Turn *left* on the tarred road to go past the Forest Office. At the end of the tarred road continue straight on past the barrier on a firm-surfaced sandy track, following the line of electric power line poles on the right. Ignore the first left-hand turn and continue straight on to rejoin the way-marked cycle route. Follow the route posts, ignoring all left-hand turns until you reach

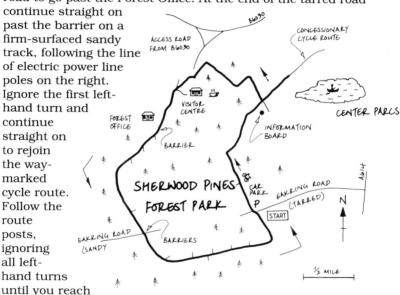

two yellow and green barriers, either side of a sandy road about 1¹/₂ miles after the Forest Office. Go straight across, following the cycle markers, for about 2 miles on a wide track which curves round to the left through an open area and then climbs gently into mixed woodland, then pine forest. At the end of the pine woodland, bear left for about 800yds and slightly downhill to a green metal barrier by **Eakring Road car park**.

If you are staying at **Center Parcs' Sherwood Holiday Village** it is possible to join the route part way round. Turn left out of the village down the slope and at the foot bear left on a firm-surfaced but untarred track – concessionary cycle way, signed *Robin Hood*

49

7

continued

Distance: about 6½ miles (or 9 including the link to and from Center Parcs' Sherwood Holiday Village)

Terrain: almost entirely **off-road on forest tracks**, with generally only slight gradients.

Refreshment opportunities: in summer, cold drinks and ices etc are available at the Sherwood Pines Forest Park visitor centre, where there are also toilets and a drinking water tap

Start: As described, the route starts at Eakring Road car park (GR 620 616). If you are on holiday there, it would also be possible to start from Center Parcs' Sherwood Holiday Village (GR 637 640) as described, or from the Visitor Centre (GR 612 642).

Ordnance Survey maps: Landranger sheet **120** Mansfield and Worksop; Pathfinder sheet **780**

Public transport links: by rail to Mansfield Woodhouse (Robin Hood Line), then follow route **23** (either outward or return legs as described) as far as Old Clipstone, then follow B6030 east for ½ or ¾ mile to the Sherwood Pines Forest Park Visitor Centre to join this circuit.

Other routes: Routes **18** and **25** give alternative 13- and 26-miles road routes east of Sherwood Pines. Route **L7** links the northern end of this route to Edwinstowe and Sherwood Forest, and so to route **23**.

Way – keeping Center Parcs perimeter fence on left. After 1¼ miles, there is a cross-tracks with an information board marked 'Start of cycle route'. Turn right and follow the route as described round as far as the Eakring Road car park and continue as far as the cross-tracks with the information board. Go straight on on the firm-surfaced concessionary cycle route back to **Center Parcs**. 🚲

8

9 miles · on-road · some hills · Southwell

Halam and Southwell

The pleasing little town of Southwell which figures on several of our routes is dominated by the Minster's twin grey square

spires, technically known as 'Rhenish caps'. The great Minster stands four-square right in the centre of the town and is the cathedral for the Diocese of Southwell, which covers most of Nottinghamshire and parts of the surrounding counties.

Southwell's other claim to fame is as the home of the Bramley cooking apple. Grown from pips by

two ladies of the town, it was commercialised by Henry Merryweather whose descendants still run a nursery and garden centre – complete with tea-room – to the west of the town. The centre also houses a display giving the history of this cook's favourite. In the town itself, down Church Street beyond the Minster, a pub called the Bramley Apple stands close to the spot where the original apple was grown.

There are many other delightful corners to Southwell, with

8 *continued*

one of the most refreshing being the wide open green of the Burgage. A 'burgage' was an area of freehold properties in an otherwise leased estate, and one of the Burgage's more celebrated residents was Lord Byron's mother. Southwell was, like many small east Midlands towns, once almost self-sufficient with its range of trades, crafts and products but now most are commemorated only in street and house names.

This route follows a short circuit round the town, visiting the attractive little village of Halam. The village's name comes from the Old English word '*halh*' meaning a hidden-away corner and, indeed, it is hidden away at the foot of its small valley. At one time it was famed for its orchards and was said to have been a sea of blossom in spring, and enough remnants are left to give a hint of what it must have been. The second part of the route swings south of Southwell giving some of the best views of Southwell's Minster.

From **Southwell Minster** car park, turn right on A612 opposite the Minster to the mini-roundabout by the Saracen's Head. Turn right into King Street, then almost immediately first left into Queen Street, and where Queen Street bears right, continue straight on on Halam Road, past Merryweather's garden centre (and tea shop). At the end of the garden centre grounds, take first right, Hopkiln Lane. After about 300yds, at T-junction, turn left into Kirklington Road, and at next T-junction after about 1/2 mile, again left, signed *Kirklington*. Follow this road for about 1 1/2 miles, still following signs to

Distance: 9 miles

Terrain: entirely **on-road**, undulating, quite hilly from Halam to Westhorpe

Refreshment opportunities: several teashops in Southwell, including the Minster Refectory; picnic area where the route crosses the Southwell Trail for the second time.

Start: Southwell Minster (car park opposite, off A612, Church Street) (GR 702 538)

Ordnance Survey maps: Landranger sheet **120** Mansfield and Worksop

Public transport links: The nearest rail station to Southwell is Fiskerton on the Nottingham to Newark Castle line, about 2 1/2 miles south-east of Southwell. Fiskerton is a request stop: trains stop there if you tell the conductor when you get on, or give a hand signal as the train approaches. Not all trains on this route will stop at Fiskerton.

Other routes: Route **22**, Blidworth and Halam, joins this one at Halam. Route **28**, Southwell Trail and the Dumbles, starts and finishes at Southwell. Route **30**, Daybrook and Southwell, gives a link to Nottingham and, at Fiskerton, by way of link route **L11** to Newark-on-Trent.

Kirklington.
Just after a
brick bridge

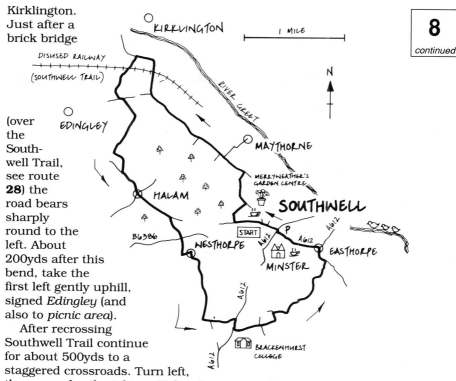

(over
the
South-
well Trail,
see route
28) the
road bears
sharply
round to the
left. About
200yds after this
bend, take the
first left gently uphill,
signed *Edingley* (and
also to *picnic area*).

After recrossing
Southwell Trail continue
for about 500yds to a
staggered crossroads. Turn left,
then very shortly right on Holme Lane, signed *Halam*. After about 1
mile at T-junction on the outskirts of Halam, turn left. At the next
crossroads, in **Halam**, continue straight up Halam Hill, signed
Southwell. Just over the crest of Halam Hill turn right into
Saversick Lane, otherwise unsignposted but opposite a bus stop
sign. At the next crossroads (*give way* sign), cross B6386 and
continue straight on downhill on an unsigned road, bearing left at
the bottom of the hill into **Westhorpe**. After about 200yds, turn
right into The Holme to leave the village and climb up Cundy Hill.
The road makes a right-angle bend to the left and about 200yds
beyond this go straight on at a T-junction where the slightly larger
of these two very minor roads goes right.

At the T-junction with the main road, A612, turn right, slightly
uphill, then after about 200yds, take the first turn left, signed
Brackenhurst College. After passing a playing-field on the left go
straight on (right then left) at the staggered crossroads. The road
bends sharp left and about 150yds later at a T-junction, turn right
(no signpost). The road winds round with some fine views across to
Southwell Minster on the left, eventually coming to a T-junction

8
continued

with Fiskerton Road, at which you learn that the road you have been on is Crink Lane. On the right is a wooden bench seat with the intriguing inscription 'This seat was donated by a cyclist'. Turn left; the road sweeps downhill to a T-junction with the A612, opposite the White Lion, turn left on A612, **Easthorpe**, past the Minster School and then **Southwell Minster** itself to complete the route. 🚲

9   10 miles • on- and off-road • undulating • Ram Inn, Eastwood

Beauvale to Bogend!

This figure-of-eight route makes use of tracks and country lanes north-east of the town of Eastwood – taking in woods, water (Moorgreen Reservoir) and Robin Hood's Well! The area is one of historical interest, with the remains of Beauvale Priory, the site of Edward III's castle, not to mention Eastwood's claim to fame as the birthplace of D H Lawrence.

Turn right out of the car park of the **Ram Inn**, along a road known as Beauvale. After approximately 300yds, just beyond Greasley Beauvale Infant School, turn right into Mill Road, which you follow

down a hill to its T-junction with Lower Beauvale. Turn right, then almost immediately left along a bridleway signed *Willey Lane*. Continue for about 1¹/₂ miles on this track, ignoring any minor paths which branch off, but following the blue arrows which indicate bridleway status. The track winds around one farm, and soon after passing a second, emerges onto a tarred road at a T-junction. Turn left and follow this – the B600, which becomes the A608 –

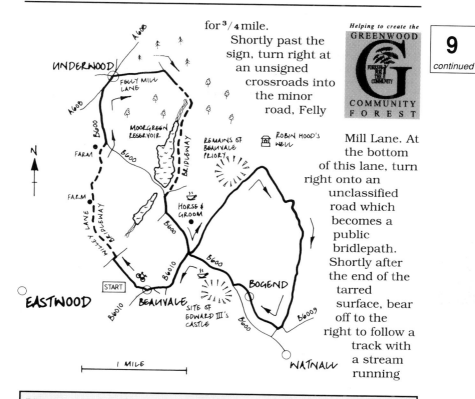

for ³/₄ mile.

Shortly past the sign, turn right at an unsigned crossroads into the minor road, Felly Mill Lane. At the bottom of this lane, turn right onto an unclassified road which becomes a public bridlepath. Shortly after the end of the tarred surface, bear off to the right to follow a track with a stream running

Distance: 10 miles

Terrain: About a third of this route is **off-road** – but on **bridleways** ridable all year round; the **on-road** sections are primarily on **B-roads**. It is fairly undulating so, with the looser surfaced off-road elements, both sturdy tyres and low gears are recommended.

Refreshment opportunities: The Horse and Groom at Moorgreen does food lunchtimes and evenings; and the route passes Minton's Tearooms.

Start: The Ram Inn, Beauvale (road), Eastwood (GR 481 471)

Ordnance Survey maps: Landranger sheets **120** Mansfield and Worksop and **129** Nottingham and Loughborough; Pathfinder sheets **795** Sutton in Ashfield and **812** Nottingham (North) and Ilkeston

Public transport links: Bogend is about 3¹/₂ miles west of Hucknall station on the Robin Hood Line. To reach the route, leave the station by the one-way system, turning left to the traffic lights by the Byron Entertainment Centre. Turn right into the High Street, then at the next traffic lights turn left on Watnall Road, B6009. Continue on this road, crossing the Hucknall bypass, A611, and the M1 to the junction with B600 at Bogend.

Other routes: The nearest of the other routes are **15** and **39** which pass through Hucknall (see 'Public transport links' above).

9
continued

along its right-hand side. Soon you will see bridleway signs for *Moorgreen*; follow the blue arrows through the woods, keeping Moorgreen Reservoir at some distance to your right. After about $^3/_4$ mile the bridleway emerges onto a tarred minor road; bear right and continue as far as the gatehouse. Turn left onto the B-road – itself known as Moorgreen – up the hill, and soon after the Horse and Groom, turn left signed *New Road leading to Narrow Road.* This virtually traffic-free lane goes past the remains of Beauvale Priory and Robin Hood's Well – hidden in the woods after about $1^1/_2$ miles.

Eventually the lane emerges at a T-junction; turn right and right again after about 50yds into Church Road – which runs parallel to the main road and takes you through the interestingly named **Bogend**! At the T-junction, the knoll on the opposite side of the main road is the site of Edward III's castle: go right and up the hill – with Minton's Tearooms on the left offering a welcome break. Opposite the same Horse and Groom, turn left down Moorgreen, B6010, signed *Newthorpe*, which leads back to the **Ram Inn**.

10

10 miles • on-road and cycle track • flattish • Nottingham Station

City Canals and Castles

Although this route is essentially an urban one – starting and finishing in Nottingham city centre, and not actually straying beyond the city boundary – it takes riders on an intricate tour through the more leafy south-west section of the built-up area. It takes in part of the Nottingham and Beeston Canal, which was opened up to cyclists by British Waterways in 1994, together with beautifully-kept Wollaton Park, which together give the route a deceptively rural feel. The route makes extensive use of the relatively comprehensive network of cycle routes in this part of the city, and finally heads back to the city centre by way of the Castle – where the Buttery cakes and view are worth a detour into the grounds. **Note** The majority of the 'signs' referred to in the directions below are the official white-on-blue cycle route signs.

With **Nottingham Midland Station** behind you, turn
right down Carrington Street. After a short way take
the ramp signed *Canal Towing Path* with a wheelchair symbol off to the left – opposite the Cosy Tea
Pot Café. Go straight on at the bottom along the
towpath of the *Nottingham and Beeston Canal*,
which you follow for nearly 2 miles. The path crosses
a number of small bridges, some with quite steep
inclines, and passes under a number of road bridges.

Eventually, the towpath goes under a very tall main road bridge
which carries the A52 Nottingham ring road, and it is at the second
smaller arched bridge after this that the route leaves the towpath
via a ramp off to the left. Bear right part way up the ramp to cross
the canal via the arched bridge and, on reaching a minor road,
turn left, signed *University (south)*. Take the first right, Cavendish
Street, and go straight on at the end under the low railway bridge,
following signs for University *(south entrance)*. Approximately
500yds beyond the railway bridge, opposite the Dunkirk Hotel,
turn left down a cycle path which runs between fenced gardens
and past Highfields Science Park. On emerging, go right and
straight over at the traffic lights, crossing the dual carriageway.
The University Arts Centre café, which is open to the public, is just
off the route to the right. Without entering the University grounds,
turn left onto the cycle track, and follow it for its entire length
along the northern side of University Boulevard.

At the end of University Boulevard, keep on the cycle track
which bears round to the right into Woodside Road, past the west
entrance to the University and straight on

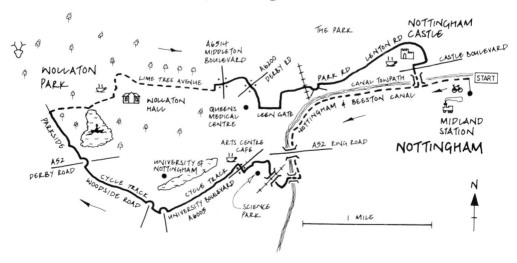

10
continued

On the canalside path near Nottingham station

following signs for *Wollaton*. The cycle track crosses numerous side-road turnings, but keep to the track, with the dual carriageway on your left. On reaching Priory roundabout – named after the nearby pub – cross Derby Road using the pedestrian crossing, then straight on into **Wollaton Vale**, continuing along the cycle track. Leave the track after a short distance, at the first right turn up Parkside. Soon after the top of the gentle climb, opposite Wollaton Rise, turn right through a pair of large brown gates into **Wollaton Park**. (Note that the Wollaton Park gates close at dusk.) Go through two more sets of gates, down a gently sloping well-defined path, then through a further wooden swing gate to emerge by a lake; turn left over a small bridge and straight on towards *Wollaton Hall*. Just beyond the Lakeside Café, follow the path which bears round to the left – skirting below **Wollaton Hall** while keeping the courtyard buildings on the left. At a 'crossroads' in the paths, marked by a telephone box, go right but ignore any further right-hand forks up to the Hall. This path leads down a gentle slope and along the aptly named 'Lime Tree Avenue' to where the route leaves the park beside the impressive main wrought-iron gates.

On reaching the A6514 dual carriageway, go left for a short distance along the shared cycle/pedestrian path, then cross the main road just before Sutton Passeys Crescent via the signalled crossings, and into Charnock Avenue. At the give-way markings bear right – although this is still Charnock Avenue – and right again at the end, between the bollards, to follow the cycle route signs for the *city centre*. Go straight over the signalled cycle crossing at the end of the shared-use path, into Hill Side, which continues as a cycle/pedestrian path behind the Queen's Medical Centre. Go left where the shared-use path meets a minor road,

Leen Gate, signed *City centre*, and left again at the T-junction opposite the White Hart. Take the second right into Church Street, bearing immediately right into Sherwin Road, passing under the railway bridge towards the far end of this quiet residential street.

Go right onto the cycle track just before Sherwin Road meets Castle Boulevard, but use the signalled cycle crossing to cross the latter after a short distance – just before Broadholme Street. Bear right to continue along the cycle track until it ends on the opposite side of the roundabout to the Grove pub. Turn left, signed for cyclists to the *city centre* and straight on at the 'dead end' with a cycle slip for *The Park*. Continue along Lenton Road, straight over at the small roundabout, to emerge from The Park residential area beside **Nottingham Castle** – there are public conveniences and The Buttery tea shop in the grounds. (Note that you can't take bikes into the Castle grounds – and that there's a charge to get into the grounds at weekends and bank holidays.)

Go right just beyond the Castle, down the cobbled street known as Castle Road, straight on at the 'no-entry' signs, where there is provision for cyclists to cut through, and down the hill signed *Canal Museum*. Just before the T-junction, turn right onto the cycle track, which meanders between trees for a short way before taking you across Castle Boulevard, via a signalled cycle crossing, signed *Lenton*. Turn right to continue along the cycle track at the far side and, just before an HSS Hire Shop, turn left up a path to cross the Nottingham and Beeston Canal via a wooden bridge. On reaching the towpath, turn right – now keeping the canal to your left – to retrace the first part of the route back to **Nottingham Midland Station**. 🚲

Distance: 10 miles

Terrain: A generally flat route, using some of the more scenic sections of the Nottingham **cycle route network**.

Refreshment opportunities: This route does not leave the City of Nottingham, so you are never very far from corner grocery shops and pubs. On the route itself there are four tea shops: Café Lautrec – at the University Arts Centre, the Lakeside Café in Wollaton Park and The Buttery in the grounds of Nottingham Castle, while the Cosy Teapot in Carrington Street is only about 150yds north of Nottingham Station.

Start: Nottingham Midland railway station (GR 574 393)

Ordnance Survey maps: Landranger sheet **129** Nottingham and Loughborough – though a street map such as the *A–Z Premier Nottingham* might be more useful.

Public transport links: Midland Main Line, Robin Hood Line and Regional Railways services go to Nottingham Midland Station

Other routes: Routes **9**, Colwick Country Park; **32**, Sutton Bonnington; **33**, Villages beginning with W; **36**, Grantham Canal; and **40**, Newark to Nottingham, all start or finish at Nottingham Midland Station. Link route **L5** joins this route to routes **4**, Attenborough Nature Reserve, and **L6**, Beeston to Strelley

11

10 miles · on- and off-road · gentle · Skegby

Pleasley and Teversal Trails

This route makes use of the track beds of disused rail lines that once served the long-since-closed local collieries and have now been turned into paths for cyclists and walkers. The tracks are generally well surfaced, but do tend to be dusty in dry weather and loose on the few short inclines. Much of the network of trails has been designated a Local Nature Reserve, containing a rich variety of plants and wild life. More information on what to look out for is available from the visitor centre – signed from various points along the route, tel (01623) 442021.

Teversal, towards the end of the route, is a surprisingly pretty village, with warm stone cottages surrounding a green open space. It is said to be the basis for the fictional home of D H Lawrence's Sir Clifford and Lady Chatterley, and the woodlands between the village and Hardwick Hall the inspiration for the setting of the book's most, er, notable happenings.

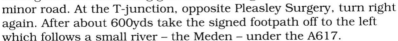

Head northward from **Skegby** trail car park along the **Teversal Trail**, and where it forks after about 400yds keep to the right-hand path. Stay on this path for a further 2 miles, crossing a couple of minor roads which involve short steep climbs and descents as the original railway bridge and tunnel have been removed. At the end of the Teversal Trail pass through a wooden kissing gate and turn right onto a minor road. At the T-junction, opposite Pleasley Surgery, turn right again. After about 600yds take the signed footpath off to the left which follows a small river – the Meden – under the A617.

Helping to create the
GREENWOOD

G

COMMUNITY FOREST

On the other side of the main road, turn left to join the **Meden Trail** keeping the river on your left. Just beyond a picnic table – a further 400yds – bear right up a fairly steep incline to join a disused railway line. Follow this track for some 1^1/$_2$ miles, until it emerges in a small car park. At the vehicle entrance to the car park, turn left into Common Lane (*the link L2 from Mansfield Woodhouse station joins her*e). Follow this minor road, which becomes

Outgang Lane, some 2 miles back through **Pleasley Vale**, past an imposing derelict mill.

Beyond Outgang Lane car park,

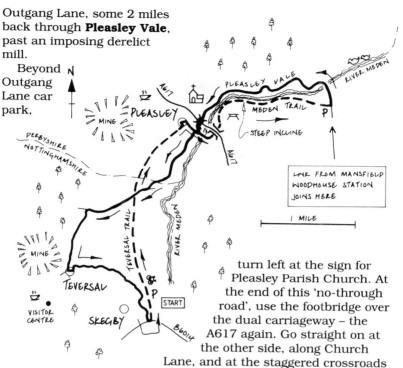

turn left at the sign for Pleasley Parish Church. At the end of this 'no-through road', use the footbridge over the dual carriageway – the A617 again. Go straight on at the other side, along Church Lane, and at the staggered crossroads 'jog-right-jog-left' into Newbound Mill Lane – signed for *Teversal* and *Skegby*. Continue along this lane – becoming Newbound Lane – for about 2¹/₂ miles, through to **Teversal**. In the village, turn left into Buttery Lane and back to **Skegby** car park. 🚲

Distance: 10 miles

Terrain: Half **off-road**, easy going with one or two steep pitches; remainder on **quite hilly minor roads**.

Refreshment opportunities: The Visitor Centre offers drinks and light snacks (open daily 11am-4pm); several pubs near the start/finish and in Pleasley – about half way along the route; bakery near the start/finish does hot and cold drinks and snacks.

Start: Teversal Trail – Skegby car park, Buttery Lane, off B6014 (GR 495 614)

Ordnance Survey maps: Landranger sheet **120** Mansfield and Worksop

Public transport links: Mansfield Woodhouse station on the Robin Hood Line (no Sunday service): see link route **L2**, Mansfield Woodhouse to Pleasley Vale,

Other routes: Route **19**, Ault Hucknall and Hardwick Hall, overlaps at Pleasley Vale and crosses again at Moorhaigh.

12 10 miles · mostly off-road · rolling · Worksop

Worksop and Thievesdale

This circuit makes extensive use of the mass of bridleways north of Worksop. These are mainly farm, park and estate roads with firm surfaces, easily ridable with any type of bike. There are one or two short stretches that are inclined to be a little loose and dusty or sandy in very dry weather. The countryside is a mixture of parkland, grazing and arable fields, with some surprisingly open views over the valley of the River Ryton to the east of Worksop.

From **Worksop** Town Hall in the corner of the Market Place, bear right at pedestrian lights into Popper Street, then at mini-roundabout turn left into Watson Road, signed *Tickhill 10 (A60)*. Continue straight on at the next two sets of traffic lights, then at the next set by McDonalds, turn right over the bridge, signed *A60, Tickhill*. At the traffic lights immediately after the bridge, get into the right-hand waiting lane then turn right into Eastgate, just in front of the King's Head. After about 600yds, at the Kilton Inn, Eastgate becomes Kilton Road.

Continue straight on to a mini-roundabout, and go straight on, still on Kilton Road. After about 500yds this bears round to the left under a railway bridge; immediately after the bridge, turn right onto a completely unnamed, unsigned minor road which starts by running close to the railway. After about ¹/₂ mile the tarred surface stops and the road continues as a firm-surfaced gravel track. In about a further 1¹/₂ miles the track crosses the grounds of Osberton Hall, which is a prominent white building to the right, visible across a small lake. The track emerges onto a tarred road,

which still only has bridleway status, with a *wooden three-way signpost* marking the junction of bridleways.

This is the hamlet of **Scofton**. Turn left on the tarred road, up a gentle slope; don't be put off by the 'No public vehicle access, no through road' notice at the next gate – it's all still a bridleway. After about ¹/₂ mile, the route comes to a former airfield runway, which is apparently used for testing – whether

Between Worksop and Scofton

aircraft or something else isn't obvious. Check that it is clear and cross to the gates on the other side. Immediately after the runway, turn left between a metal gate and a concrete plinth, to follow a firm-surfaced track which runs to the left of a fir plantation. After about 700yds the firm track bears round to the left by a notice warning *'Soft verges – no cars'* and some $^1/_2$ mile later reaches a T-junction of tracks (which is actually a 'crossroads' of bridleways – the one straight on just crosses a grassy meadow). Turn left up hill to a line of trees, and at the top of the hill follow the track round to the right between wooden fences to what appears to be a small pumping station, where the track jogs right and left.

About 700yds beyond this

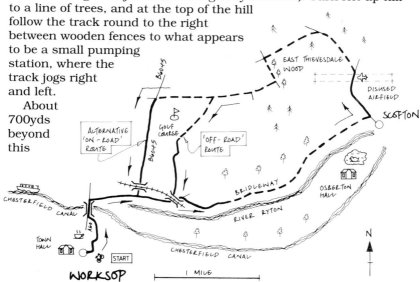

12
continued

point there is a crossing of tracks. The right-hand leg aligns with a radio mast, and to the left there is a misleading green, grassy track. A bridleway (unsigned) strikes off to the left at this point, in the angle between the green track and the track you are already on and about midway between the two. At the time we prospected this route, the field it crosses was newly ploughed and harrowed and only a couple of lines of footprints and a mountain-bike tyre imprint revealed its line. It is probable that at other seasons it is more obvious.

(If you **don't want to try the cross-country bridleway**, continue straight on to the junction with the B6045 at the exit to the Kilton Forest Golf Club, then left down hill on B6045 into Worksop, following signs for the town centre.)

The alternative bridleway carries on across open country, then across a golf course. Aim for three blocks of five-storey flats; the bridleway passes between the two left-hand blocks. At the edge of the golf course there are two wooden posts and the bridleway goes between these and then between some green metal railings to emerge onto Osberton View, a short dead-end road. At the head of Osberton View, turn left onto Browning Close (not signed at this point) to the T-junction with Coleridge Road (not signed at this point). At the next T-junction, turn left down Plantation Hill (also not signed at this point) past a pub called the Lord Byron. At the second road after the Lord Byron, turn left on Rayton Spur, signed *Bracebridge and Town Centre* and follow the road round under the railway bridge into Kilton Road. At the T-junction with the B6041 (not signed) turn right, then immediately left at the mini-roundabout, still on Kilton Road. This becomes Eastgate. At the traffic lights by the King's Head, turn left over the bridge, and left again at the next set of lights by McDonalds into Watson Road. Continue straight on at all traffic lights to the mini-roundabout junction with Popper Street, turn right, signed *Ollerton and Nottingham*, to return to **Worksop** Town Hall. 🚲

Distance: 10 miles

Terrain: a large proportion is **off-road** on untarred **farm and estate roads** which have the status of **bridleways**; they are for the most part firm-surfaced and easily ridable. The terrain rolls a little but there is only one appreciable short hill, towards the end of the bridleway section.

Refreshment opportunities: Worksop

Start: Worksop Town Hall (GR 584 786)

Ordnance Survey maps: Landranger sheet **120**, Mansfield and Worksop

Public transport links: Regional Railways services run from Sheffield, Retford and Gainsborough to Worksop. At the time of writing it was also intended that the Robin Hood Line should be extended as far as Worksop by 1998.

Other routes: Routes **14**, **17** and **21** also start from Worksop.

Above: Papplewick Pumping Station – stained-glass windows, polished brass, gleaming oiled steel and warm, rich woodwork make this an ornate Victorian temple to the gods of industry (see route 15).

Left: relics of an earlier industry – the long windows of former frame-knitters' cottages in Windles Square, Calverton (see routes 5 and 30)

Two Nottinghamshire skyscapes

Above: a misty winter morning from the road between Dorket Head and Calverton (see routes 5 and 30).

Right: One of Nottinghamshire's Trent valley power stations at dusk.

CIRCULAR ROUTES FROM 11 TO 20 MILES

A tour round Bingham

This short on-road circuit based on Bingham has some surprising delights. The little hamlet of Tithby is charming – and seems so remote that you wonder why the AA felt it necessary in the 1920s to put up one of its yellow circular signs, giving the distance to London! The next village, Cropwell Butler, is larger and perhaps a little self-consciously picturesque with its shaded green and old water pump preserved in the village centre. About three miles later you come out onto a tiny open hedgeless road that crosses a gentle rolling hill – in high summer, nothing to be seen but the corn and the sky – and then as it rolls over the brow reveals

In Cropwell Butler

one of the most attractive views in south Nottinghamshire, across the village of Shelford, nestled in a bend of the Trent.

From **Bingham** station go south on Station Street, then right along the edge of Market Place to Market Street. This becomes Fisher Lane and continues to T-junction with The Banks. Turn right to T-junction with Tithby Road, then left to A52. Cross the main road at a staggered crossroads, right and left, still on Tithby Road.

Head southwards and after about $1^{1}/2$ miles take the first right,

65

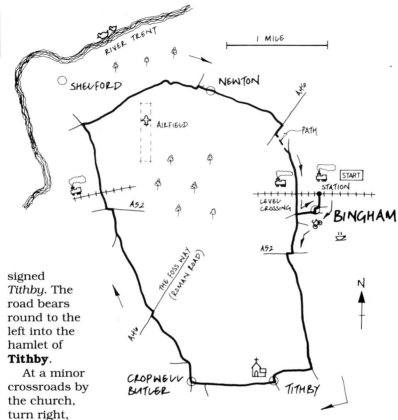

13
continued

signed
Tithby. The
road bears
round to the
left into the
hamlet of
Tithby.

At a minor
crossroads by
the church,
turn right,
signed *Cropwell Butler*. After 1 mile, turn
right at T-junction. (The sign at this junction, for *Radcliffe*, is
rather hidden, on the right-hand side of the road after you've gone
round the corner.) The road bears right through the centre of
Cropwell Butler: follow signs for *Bingham*. At the staggered
crossroads over the A46 go right then left — effectively straight on
— on an unsigned, unnamed minor road. After about 1 mile at

junction with the A52, go left, then almost
immediately right, signposted *Shelford*. Follow this
open unfenced road with its fine views over the Trent
valley for about 1 mile to a crossroads.

Turn right, signposted *Newton*, and continue
through **Newton** to the junction with the A46. Turn
right (care), or cross over to the footway on the
south-east side of the road, riding or walking as
appropriate for about 250yds, then turn left at a

footpath fingerboard just before a white house to join a blocked-off track. Follow this track which becomes tarred, to T-junction with minor road. Turn right (no signs) to go over the level crossing up a slight hill into **Bingham**, then left into Newgate Street, signed *library and health centre*. Just after the road bears round to the right, turn left along the edge of Market Square, then first left by two telephone boxes into Station Street; the station is at the end of this road. 🚲

Distance: 11 miles

Terrain: entirely **on-road**, gently rolling

Refreshment opportunities: Bingham

Start: Bingham station (GR 705 401)

Ordnance Survey maps: Landranger sheet **129** Nottingham and Loughborough

Public transport links: Regional Railways services to Bingham on the Nottingham-Grantham line (not all services on this line stop at Bingham)

Other routes: Route **31** is a longer (31-mile) version of this one; route **40**, Newark to Nottingham, meets this one at the crossroads above Shelford;

13
continued

---

11 miles • on- and off-road • moderate • Worksop Town Hall   **14**

Rhodesia and the Manor Hills

Note: do not confuse Worksop Manor South Lodge (this route and link L4) with Clumber Park South Lodge (route 27)

This route can be used either as a short circular trip south and west of Worksop, or as an alternative route (to route **17**) from Worksop to Clumber Park. Used with link route **L4** it can also be used to reach the Creswell Crags archaeological site. The forested section of the route includes some fine trackways through the western remnant of the once-continuous Sherwood Forest.

From **Worksop** Town Hall in the corner of the Market Place, bear right at pedestrian lights into Popper Street, then at mini-roundabout turn left into Watson Road, signed *Tickhill 10 (A60)*. Continue straight on at the next two sets of traffic lights, then

14
continued

at the next set by McDonald's, turn right over the bridge, signed *A60, Tickhill.* Keep in the left-hand lane, signed *The North, Sheffield.* After about 400 yds, turn left at a

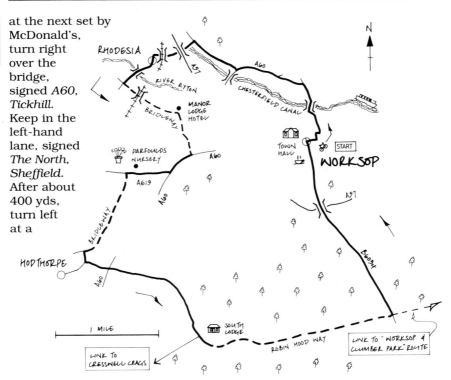

mini-roundabout into Sandy Lane, signed *Shireoaks.* At the next T-junction, opposite the football ground, turn left, still on Sandy Lane, and at the next mini-roundabout turn right, once more still on Sandy Lane, this time marked as *leading to Shireoaks Road,* with the Chesterfield Canal to the left. Take the first turning on the left after about 600yds, Tylden Road, signed *Rhodesia,* to pass almost immediately under the A57.

After **Rhodesia** village centre the road bears round to the right and under a railway bridge, then bends immediately round to the left. In about 600yds there is a bridge over a stream, the infant River Ryton, and immediately after that, turn left on an untarred track signed *Public bridleway Lodge Farm,* opposite a road signed to Shireoaks. Pass some farm buildings at the entrance to the bridleway, then go through a wooden gate beside a large metal swing gate and under a high railway arch. Go through the next metal gate after the bridge and continue on this firm-surfaced track. About ¹/₂ mile later pass round another white metal gate onto a minor tarred road opposite the Manor Lodge Hotel. Turn right (the surface improves) as far as the T-junction with the A60.

Turn right on the A60 for about 400yds, then turn right on A619, signed *Chesterfield*. *If you do not wish to ride on the A60 and A619, there is a footpath on the north side of the road which avoids the main roads and right turn*. About 500yds further on, just after Darfoulds Nursery on the right, turn left on a well-surfaced track which is a bridleway (unsigned), opposite a red pillar box. After about a mile the track passes between two farm buildings and then

bends sharply round to the left as far as a minor tarred road. Turn left for about 300yds to a crossroads with the A60. Go straight across on a minor road (unsigned) which winds gently for about 1¹/₂ miles up to the forest, eventually reaching Worksop Manor **South Lodge**. (*Link route L4 to Creswell Crags joins/leaves here.*) At the Lodge, go straight ahead following a bridleway fingerpost beside a metal fence. The path climbs quite steeply for a while, then becomes flat. The path is well-defined and marked with *bridleway posts, blue arrows and Robin Hood Way bow-and-arrow signs* – ignore all turnings to either side. After about 2 miles the track reaches the B6034.

Distance: 11¹/₂ miles if used as a circuit starting and finishing in Worksop; about 9¹/₂ miles if ridden from Worksop to its junction with route **17**.

Terrain: the first section is **relatively flat** but there is quite a stiff climb for a short distance from South Lodge on the Robin Hood Way into the forest. The **off-road** sections are firm-based and reasonably surfaced.

Refreshment opportunities: Worksop

Start: Worksop Town Hall (GR 584 786)

Ordnance Survey maps: Landranger sheet **120**, Mansfield and Worksop

Public transport links: Regional Railways services run from Sheffield, Retford and Gainsborough to Worksop. At the time of writing it was also intended that the Robin Hood Line should be extended as far as Worksop by 1998, with a possible station at Whitwell, near to the route at Hodthorpe.

Other routes: This route joins route **17**, Worksop and Clumber Park near Truman's Lodge. Routes **13** and **21** also start from Worksop. Link route **L4** joins Worksop Manor South Lodge to the Creswell Crags archaeological site, by way of Welbeck Park.

To return direct to Worksop, turn left on B6034 for about 1 mile, then turn left on an unclassified road where the B6034 swings right, signed *Worksop Town Centre*. Go down the hill, Sparken Hill; the road becomes Park Street, leading to **Worksop** Town Hall.

To continue to Clumber Park go straight across the B6034, signed as a bridleway. This emerges after some 500yds on a minor tarred road to join route **17**, Worksop and Clumber Park. Turn right for Clumber Park. 🚲

69

15 | **12 miles • on-road and cycle track • gentle • Hucknall station**

Hucknall, Newstead and Papplewick

This gentle circular route inevitably has strong Byron connections. Newstead Abbey became the home of the Byron family in 1539, although there had been an Augustinian priory on the site since the 12th century. The Byrons seemed always to be plagued by financial problems, and when the poet inherited the place and the title as the 6th Lord Byron only one room, the scullery, was habitable. Byron was fond of the place and brought more of it into use – living there, on and off, from 1809 to 1814. However, his lifestyle once more resulted in money problems and he was forced to sell it in 1817. He died in 1824 in exile in Greece, a country which still reveres him for his support of the cause of Greek independence. He is buried in the Byron family vault in Hucknall church.

Another landmark on the route is Papplewick Pumping Station, a prominent Victorian building whose tall chimney is visible for miles. Built around 1880 as one of several to supply water to the city of Nottingham, it contains a superb restored steam beam-engine, which worked the pumps, housed in an ornate temple to industry. It can be seen working at specified times, mainly on summer Sundays and Bank Holidays. It is actually about $2^1/2$ miles from Papplewick, at the time it was built the nearest identifiable village.

The little village of Papplewick sits around what is at times a rather busy crossroads, with some attractive runs of light stone-built cottages leading towards the imposing Papplewick Hall. Just west of the village centre lies Castle Mill Farm. In the 17th century Castle Mill was a large employer of child labour, with children being brought from as far as London to toil over the machines. Many died and are buried in Papplewick churchyard. What is now a pleasant small patch of wetland north of the road was the site of the dam impounding the waters of the River Leen to power the mill.

15
continued

From **Hucknall** station platform, turn left and follow the one-way route out via Baths Road to cross Station Road by the Station Hotel into Linby Road. After about ¹/₂ mile the road passes over a level crossing, then after another 700yds, just after a turn (unsigned) for Linby village on right, join the signed cycle/pedestrian path on the right which brings you to the B6011, just east of a roundabout. Cross the B6011, onto the cycle path following blue cycle route signs to *Newstead*, passing a wooden barrier. Just beyond a

Helping to create the
GREENWOOD
G
COMMUNITY
FOREST

second wooden access control barrier after about a mile continue straight ahead and in¹/₂ mile or so the path bears round to the right between two wooden fences to join a tarred road.

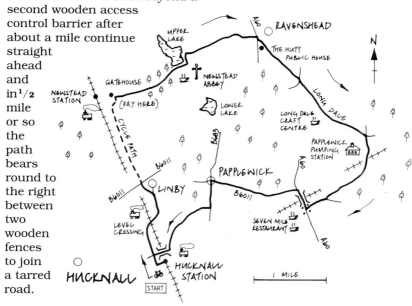

71

15
continued

Distance: 12 miles

Terrain: mostly **on-road** but making use of the **cycle track** from Linby to Newstead. Nearly all gradients are gentle, with the exception of the climb from Newstead Abbey to the east gatehouse opposite The Hutt.

Refreshment opportunities: there is a tea shop at Newstead Abbey and another at the Longdale Craft Centre, and two restaurants, Seven Mile House and the Seven Mile Beefeater, at the Seven Mile traffic lights on the A60. There are also cafés in Hucknall.

Start: Hucknall Station (GR 540 493). Alternatively you could start at Newstead station (GR 522 528), following the cycle route signs for Newstead Abbey to join the circuit, or start at Newstead and finish at Hucknall, to give a total of about 9 miles.

Ordnance Survey maps: Landranger sheets **120** Mansfield and Worksop, **129** Nottingham and Loughborough; Pathfinder sheets **795** Sutton in Ashfield, **812** Nottingham (North) and Ilkeston.

Public transport links: Robin Hood Line from Nottingham, Bulwell, Sutton Parkway, Mansfield, Mansfield Woodhouse to Hucknall or Newstead stations (no Sunday service)

Other routes: Route **39**, Leen Valley Path, follows the same line as this one from Hucknall station to near Newstead station. Route 39 also gives a link (just over 1 mile) to route **2**, Bestwood Country Park.

Turn right on this road past the gatehouse into Newstead Abbey grounds (*note: there is a charge to enter the Abbey grounds*). Go straight ahead along a tree-lined avenue for $1/2$ mile or so, then between the stone pillars of another gateway. Continue straight on, up a slope and then down to some lakes, with a waterfall on the left; the remains of **Newstead Abbey** (and the far-from-ruined tea shop) are on the right. The road sweeps round to the left, then right, with traffic-calming humps, then climbs between rhododendrons to the east gateway where the route leaves the Abbey grounds. Keep left at the small grassed triangle after the park gates to the main road, A60.

Go straight over the A60 into Longdale Lane, which bears round to the right. After about $2 1/2$ miles turn right at a minor crossroads, signed *Papplewick Pumping Station*. Pass this Victorian **pumping station** on your right and follow the road for about 1 mile to a T-junction. Turn right (unsigned) to traffic lights at the A60 junction opposite the Seven-Mile Restaurant. Turn right on A60, signed *Mansfield*, over the railway bridge, then first left into Forest Lane, B6011, signed *Hucknall*. Continue for about $1 1/2$ miles to **Papplewick**, then left at the Griffin's Head on B683, signed *Hucknall*. After about 500yds, turn right into Papplewick Lane, signed *Hucknall*. After about 1 mile turn right at a mini-roundabout just before the railway bridge into Station Road. Continue over the railway bridge, then right just after the bridge into Linby Road, and immediately right again into Station Terrace in front of the Station Hotel, following signs for *station* to complete circuit at **Hucknall** station. 🚲

12 miles · on- and off-road · flat · Retford

16

Retford wetlands

Just as in the south of the county – at Attenborough beside the River Trent on route **1** – gravel extraction beside the River Idle, north of Retford has left an array of lakes in the flat landscape. This route goes round them on a mixture of mostly minor roads and gravel tracks – though the first couple of miles follow in the hoofmarks of characters such as Dick Turpin: along the old Great North Road, the old coaching route between London, York and Edinburgh. Now the broad road is relatively quiet, with today's traffic hurtling along a mile or two to the west on the tarmac wastelands of the near-motorway A1.

Just under half-way round, on the first section of gravel track, the route passes the Wetlands Waterfowl Reserve, which now offers a habitat for many varieties of waterfowl in a series of lagoons created from the old gravel workings. There are nature trails and hides from which the birds can be seen. There is a charge for admission – and also a teashop (which you don't have to pay to get to).

The River Idle, beside which an optional section of the route runs, begins only four or five miles south of Retford, where the Rivers Maun and Meden that feature on several of the other routes come together and lose their names. As in all really flat landscapes, the sky dominates the scene and this area is a great place to be on a breezy showery day with tall cumulus clouds sweeping across the sky.

Leave **Retford** Market Square at the northern end, turning left at the mini-roundabout by the White Hart into Bridge-gate to cross the River Idle. At the next roundabout take the second exit, signed *Bawtry A638* and *Ranskill*; this is the old Great North Road, the original coaching route from London to York and Edinburgh. After about 1¹/2 miles, just before the main road begins to climb to a railway bridge, fork right at an oblique crossroads onto a minor road, Sutton Lane, signed *Sutton* and *Wetlands Wildfowl Reserve*. Follow

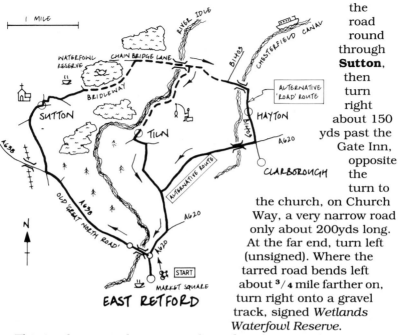

16
continued

EAST RETFORD

the road round through **Sutton**, then turn right about 150 yds past the Gate Inn, opposite the turn to the church, on Church Way, a very narrow road only about 200yds long. At the far end, turn left (unsigned). Where the tarred road bends left about $3/4$ mile farther on, turn right onto a gravel track, signed *Wetlands Waterfowl Reserve*.

This track passes the reserve, then after about a mile, just past Sutton Grange Farm, there is a junction of tracks. Turn right (this is Chain Bridge Lane, unsigned at this point). Just under a mile later, the track crosses the River Idle by a rather prosaic bridge, presumably replacing the original Chain Bridge. Just beyond the bridge, a firm sandy track on the right follows the river bank: it is signed *'Private fishing'* but appears to be in common use as a footpath and bridleway, although we have to emphasise that its status is not clear. After about $1/2$ mile there is a gateway marking the limit of the private fishing and vehicle access, and after about a further $3/4$ mile the track reaches a gate, marking the limit of vehicle access, onto a tarred road at **Tiln** Farm. From here, follow this road for about 1 mile until it joins a larger road on a bend.

Alternative road route from Chain Bridge to this point: continue straight on along Chain Bridge Lane, which now becomes a firm earthy track passing between wide, open fields. After about $3/4$ mile, this reaches the B1403 at a very sharp bend in the B-road. Continue straight on on B1403 to cross the Chesterfield Canal by the Boat Inn. Follow the B1403 round to the right through the long village of **Hayton**. Just before the give way sign at the approach to the A620 crossroads, opposite Corner Farm, turn right on Smeath

Lane (not otherwise signed at this point).

At the junction with the lane from Tiln, turn left, signed *Retford Market Place 1*. This soon enters the built-up outskirts of Retford and after about ³/₄ mile joins the A620, Moorgate. Turn right downhill, turn left at the traffic lights at the foot of the hill onto Arlington Way, then right at the next set of lights into Chapelgate to return via the short pedestrianised section to **Retford** Market Place. 🚲

> **Distance**: 12 miles following the road version through Hayton; 10 miles following the River Idle bank to Tiln.
>
> **Terrain**: virtually flat; **minor roads** with the **off-road** sections **firm-surfaced tracks**.
>
> **Refreshment opportunities**: there is a tearoom at the Wetlands Waterfowl Reserve.
>
> **Start**: Market Square, Retford (GR 704 811)
>
> **Ordnance Survey maps**: Landranger sheet **120,** Mansfield and Worksop
>
> **Public transport links**: East Coast Main Line trains (well, some of them) stop at Retford, and the Regional Railways service from Sheffield to Lincoln via Worksop and Gainsborough calls at the lower station at Retford.
>
> **Other routes:** Routes **24** and **29,** and the longest one in the book, **37,** also start from Retford and use some of the same roads .

16
continued

---

12 miles • mostly on-road • gentle • Worksop

17

Worksop and Clumber Park

Worksop lies at the heart of what has come to be known as the Dukeries. Two centuries and more ago, wealthy titled families created their parklands out of the rapidly-shrinking Sherwood Forest: Clumber Park was the domain of the Dukes of Newcastle, Welbeck Abbey the family home of the Dukes of Portland, Thoresby of the Dukes of Kingston, while Worksop Manor was owned by the Dukes of Norfolk. (And when you consider that Chatsworth over the border in Derbyshire is the seat of the Dukes of *Devonshire* you begin to despair of the ducal mapreading!) The result is that the natural landscape is enhanced by great houses, fine parks and enlarged or artificial lakes. The 3800 acres of the largest of the parks, Clumber, is now without its

17
continued

great house but safe in the hands of the National Trust, under whom it is open to the public. There is a fine network of tarred and untarred roads and paths in the parks – and, best of all, cyclists can go anywhere free, while car-drivers have to pay. We suggest a pleasant route to, from and round the park, but there is plenty of scope for other rides in this mixture of heath, open space and fine woodland, including some spectacular avenues.

From **Worksop** Town Hall, go south on Park Street. This becomes Sparken Hill, which crosses the A57 by an overbridge and climbs quite steeply through woodland to a T-junction with the B6034. Turn right on B6034 for just over $1/2$ mile, then fork left onto an unclassified road signed *Clumber Park* with a brown National Trust sign. After $3/4$ mile this reaches **Truman's Lodge**, the entrance to the Park. (*The short bridleway link from route* **14** *Rhodesia and Manor Hills, joins here.*) Just after a road forks to the left, go straight ahead on a tarred road through a stone arch into the Park. Continue gently downhill for about 1 mile to a crossroads, marked with a *'Give way'* sign. Go straight across, continuing downhill. At the foot of the hill, the road bears round to the left, signed *Car park, cycle hire and chapel.* (To visit the **Clumber Park** shop, restaurant and toilets, go straight ahead on a firm-surfaced track.)

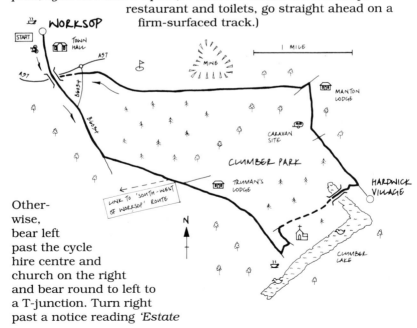

Other-
wise,
bear left
past the cycle
hire centre and
church on the right
and bear round to left to
a T-junction. Turn right
past a notice reading *'Estate*

The Victorian Gothic chapel at Clumber

Office only – no access for other vehicles'; this refers specifically to
motor vehicles. Leaving the garden tools and vineries exhibition on
the right continue to pass a vehicle barrier. Shortly afterwards the
tarred surface changes to a firm-surfaced but untarred track.
Continue straight on, ignoring crossing tracks and passing
occasional wooden barriers downhill to cross the lake by a
causeway to a tarred road. Turn right uphill to a T-junction, with
Hardwick Village to the right. Turn left (unsigned) for just over ³/₄
mile to a crossroads. Go straight across, signed *Clumber Park
Caravan Site*, ignore the turning to the caravan site and continue
to a barrier and through the white wooden gates by Manton Lodge,
the northernmost entrance to Clumber Park.

Immediately after passing through the gates, turn left on a
minor road, then after about 150yds fork right (unsigned) on a
minor road for about 2¹/₂ miles to a T-junction with the B6034, just
south of a roundabout junction with the A57. Go straight over the
B6034 (well, slightly left-and right) between concrete bollards next

17
continued

Distance: 12 miles

Terrain: **mostly on-road**, with some **stone-surfaced track** in Clumber Park; mostly gently rolling, although there's quite a determined hill to be conquered right at the start as you leave the centre of Worksop.

Refreshment opportunities: Worksop and Clumber

Start: Worksop Town Hall (GR 584 786)

Ordnance Survey maps: Landranger sheet **120**, Mansfield and Worksop

Public transport links: Regional Railways services run from Sheffield, Retford and Gainsborough to Worksop. At the time of writing it was also intended that the Robin Hood Line should be extended as far as Worksop by 1998.

Other routes: This route is joined by route **14**, Rhodesia and Manor Hills near Truman's Lodge, and joins route **27**, Clumber Park and Meden Vale in Clumber Park, route **38**, Hardwick and Ollerton in Hardwick village, and link route **L8**, Clumber and Walesby in Clumber Park. Routes **12** and **21** also start and finish in Worksop.

to the speed limit derestriction sign onto a bridleway (unsigned). Continue straight ahead for about 300yds to a tarred road. This is the foot of Sparken Hill; turn-right to cross the A57 by the overbridge to Park Street and **Worksop** Town Hall in the Market Place. 🚲

---

18. 13 miles · forest track and on-road · rolling · Sherwood Pines

Wellow and Rufford from Sherwood Pines Forest Park

This route – and the longer version, route **25** – reach out into the pleasant and remarkably quiet rolling farmlands to the east of Clipstone Forest. The first village on the route, Eakring, was at one time, particularly during the 1939-1945 war years, the unlikely centre of the British oil industry; even up to the 1960s

the 'nodding donkey' pumps, scattered around the fields and nodding into action when the oil level was high enough, were a feature of the surrounding countryside. One is preserved as a memorial in Duke's Wood above Eakring, while you can see two still working near Bothamsall (on route **38** and link route **L8**).

Eakring is also the village to which the

Reverend William Mompesson moved from Eyam in Derbyshire in 1670. Five years earlier Mompesson had been the hero of the plague-stricken village of Eyam, closing it off from the outside world and preventing the spread of the disease. Because of Eakring villagers' fear of the plague, then only four years in the past, he had to preach in the open air for the first few years of his ministry here, at a spot now marked by a monument which is signed from the village.

18

continued

A 'nodding donkey' at work

The next village on the route, Wellow, is one of only three in England to have a permanent traditional maypole on the village green – though the tubular steel of the current 55ft mast is hardly the traditional material! The May Queen is still crowned and children dance their intricate interweaving steps round the pole at the Spring Bank Holiday at the end of May.

The route returns through Rufford. Rufford Country Park is based on the grounds of the ruined Rufford Abbey, part wild with lakes and woodland, part lawn and formal garden. The coach-house in the grounds near the Abbey ruins now houses a craft centre, a café and restaurant. Although Rufford lies in the area of the 'Dukeries', it was however really a step down the league table, being owned not by a Duke but a mere Marquess.

Turn left and right out of **Eakring Road car park** eastwards along Eakring Road for about 1¹/₂ miles to the A614. Cross the A614, and continue straight on, signed *Eakring 2¹/₄*. After climbing a longish hill, this road becomes Bilsthorpe Road, **Eakring**, where you turn left at the Savile Arms, into Wellow Road, signed *Wellow*, for about 2¹/₂ miles. In **Wellow**, at the T-junction at the far end of the green, turn left on the A616; follow the main road as it swings round left and right, then after about 500yds turn first left on a minor road, signed *Rufford*. Follow this road for about 1¹/₂ miles, then down the hill to **Rufford** and through the ford (there is a footbridge). After about 200yds turn left, signed *Rufford Mill and Country Park*, into the car park area.

Keep round to the left of the car park to join a path by the **Rufford Country Park** noticeboard. Cycling isn't permitted in the Park, so you'll have to walk the next 800yds or so as far as the Old

18
continued

Coach House. Bear right on the lakeside path, with the lake on the left, and at a junction of paths, bear right, signed *Rufford Abbey*. The path follows the fence

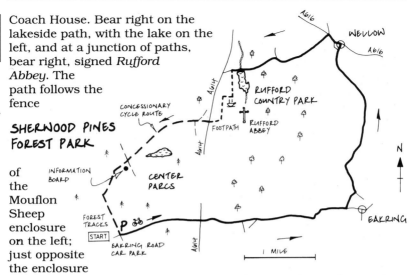

SHERWOOD PINES FOREST PARK

of the Mouflon Sheep enclosure on the left; just opposite the enclosure information board, turn right up a path between lines of trained trees, then follow it round to the left (ramp beside steps) towards Rufford Abbey. Continue between the shaped yew trees onto a tarred path. The second – and more modern – building on the left is the Old Coach House craft centre and tearooms.

To leave Rufford Park continue straight on across the access road to a small wooden gate in the brick wall. Go through the gate onto a gravel road (you can start riding again though the loose gravel makes it tricky!), bear right at the end of this on a concrete-surfaced road, then take the first left opposite Rufford Parish Council noticeboard for about 200yds. Shortly after a tennis court on the right, turn right and follow the road, signed *Robin Hood Way,* past a metal barrier, to the T-junction with A614. Go straight over on the old road (now bridleway, signed *Road closed*) for about 300yds to a set of metal gates. Go through the gap to the right of the gates and cross the tarred road which leads to Center Parcs Sherwood Holiday Village onto a firm-surfaced but untarred track – concessionary cycle way, signed *Robin Hood Way* – keeping Center Parcs' perimeter fence on the left. After about $1^1/_4$ miles, at a cross tracks with information board marked 'Start of cycle route', go straight on, past the green metal barrier, for about 1 mile, then left up a slight hill. (This is part of the waymarked cycle route *in reverse*: you can check that you're on the right track by means of the red cycle route signs, which are mounted on short wooden posts, also painted red.) Follow this track to a green metal barrier at the T-junction of tracks and car parking area. Turn left into **Eakring Road car park**.

Distance: 13 miles

Terrain: Except for the finish section through Clipstone Forest on **forest tracks** and a short section which has to be walked through Rufford Country Park, entirely **on-road** through rolling countryside.

Refreshment opportunities: There are pubs serving food in several of the villages and a teashop in Rufford Park.

Start: As described, the route starts from the Eakring Road car park (GR 620 616). It would also be possible to start from either of the Rufford Abbey car parks (GR 643 647 or 646 656) or, if you are staying there, from Center Parcs' Sherwood Holiday Village (GR 637 640).

Ordnance Survey maps: Landranger sheet **120** Mansfield and Worksop

Public transport links: by rail to Mansfield Woodhouse (Robin Hood Line), then follow route **23** (either outward or return legs as described) as far as *Old Clipstone*, follow B6030 east for 1/2 or 3/4 mile to the Sherwood Pines Visitor Centre, then follow link **L7** to the cross-tracks west of Center Parcs' holiday village to join this route.

Other routes: Route **7** is a circuit in Sherwood Pines Forest Park. Route **25** is a longer (26-mile) version of this one; link **L7** leads from Sherwood Pines to Edwinstowe and Sherwood Forest, giving another link to route **23**. Route **28**, Southwell Trail and the Dumbles, shares a short stretch of road with this one, west of Eakring.

18

continued

---

17 miles • mostly on-road • undulating • Mansfield Woodhouse

19

Ault Hucknall and Hardwick Hall

This route is one of several which makes use of the Robin Hood Line to get out to a different part of the county – and it's also one of the routes to venture a mile or two over the border into a neighbouring county, in this case Derbyshire. Although it is never more than five or six miles from the large town of Mansfield the route ventures into some remarkably quiet – and quite hilly – country.

There are several attractive warm stone-built hamlets on the route – such as Ault Hucknall and Rowthorne – but the obvious star of the show is Hardwick Hall and its park. There are in fact *two* halls at Hardwick: the partially ruined Old Hall, which is in the care of English Heritage, and the better-known 16th-century Hardwick Hall, which belongs to the National Trust. It is the latter with

its six towers that is such a landmark in its commanding position overlooking the valley of the River Doe Lea (and nowadays the M1, too). The great west-facing windows are taller on the upper storeys than the lower – giving rise to the local jingle when it was built: 'Hardwick Hall – more glass than wall'. As well as the rooms which are still furnished much as they were in the days of Elizabeth Shrewsbury ('Bess of Hardwick') for whom it was built, there is a fine formal garden and recreated herb garden. There is a charge for entry into the house and garden. The Old Hall can also be visited, and a combined ticket is available. Both are open Wednesday to Sunday (plus Bank Holidays) from the end of March to the end of October. The park, formerly a deer park but now used for cattle and sheep grazing, is open free throughout the year from dawn to dusk.

From **Mansfield Woodhouse station**, walk down the ramp and turn left through the pedestrian exit beside steel gate at the north end of the station car park into Oxclose Lane (unsurfaced and unnamed at this point). Turn right on Oxclose Lane, then at a diagonal crossroads where the road bears round to the right, sharp left and left again into Thoresby Road (sign on wall on left by pillar box). At the end of the houses, just before the railway embankment, turn right into Manor Road. At a T-junction, turn left into Vale Road (not signed). Where Vale Road bears round to the right as Brown Avenue, continue straight on under a low railway bridge on Common Lane (not signed). Follow this road for about 1¹/₂ miles to the foot of Pleasley Vale, then up the valley of the River Meden to **Pleasley Mills**.

Pass to the right of the road barrier and continue up Pleasley Vale past the disused mills. Just after the exit barrier turn right through a small gate to the left of a steel gate marked *J Thompson Engineering (Mansfield) Ltd*, where there are also metallic gold-coloured arrows marking the *Archaeological Trail*. Continue past the buildings to a second steel gate, pass to the left of it, and go straight on. The path continues as a full-width tarred road, then becomes a tarred path, which reaches a road (B6407 but unmarked at this point) at a wooden gate. Cross the B-

19
continued

road onto an unsurfaced bridleway, still following the metallic gold-coloured arrows of the *Archaeological Trail*. The surface of this $^3/_4$ miles of track is grassy, with a possible slightly muddy patch after wet weather halfway along it. After this the surface improves. Continue to a T-junction with a tarred road. Turn left for about 1 mile up a steady climb, then about 200yds after the electricity pylons, where the major road goes right and is signed *Bolsover 3 Clowne 6*, turn **left** on an unsigned road into **Stony Houghton**. The road drops and curves round to the right through the hamlet, meeting the B6417 at a 'Give way' sign. Turn right on B6417, then straight on on Green Lane where the B6417 bears right. Continue on Green Lane to a T-junction with the A617. Turn right for about 300yds, then first left left on an unsigned minor road. **(If you don't want to ride on the A617, which can be quite busy, you can wheel your bike along the pavement on the north (right-hand) side of the road briefly until you are opposite the turn.)**

Continue for about $^3/_4$ mile, following the road round to the right to a T-junction on the outskirts of **Rowthorne**. Turn right under pylons and then first left after about 300yds, signed *Ault Hucknall and Stainsby*. From this road there are views to the right across to the Peak District hills, with Hardwick Hall's towers clearly visible to the left. Follow *Hardwick Hall* signs for about 1$^1/_2$ miles through **Ault Hucknall,** then down a quite steep winding descent, with a double bend at the bottom. Immedi-ately after the bend and stone bridge, bear left through some blue-grey gates towards *Hardwick Hall.* Cross cattle grids and climb for about 1 mile through the park to a T-junction about 300yds before **Hardwick Hall.** (To visit the Hall turn right: **note that a one-way traffic system operates here – if you visit the Hall, you must**

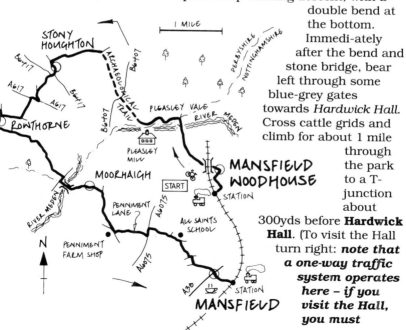

19
continued

exercise extreme care when retracing against the traffic flow to this junction to rejoin the route.)

The route itself turns sharp left at this junction, along a broad avenue signed *No Entry or Exit* (this refers explicitly to car traffic). Continue on this broad straight avenue for about ³/₄ mile to the lodge and another set of blue-grey gates. Go through the swing wicket gate to the left of the main gates and continue for about 300yds to a T-junction at a small triangular green; turn right, signed *Rowthorne*. In **Rowthorne**, by a large house and stone wall on the left, turn right (unsigned) and follow this road for nearly 2 miles. Eventually it drops in a winding descent between high banks. At the T-junction at the foot of the hill, turn right and immediately left, signed *Skegby*, over a small river bridge and then first left (unsigned – but just after a sign warning of horses for 2¹/₂ miles) along the flank of the stream valley. This road eventually climbs away from the stream and valley; keep round to the right where a road joins from the left, along the road signed *Penniment Lane* and up to a T-junction with Top Lane opposite a farm shop.

Turn left on Top Lane and immediately left again, opposite Penniment House Farm, on an unsigned road. This is still Penniment Lane, signed at the far end where it meets the A6075 at a T-junction. Turn left for 200yds along the A6075, then right (there is a separate right-turn waiting lane) into Westfield Lane. (**If you do not feel confident enough to do this, walk along the pavement on the left of the A6075 for the 200yds until you are opposite Westfield Lane, then cross on foot.**)

This is the beginning of the **Mansfield** built-up area (*for alternative route from All Saints RC School through **Mansfield town centre**, see below*). After about ¹/₂ mile, by the entrance to All Saints RC School on the left, turn right into Harrop White Road. At the end of the road, after about 400yds, turn left into Ladybrook Lane and almost immediately first right into Oardale Road. At the T-junction at the end of Oardale Road, turn left on Bancroft Lane (not signed at this point). Follow Bancroft Lane to its junction with Stockwell Gate, A38. Cross the A38 into Dallas Street and at a T-junction turn left into Peacock Lane and immediately right into Rooth Street to its T-junction with Victoria Street (unsigned at this point but marked as *no through road*). At the end of this road follow the ramp down to the left to a light-controlled pedestrian crossing of the A6009 dual carriageway. Cross on foot to the opposite side, then still on foot left to the junction with Station Road (unsigned). Take the first turn on the right behind the Midland Hotel and Rumours Wine Bar to the old station buildings, now a pub named Brunel's. Follow signs under the subway to the far platform of **Mansfield Station** for Nottingham trains, or remain on the nearside to return to Mansfield Woodhouse.

19
continued

If you want to visit **Mansfield town centre**, there is an alternative route but it involves a considerable amount of walking through a pedestrianised area:

From All Saints RC school entrance, continue straight over the inner ring road at traffic lights, still on Westfield Lane. At the next T-junction, with compulsory right turn sign, dismount and walk to the street opposite, Westgate, and continue on foot through the pedestrianised area to Market Square. Opposite Leeming Street turn right across Market Square, following pedestrian signs to *Mansfield Station*. Go up Market Street which becomes Queens Walk. Cross the road, still on foot, into a subway marked *Crown Walk to buses*. At the far end of the subway, turn sharp left, then to the right into the car park. Follow car park exit arrows up a steep pitch and under a yellow barrier to the T-junction with Station Road (unsigned). Turn right and then almost immediately first left into a road signed to *Station Road South car park*, and marked as *no through road*. This leads to the old station buildings, now a pub named Brunel's. Follow signs under the subway to the far platform of **Mansfield Station** for Nottingham trains, or remain on the nearside to return to Mansfield Woodhouse.

Distance: 17 miles

Terrain: Except for the ³/₄-mile stretch of **bridleway** between Pleasley Mills and Stony Houghton, entirely **on-road** through rolling countryside.

Refreshment opportunities: There are few pubs on the route, but there is a restaurant (seasonal opening) at Hardwick Hall and a number of refreshment places of different kinds in Mansfield. The teashop at the Herb Garden, Hardstoft, is about 2 miles west of the official car exit from Hardwick Hall.

Start: As described, the route starts at Mansfield Woodhouse station (GR 534 633).

Ordnance Survey maps: Landranger sheet **120** Mansfield and Worksop

Public transport links: by rail to Mansfield Woodhouse, returning from Mansfield (both Robin Hood Line)

Other routes: Route **23,** Mansfield Woodhouse to Sherwood, also starts from Mansfield Woodhouse station, while link route **L10** leads from the station to route **27,** Clumber Park and Meden Vale.

20

15 miles • on- and off-road • some hills • Gunthorpe

Lambley and Lowdham

This circular route to the east of Nottingham gives a chance to follow the north bank of a rural section of the River Trent for some distance on easily ridable and mainly grassy bridleways.

Gunthorpe, where the route description starts, has been the site of a crossing of the River Trent for millennia. Long before the first bridge (which wasn't built until 1875), and before the rapids were tamed with a weir and lock, the Trent was fordable here. In Roman times it lay on a route between the town of MARGIDVNVM (on the Fosse Way between what are now East Bridgford and Bingham) and the lead mines of Derbyshire. Later it was here that the Iceni tribal queen Boudicca (or Boadicea) saw off the Romans' Tenth Legion.

The first stretch of bridleway leads to Burton Joyce, then by way of quite a stiff climb over the ridge to Lambley. There's a particularly fine view of Lambley and the hills and valleys behind it at the point where the bridleway crests the hill. Considering its closeness to Nottingham, Lambley remains a secluded village nestling in the narrow valley alongside the tumbling waters of the Cocker Beck. Its sheltered position must have given it its name – the 'lea' or field in which lambs were raised. Like many other Nottinghamshire villages it grew in the early 19th century with the advent of cottage frame-knitting machines: local records number 381 in 1844!

The road beside the Cocker Beck leads gently down to Lowdham, a village separated from its parish church by the main A6097, which the route crosses safely at traffic lights. Lowdham Mill, to the north of the village, is one of the dozen  which once surrounded Lowdham; it is now a private house. The bridle path which the route follows passes close to the mill and its millpond, and you can see the mill race where the wheel once turned. From Lowdham Mill the route follows very quiet byroads until it reaches the Trent once more, to embark on a fine stretch of riverside path through wide grassy meadows.

Start on the northern side of **Gunthorpe Bridge** over the River Trent and on the west side of the main A6097, opposite the road leading to the hotel and lock. Go west along the north bank of the river, taking the unsigned bridleway that follows the river bank. Go through the anglers' car park, and straight on along the riverside track for about a mile; the surface improves to a firm broad track, which then leaves the bank of the river as the Trent meanders off to the south (although, after a further mile of so, the two rejoin briefly before you bear inland towards Burton Joyce). Ignore the minor surfaced road that comes in from the right, instead continuing ahead on along the track to cross the railway at the level crossing. The large vehicle gates are normally shut: use the small swing gates to the side of them, then go straight on at the far side to cross the main A612 into Meadow Lane, **Burton Joyce**. At the T-junction by Burton Joyce Methodists' Church, turn left, then take the third minor road on the right – Padleys Lane. Go up to the top of the road, left at the T-junction into Foxhill Road, then at the next T-junction after a short way, right onto Bridle Road which you follow up and over quite a steep hill, signed *Stockhill Farm*. The surfaced road becomes an open grassy track which descends steeply across an open field into **Lambley**.

20
continued

When the track eventually emerges onto a tarred road, turn right and continue along the valley of the Cocker Beck for a couple of miles into Lowdham. Cross straight over the dual carriageway (A6097) at the traffic lights into Ton Lane, which leads into **Lowdham**. At the T-junction, almost opposite the old school building which has a prominent clock, turn left onto Main Street (not signed at this point). At the top end of

Helping to create the
GREENWOOD
COMMUNITY
F O R E S T

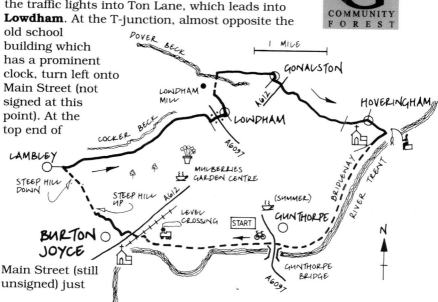

LAMBLEY
STEEP HILL
DOWN
STEEP HILL
UP
BURTON
JOYCE
LEVEL
CROSSING
START
GUNTHORPE
GUNTHORPE
BRIDGE
A6097
MULBERRIES
GARDEN CENTRE
A612
COCKER BECK
DOVER BECK
1 MILE
GONALVSTON
A612
LOWDHAM
MILL
LOWDHAM
A6097
HOVERINGHAM
BRIDLEWAY
RIVER TRENT
(SUMMER)
N

Main Street (still unsigned) just

20
continued

before the road rejoins the dual-carriageway Lowdham bypass, A6097, and immediately before the '50' speed limit sign, turn right on what is obviously a short section of the old road by a small silver birch tree. After about 40yds, turn right into the entrance to Lowdham Mill (signed *public bridleway* on a wooden finger post), then about 150yds down this track, go through the small white wicket gate to the right of the track, marked with a blue bridleway arrow (the larger white gates to the left mark the private entrance to Lowdham Mill). This attractive little firm-surfaced path looks almost as though it's going through somebody's garden as it goes over a little wooden bridge and then passes between the lower mill pool on the left and a tennis court on the right, to emerge by the upper millpond. After crossing a small stone bridge over a weir there is a second gate; go through this and 150yds later reach the tarred road.

Turn right on the road through **Gonalston** to a crossroads with the A612. Go straight across on a minor road signed *Hoveringham light traffic only*. Go into **Hoveringham** and at a T-junction with the church on the right, turn right (effectively straight on) on Boat Lane, signed *Caythorpe* and *Lowdham*. After about 500yds the road meets the River Trent and turns sharp right to leave the river on the left, then about 400yds later there is a car parking area on the left as the road bears to the right away from the Trent. Go left

---

Distance: 15 miles

Terrain: Fairly flat with one steep hill, about two-fifths is **off-road** on bridleways – most of the off-road section is along the banks on the River Trent; otherwise on **minor roads**.

Refreshment opportunities: Although fairly short, this route passes through a number of villages offering pubs and shops. In the summer months the church hall in Gunthorpe where the route starts and finishes offers teas on Sunday afternoons from Easter to autumn. It's in the village: from the Unicorn Hotel on Trentside, go north (away from the river) up Main Street for about 600yds – the church of St John the Baptist is on the right-hand side of the road, just where the village street begins to bear round to the left to rejoin the main road. There is also a tea room (Mulberries Coffee House, if that isn't a contradiction) at the Tall Trees Garden Centre, about 1 mile east of Burton Joyce on the A612.

Start: Gunthorpe Bridge, north side of the River Trent (GR 681 437). You could also start in Burton Joyce, Lambley or Lowdham.

Ordnance Survey maps: Landranger sheet **129** Nottingham and Loughborough

Public transport links: Burton Joyce and Lowdham stations are on the Nottingham to Newark line. Not all services on this line stop at all the stations.

Other routes: The westernmost point of this route, where the bridleway comes down to the road in Lambley village, is only about 200yds from the nearest point of route **5**, the Woodborough rounds. Route **30**, Daybrook to Southwell, uses the same roads as this one between Gonalston and Hoveringham, while route **40**, Newark to Nottingham, passes on the south side of Gunthorpe Bridge.

through a white swing gate to join a bridleway which runs along the northern bank of the river; there is no bridleway sign but the gate is by a board reading 'Midland AS Private Fishing'. This bridleway is not so much a well-defined track as an open grassy area popular with walkers and anglers. Pass through a number of distinctive swing gates, keeping the river on your left, to reach a tarred path at Gunthorpe Lock. Continue straight on to return to **Gunthorpe Bridge** over the Trent where the route started. 🚲

20
continued

---

16 miles • on- and off-road • gentle • Worksop

21

Worksop, Scofton and Bilby

Like route **17**, this route makes extensive use of the network of farm and estate roads north and east of Worksop. These have the status of bridleways and range from tarred roads to firm-based stone-surfaced tracks. Although this countryside is no more than a couple of miles from the busy A1, some of the little settlements, such as the hamlets of Scofton and Bilby, set in their wide open fields and copses, seem incredibly remote. This is not the pretty parkland of the Dukeries but a working landscape which nevertheless has its picturesque corners.

From **Worksop** Town Hall in the corner of the Market Place, bear right at pedestrian lights into Popper Street, then at mini-roundabout turn left into Watson Road, signed *Tickhill 10 (A60)*. Continue straight on at the next two sets of traffic lights, then at the next set by McDonald's, turn right over the bridge, signed *A60,*

Tickhill. At the traffic lights immediately after the bridge, get into the right-hand waiting lane then turn right into Eastgate, just in front of the King's Head. After about 600yds, at the Kilton Inn, Eastgate becomes Kilton Road. Continue straight on to a mini-roundabout, and go straight on, still on Kilton Road. After about 500yds this bears round to the left under a railway bridge; immediately after the bridge, turn right onto a completely unnamed,

21 continued

unsigned minor road which starts by running close to the railway. After about ¹/₂ mile the tarred surface stops and the road continues as a firm-surfaced gravel track which crosses the grounds of Osberton Hall after about 1¹/₂ miles. The Hall is a prominent white building to the right, visible across a small lake.

The track emerges onto a tarred road, which still only has bridleway status, with a wooden three-way signpost marking the junction of bridleways. Turn right on the tarred-surfaced bridleway through the hamlet of **Scofton**, leaving the church to the right. If you're feeling adventurous there is a ford through the River Ryton as well as the much more obvious bridge. The road crosses the Chesterfield Canal at a lock on a double bend and then climbs through an avenue of trees towards the B6079. As you emerge from the avenue, there is an obvious left turn which leads shortly to the B6079. The official bridleway, however, continues about 150yds to the B-road.

Turn left on B6079 to pass under the A1 dual carriageway. About 300yds past the A1 bridge, turn left into **Ranby** village, signed *Ranby*. Follow the road round to the right into the village, then continue to follow it as it sweeps round to the right in front of the Chequers Inn, signed *Retford 4*, to rejoin the main road, which has now become the A620. Turn left on the A620 (no sign) past Ranby House school and Ranby Prison. About 300yds past the prison entrance, turn left on a minor road, signed *Barnby Moor*. After just over a mile, and just past Green Mile Farm, by a very striking tall beech hedge, fork left (no sign) onto a very minor road by some farm cottages. (You can check that you're in the right place because this small road continues as a grassy track on the opposite side of the road behind you – possibly the 'green mile' that gives the farm its name.) After about 200yds the road becomes a firm earth-based track that leads to a picturesque willow-fringed bridge over the Chesterfield Canal. The track continues for about 1¹/₂ miles, with the surface improving for a while near a junction of tracks by Ranby Hall, eventually emerging onto a tarred road about 150yds short of the A1.

Turn left to cross the A1: ***take great care, since this road carries heavy, fast traffic. You may find it easier to walk (or run) across wheeling your bike.*** There is a central reservation between the traffic streams, with a waiting gap. On the far side of the A1, turn right along the deceleration lane for about 100yds, then turn left on a minor tarred road, signed *Bilby ¹/₂*. This is firmly marked with discouraging notices stating that it is a private road.

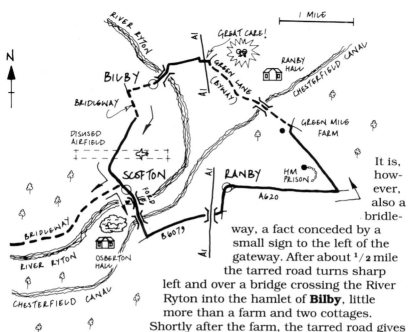

It is, however, also a bridleway, a fact conceded by a small sign to the left of the gateway. After about ¹/₂ mile the tarred road turns sharp left and over a bridge crossing the River Ryton into the hamlet of **Bilby**, little more than a farm and two cottages.

Shortly after the farm, the tarred road gives way to a firm gravel track between open fields. After about 500yds, there is a T-junction of tracks, with a *blue bridleway arrow* pointing left. Turn left (the track to the right is firmly marked 'Private road, keep out') for about ¹/₂ mile to join a tarred road at a double set of metal gates. Go straight on on the tarred road, still a bridleway, for about 600yds to a former airfield runway, which is

---

Distance: 16 miles

Terrain: a mixture of **minor road** and **farm and estate roads** with the status of **bridleways**, some untarred but firm and easily ridable. The route rolls gently but the biggest hill is climbing up from the underpass below the A1.

Refreshment opportunities: Worksop; in Ranby there's the Chequers Inn, and to the north of the village there's a regular refreshment van in a layby on the east side of the A1 (at least, on weekdays), approachable from the old Blyth Road (to get to it, turn left at the Chequers Inn into Blyth Road, signed *Village Hall*; ignore the left turn onto the A1 and continue on the old Blyth Road; the van's on the left).

Start: Worksop Town Hall (GR 584 786)

Ordnance Survey maps: Landranger sheet **120**, Mansfield and Worksop

Public transport links: Regional Railways services run from Sheffield, Retford and Gainsborough to Worksop. At the time of writing it was also intended that the Robin Hood Line should be extended as far as Worksop by 1998.

Other routes: Routes **12**, **14** and **17** also start from Worksop.

21

continued

apparently used for testing – whether aircraft or something else isn't obvious. Check that it is clear and cross to the gates on the other side. Continue on the tarred road for about ¹/₂ mile to the three-way junction of bridleways in **Scofton**. Turn right and retrace the outgoing route to the outskirts of Worksop, turning left under the railway bridge into Kilton Road. At the T-junction with the B6041 (not signed) turn right, then immediately left at the mini-roundabout, still on Kilton Road, which becomes Eastgate. At the traffic lights by the King's Head turn left over the bridge, and left again at the next lights by McDonald's into Watson Road. Carry straight on at all traffic lights to the mini-roundabout junction with Popper Street, signed *Ollerton and Nottingham*; turn right to return to **Worksop** Town Hall. 🚲

22

18 miles • on-road • mostly gentle • Blidworth

Blidworth and Halam

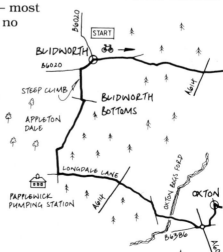

This compact circular route follows some intricate country lanes – most of which carry no more than very light traffic – in a pocket of countryside to the north-east of Nottingham, known as the Dumbles. ('Dumble' is a local word for a usually narrow stream valley.) The going is not entirely flat, but any climbs are rewarded by fine views over rolling farmland.

The route leads through the large village

22

continued

of Farnsfield past the trim fields of a stud farm, and then on through Edingley to Halam. The name of this little village, the easternmost point of the route, comes from the Old English word '*halh*' meaning a hidden-away corner and it is certainly hidden away at the foot of its small valley. At one time it was famed for its orchards and was said to have been a sea of blossom in spring. Enough remnants are left to give a hint of what it must have been. The little valley road that leads up to the B6386 above Oxton is a delight at any season and well worth the stiff little pitch you have to climb at the end. And of course there's the reward of swooping down Oxton Bank on the other side: mind the S-bend halfway down! Oxton, at the foot of the hill, is a pleasant light stone-built village, now quietly bypassed.

From the car park of the Jolly Friar, turn left along Dale Road up the hill leaving **Blidworth** behind. After 1^1/$_2$ miles there is a cross-roads with the A614; go straight over onto the minor road opposite, and follow this for a further 1^1/$_2$ miles into **Farnsfield**. At the T-junction, opposite the Red Lion, turn right along Main Street. Leave Farnsfield and continue on this road for about 2 miles – through **Edingley**, then to Halam.

Helping to create the
GREENWOOD

COMMUNITY
FOREST

Just after the Wagon and Horses in **Halam**, turn right into Bradley Road. Follow this as it winds out of the village and up a quiet valley, climbing to the Southwell–Oxton ridge road, B6386. At the T-junction, turn right, signed *Oxton*. Having descended Oxton Bank, take the first turn on the right – Blind Lane – into **Oxton** village. Go past the Green Dragon pub, then left at the T-junction, signed *Nottingham*. Turn right onto Nottingham Road at the T-junction just after Ye Olde Bridge Inn, and straight over at the roundabout – crossing the A6097 – onto the B6386, then, after a very short distance, first right. This unsigned, unnamed

N

FARNSFIELD

EDINGLEY

I MILE

HALAM

SOUTHWELL

OXTON – SOUTHWELL RIDGE ROAD

B6386

B6386

OXTON BANK – NICE SWOOP DOWN !

22
continued

road is, in fact, Beanford Lane – as you'll discover at the far end – and goes through a ford, which is part of 'Oxton Bogs'. Turn right at the T-junction onto Whinbush Lane, which meets the A614 after about 1^1/$_2$ miles. Cross straight over the main road to Longdale Lane – which is long and straight and slightly uphill! After approximately 1^1/$_4$ miles there is a minor cross roads: *Papplewick Pumping Station* is signed off to the left, but turn **right** onto an unnamed minor road. This climbs to one of the car parks for Blidworth Woods, Blidworth Tower, and then swoops down Appleton Dale to **Blidworth Bottoms**. At the junction opposite the Fox and Hounds, go left then first right after a short distance to climb the hill back into **Blidworth**. At the top, turn right at the T-junction on the B6020, signed for *Mansfield* and *Rainworth*. Just after the petrol station at the bottom of the hill, right into Dale Road – signed for *Sherwood Forest*, and back to the Jolly Friar. 🚲

Distance: 18 miles

Terrain: Entirely **on-road**, making use of quiet country lanes; fairly easy going with one or two short climbs.

Refreshment opportunities: The villages the route passes through offer a good selection of pubs, most of which offer food. Slightly off the route there are numerous tea shops in Southwell.

Start: Jolly Friar pub, Dale Road, Blidworth (GR 603562)

Ordnance Survey maps: Landranger sheet **120** Mansfield and Worksop

Public transport links:

Other routes: Route **8**, Halam and Southwell, also visits Halam, and route **15**, Hucknall and Newstead, just touches this one at the crossroads between Blidworth Bottoms and Papplewick Pumping Station. Route **30**, Daybrook to Southwell, shares a short stretch of the B6386 near Oxton.

23

15 miles · on- and off-road · gentle · Mansfield Woodhouse

Mansfield to Sherwood Forest

This route skirts the eastern fringes of Mansfield, using a bridleway as a traffic-free exit to the countryside. For the first few miles the route picks its way round the workings of Clipstone colliery, one of Nottinghamshire's remaining working pits, but you might hardly realise it unless you glimpse the

23

continued

In Sherwood Forest

great towers of the pithead gear to your left. The little path ducks though tunnels and follows a series of water features – ponds, streams – in effect a linear park. A minor road section leads to Edwinstowe, then on into Sherwood Forest, tracing a semi-circular route on delightful woodland tracks. Another section of minor road leads to Old Clipstone, from where there are two bridleway possibilities before you reach the last couple of road miles back to Mansfield Woodhouse station.

Edwinstowe gets its name from King Edwin of Northumbria, who was killed in battle nearby in 632. It became quite a popular Victorian resort on the edge of Sherwood Forest, and in early cycling papers is frequently noted as the destination for cycle rides from Nottingham. Local members of the Cyclists' Touring Club (CTC) would ride out from Nottingham and the other towns on a Saturday afternoon (no Sunday riding then), enjoy a tea and evening sing-song followed by a ride home by lamp-light. Edwinstowe did not become a mining village until 1925, but nearby Thoresby Colliery is another of the last remnants of the once-great Nottinghamshire coalfield.

From **Mansfield Woodhouse station**, go down the ramp at the end of the platform and left through the pedestrian exit beside a steel gate into Oxclose Lane (unsurfaced and unnamed at this point). Turn right on Oxclose Lane and continue to follow it round to the

23

continued

right as Grove Way and Grove Street, eventually becoming Station Hill. At the T-junction at the end, turn left into Station Street, which becomes High Street, and follow this road through the centre of **Mansfield Woodhouse** and round to the right where it becomes Portland Street, signed *Alsop and Worksop*. After a short distance you reach a crossroads with traffic lights; go straight over into New Mill Lane. At a second set of traffic lights, at the crossroads with the A60, go straight on again, still on New Mill Lane for about 2 miles. The road leaves the built-up area and climbs to an oblique T-junction with B6030, Clipstone Road East.

Go right and left across the B6030 into Lime Grove. At the bottom of this residential road, turn left onto Newlands Road. Continue eastwards along Newlands Road, with the embankment of a dismantled railway on your right. When the tarred road stops, continue straight on along a firmly surfaced track which is also a bridleway. After about $^1/_2$ mile pass round a metal gate, ignoring a turning off to the left. Keep to the right of Newlands Farm, continuing along the valley – passing various ponds and an attractive willow-lined stream on your right. Negotiate the odd cycle-unfriendly gate and pass through a fairly long tunnel. **Vicar Water** – a popular fishing spot – appears on the right. At the far end of this small lake, bear round to the right – through the car park – then left at the far side of the head of the water to continue along the bridleway, signed by a *blue arrow*. Go under a couple of bridges, passing fairly close to the pithead gear of Clipstone Colliery, visible to the left. Follow the *blue bridleway arrows* – essentially straight on – for a further mile until you reach the B6030 beside the car park of the Dog and Duck. Turn right on the B6030, under a railway bridge, past the tourist information sign for Sherwood Pines Forest Park, then first left – signed *Edwinstowe*.

At the T-junction, after about 1$^1/_2$ miles, turn left into **Edwinstowe**. The village has a one-way system through its narrow streets, and northbound traffic (the direction you are travelling) is diverted to the left on West Lane. You may find it easier when you reach the 'no-entry' signs into the High Street to get off and wheel your bike up this main shopping street – not only is it shorter, but here's where you'll find several of the tea and cake shops. If you follow the one-way system, turn right at the junction with Mansfield Road, A6075, then left at the traffic lights at the top of High Street into

MANSFIELD
WOODHOUSE
[START]
A6075
STATION
A60

Helping to create the
GREENWOOD
COMMUNITY
FOREST

Church Street. (If you've walked up the High Street, go straight on at these traffic lights into Church Street.) After about 300yds, turn left signed *Amusement Park*, past some public conveniences on the right. When

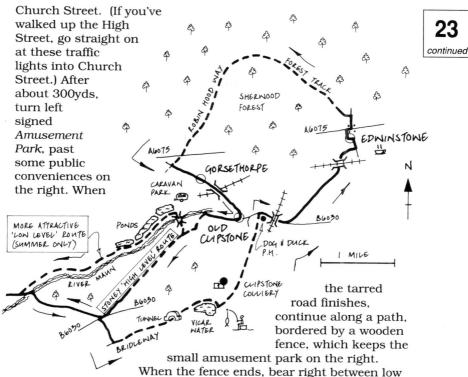

the tarred road finishes, continue along a path, bordered by a wooden fence, which keeps the small amusement park on the right. When the fence ends, bear right between low wooden posts onto a path which bears left and up a gentle incline – signed *bridleway to Gleadthorpe*.

This bridleway continues for about 1¹/2 miles through **Sherwood Forest** before you turn off. There is at least one further signpost for *Gleadthorpe*, and occasional *bridleway* signs; otherwise follow the posts marked with a *yellow horseshoe*. Eventually, you will pass round a low wooden barrier, and come to a crossing of wide tracks. The Robin Hood Way is signed to the left and right, but continue straight ahead along an unmarked forest track. Ignore the first significant turning off to the left, but after about ³/4 mile – where the track forks – take the left-hand fork (the right is signed as a public footpath). This track has a hard surface, which is badly crumbling in places, and meanders through the forest for about 1¹/2 miles. Ignore any minor tracks which head off at right angles, and where the track forks, keep right. Eventually, you will emerge onto a road (A6075). Go straight over into the track opposite, which emerges after a short way onto a minor road, opposite the entrance to Sherwood Forest Farm Park.

Turn left, through the small settlement of **Gorsethorpe** and over

23
continued

a railway bridge and the River Maun. On the left-hand bend in **Old Clipstone** – shortly before the junction with the B6030 – turn right into Squires Lane. This 'no-through' road becomes a bridleway, bearing left in front of Cavendish Lodge to become Clipstone Drive, then right after a short stretch between hedged fields. The bridleway continues as a wide, if rather stony track – with woods to the right and hedged fields on the left.

There is an attractive alternative return route from this point along another parallel bridleway, following close beside the River Maun. However, the surface can be muddy after wet weather, so we would only recommend it for summer use (or for adventurous mountain-bikers). To reach it from Clipstone Drive, about 400yds after the wood (Cavendish Wood) begins on the right, turn right into the wood opposite a post on the left marked with a *blue bridleway arrow.* After about 100yds, bear left downhill to cross the River Maun by a small bridge. Immediately after the bridge, with the white gateway entrance to Sherwood Forest Caravan Park on the right, turn left following *blue bridleway arrows,* leaving the River Maun on the left and a series of ponds on the right. After about 1 mile, the bridleway bears round to the right round another pond to leave the river and goes slightly uphill. After about 200yds, turn left, still following *blue bridleway arrows.* At a crossing of bridleways after about $^3/_4$ mile, and again at a junction of paths about 500yds farther on, continue straight on, always following the *blue bridleway arrow* signs. At the end of

Distance: 15 miles

Terrain: Well over half this route is **off-road**, on bridleways and forest tracks. With the exception of parts of the River Maun alternative bridleway section, the majority of these off-road sections are well-drained, and should be ridable throughout the year, although the loose or sandy surface material makes the going a little bumpy in places, so sturdy tyres are advisable. There are a few gentle slopes, but no tough climbs. The road sections are mainly on **minor roads.**

Refreshment opportunities: Nearly half-way round, Edwinstowe has made a virtue of its nearness to Sherwood Forest, and is well endowed with tea shops (e.g. Bentley's Bakery, Limetree Pantry, Church Farm Tea Shop), pubs, fish-and-chipperies and shops selling all the necessary ingredients for a picnic in the woods.

Start: Mansfield Woodhouse station (GR 534 633).

Ordnance Survey maps: Landranger sheet **120** Mansfield and Worksop

Public transport links: by rail to Mansfield Woodhouse (Robin Hood Line)

Other routes: Route **19**, Ault Hucknall and Hardwick Hall, also starts at Mansfield Woodhouse station. Link route **L2** leads from the station to route **11**, the Pleasley trails, and link route **L10** leads from the station to join route **27**, Clumber Park and Meden Vale. Link route **L7** joins this one at Edwinstowe to Sherwood Pines Forest Park and Center Parcs.

the bridleway, turn right on New Mill Lane for about 500yds to the traffic lights at the junction with the A60.

23
continued

If you continue on the upper stony bridleway, after about 1¹/₄ miles houses start appearing on the left, the track becomes a tarred road –

The new Robin Hood Line station at Mansfield Woodhouse makes elegant use of the stone-built goods shed from the original station on the same site.

still Clipstone Drive – and you're well and truly back in civilisation. From the end of Clipstone Drive, turn right into Clipstone Road East, B6030, then after about 20yds, first right again, signposted *Mansfield Woodhouse*, into New Mill Lane. (You may prefer just to walk the few yards on the right-hand pavement, rather than have to cross the B6030 twice.) Follow New Mill Lane for about 2 miles, past the point where the alternative bridleway rejoins the road, to traffic lights at the junction with the A60.

Go straight across the A60, still on New Mill Lane. After about 200yds at a second set of lights, at the junction with the A6075, go more or less straight ahead into Portland Street. Follow Portland Street round to the left; it becomes High Street, **Mansfield Woodhouse**, which in turn becomes Station Street. After about 200yds after it becomes Station Street, opposite Castle Street and a small green, turn right into Vale Road, then first left into Oxclose Lane. There's a bit of a dogleg where Oxclose Lane joins Grove Way at the top of the slope, but the route is effectively straight on, still on Oxclose Lane which becomes unsurfaced. At the steel gate shortly before the railway bridge, turn left (signposted as pedestrian way to station) into **Mansfield Woodhouse station** car park and up the ramp to the platform. 🚲

CIRCULAR ROUTES OVER 20 MILES

25 miles • on- and off-road • flat • Retford

Retford round

North of Retford, Nottinghamshire takes on quite a different character. This part of the Trent valley and the neighbouring part of South Yorkshire were once marshland, not unlike the Fens of Lincolnshire and Cambridgeshire. Like the Fens, this area was drained to yield fertile grazing and arable land. In the far north of the county (touched on by route **37**) the flat landscape has the same geometrical pattern of drains, large hedgeless fields and roads as the Fens, but on this route roads follow the more gentle curves of the natural landscape. There are several pleasant villages, such as Mattersey and North and South Wheatley, while the little hamlet of Wiseton is well worth the detour we suggest.

It is in Wiseton that the route makes its second acquaintance with the Chesterfield Canal, originally built in the 1770s to link Chesterfield with the Trent. The route first meets it at Drakeholes, about 1¹/₂ miles before Wiseton, where the canal passes through a tunnel a little over 150yds long. Unlike many canal tunnels, this one was hewn directly out of the sandstone ridge it cuts through and has no brick lining. In most low brick-lined tunnels, boats were 'legged' through: the bargee lay on his back and walked – almost pedalled – his way along the tunnel roof. This tunnel was too high, so boats had to be poled or 'shafted' through, while the horses who towed the boats in open country had to be walked over the top.

After crossing the canal just before Clayworth the route climbs (only a few feet!) away from the marshlands into a more rolling countryside, passing through several villages, including

Sturton le Steeple, which has Pilgrim Fathers connections (see route **37**). Oddly, the church at Sturton le Steeple has a prominent *tower*, crowned by a large number of miniature steeples! The most notable feature of the next village, North Leverton, is the windmill, dating from 1813, which lies to the west of the village. It is one of the country's relatively few remaining working mills. It can be visited and you can buy stone-ground flour milled on the spot.

24
continued

From **Retford** Square, leave the town centre via Chancery Lane and Carolgate. Turn right at the traffic lights at the end of Carolgate into Albert Road, B6044, then after about 150yds first left into Thrumpton Lane and over the level crossing. About 300yds farther on, turn right after the New Inn and just before the primary school into Thrumpton Close. Follow the bridleway at the side of the school field under the railway past playing fields into Goosemoor

Lane (a chicane means that tandems, trailers etc will need to make a diversion via Whinney Moor Lane (the continuation of Thrumpton Lane), turning right at the end onto London Road, A638, to pass over the railway, then first right into Goosemoor Lane.) From the bridleway, turn right on Goosemoor Lane and over the bridge over the River Idle, then left into High Street. Follow High Street to a T-junction, where turn left and follow this road for about 3 miles past the airfield to Jockey House. Turn right to *Little Morton.*

Go by **Little Morton** Farm, then over the level crossing and briefly join the B6240, Mansfield Road, signed *Babworth*, then after about 150yds, go straight ahead on a minor road where the B6420 turns sharp right. This road quickly becomes a track and climbs to woods at the top of the hill, where it meets the A620. Go straight across the A620 on a minor road to *Green Mile* and *Barnby Moor*. At the village of **Barnby Moor**, turn right onto the A638, the Great North Road, signed *Retford*, and then after about 600yds just after leaving the village, turn left to *Sutton-cum-Lound*. Go over the level crossing to **Sutton**. At the first T-junction turn left through the village, then right at the Gate Inn to *Lound*, following the road round to the left where the entrance to the Wetlands Waterfowl Reserve lies straight ahead. In **Lound**, go straight over the crossroads in the centre of the village on Town Street, then follow this road as it bears round to the left to a T-junction. Turn right to *Mattersey*.

In **Mattersey** follow the road round to the left by the church to a crossroads with Main Street, B6045. Turn right on the B6045 to

101

24
continued

pass over the River Idle, then take the next turning right, Eel Pool Road, still B6045, to **Drakeholes**. Bear right where the B6045 swings round to the left on a minor road, signed *Clayworth*. (It is worth making a detour into the picturesque hamlet of **Wiseton**, about ³/₄ mile after

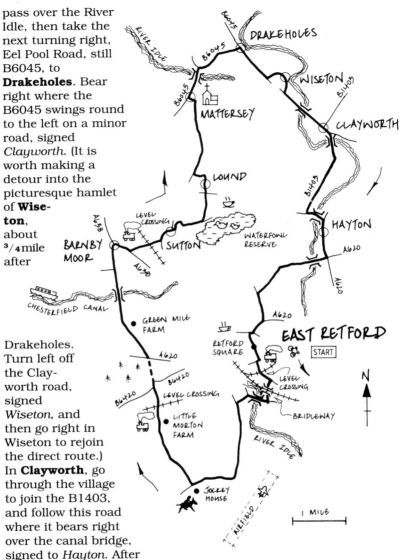

Drakeholes. Turn left off the Clayworth road, signed *Wiseton*, and then go right in Wiseton to rejoin the direct route.) In **Clayworth**, go through the village to join the B1403, and follow this road where it bears right over the canal bridge, signed to *Hayton*. After about 2 miles the B1403 turns sharp left to cross the Chesterfield Canal again, then right into Main Street, **Hayton**.

At the southern end of Hayton, just before the junction with the A620, turn right on an unclassified road, Smeath Lane. Follow Smeath Lane, which becomes Smeath Road, for about 2 miles to a T-junction with Tiln Lane. Turn left on Tiln Lane, signed to *Retford*, turning right at the junction with the A620 out of Tiln Lane into Moorgate. Go down the hill, turn left at the traffic lights, then first right into Chapelgate and Cannon Square and back either walking via the pedestrianised section, or taking the second right into Grove Street to Market Square, **Retford**. 🚲

Distance: 25 miles

Terrain: mostly flat on quiet **roads**; short section of **track** near Babworth.

Refreshment opportunities: there are tea shops in Retford and a tea shop/café at the Wetlands Waterfowl Reserve, between Sutton and Lound. Most of the villages also have pubs.

Start: Market Square, Retford (GR 704 811)

Ordnance Survey maps: sorry, you'll need three Landranger sheets – **111** Sheffield and Doncaster, **112** Scunthorpe and **120** Mansfield and Worksop

Public transport links: East Coast Main Line trains (well, some of them) stop at Retford, and the Regional Railways service from Sheffield to Lincoln via Worksop and Gainsborough calls at the lower station at Retford.

Other routes: Routes **16** and **29**, and the longest one in the book, **37**, also start from Retford and use some of the same roads into and out of the town.

24
continued

---

26 miles · forest track and on-road · rolling · Sherwood Pines **25**

Laxton, Ollerton and Rufford from Sherwood Pines Forest Park

For the first few miles this route follows the same tracks and roads as the shorter version, **18**, as far as Eakring, which is described in the account of that route.

A few miles farther on, Laxton is unique – it is the last village in England to practise mediaeval strip cultivation, with strips of each of the great open fields allocated to farmers on a rotating basis by a traditional meeting known as the 'Court Leet'. There is a visitor centre describing the system and its history next to the Dovecote Inn in the village.

Fine open roads lead through Egmanton to Kirton, with the little winding road from Kirton towards Walesby a further delight. In coaching

103

At Ollerton Mill

days, the next village, Ollerton, occupied a very strategic position: where the Worksop to Newark road – the Worksop to Kelham turnpike, freed from tolls in 1878 – crossed one of the London to York routes, as well as lying on the Mansfield to Lincoln route. The village's two coaching inns were the changing points for horses for the London to Glasgow coach, travelling via Newark. The Hop Pole and the White Hart still dominate the centre of the village. The name of the Hop Pole also commemorates what was another feature of the village – its hopfields; these provided the major employment until the turn of the century, when hop-growing was superseded by mining. In Ollerton village, the watermill, on the site of one mentioned in the *Domesday Boke* of 1086, still grinds flour and meal, the fruit of an award-winning restoration. You can see the wheel and the mill-race through a convenient viewing panel – on your way to the upstairs teashop!

Turn left and then right out of **Sherwood Pines Forest Park** Eakring Road car park eastwards along Eakring Road for about 1¹/₂ miles to the A614. Cross the A614, and continue straight on, signed *Eakring 2¹/₄*. After climbing a longish hill, this road becomes Bilsthorpe Road, Eakring, and then Newark Road.

Continue straight through the village of **Eakring**, following signs for *Kneesall*. After about ³/₄ mile, take the first left, signed *Kneesall*, for about 2 miles to the T-junction with the A616 in **Kneesall**; turn right here, signposted *Newark*. After about 150yds, turn first left just after the church into School Lane. Follow School Lane to a T-junction just after the school. Turn right, and follow the road down the hill for about 1¹/₂ miles to a crossroads; turn left, signed *Laxton*. Continue for about 1¹/₂ miles into **Laxton** village, climbing to a small triangular green with the Dovecote Inn and Laxton Visitor Centre on the right. Turn right just after the pub, signed *Egmanton*, for about another 1¹/₂ miles.

In **Egmanton** village, just after a bridge over a little stream, turn left into Kirton Road, signed *Kirton* and *Ollerton*. Follow this road for about 3 miles to a T-junction with the A6075, opposite the Littlemore pub. Turn left on the A6075 down the hill into **Kirton**, and where the A6075 bears left, turn right just after the church, signed *Walesby*. At the next T-junction, after about ³/₄ mile, turn left (unsigned) and at the second T-junction, after about 200yds, turn left again, signed *Walesby*. Just past the church in **Walesby**, turn left opposite the 3D petrol station into Main Street. Follow Main Street round to the right past the Post Office and at the crossroads with the B6387, Retford Road, go straight across into Brake Road, signed *Thoresby*, past the Carpenter's Arms. After about 1¹/₄ miles, at the end of the wooded section on the left, turn left (no sign). After about 1 mile, just after the start of the built-up area of Ollerton, fork right into Walesby Lane, over a rise and down a hill to the junction with Forest Road, A6075. Turn right on Forest Road for a few yards to the roundabout junction with the A616.

Bear right on Ollerton Road, signed *Ollerton village*, then shortly first left onto Main Street (no road name sign, but signed *Watermill Tea Shop*).

In **Ollerton** village centre bear round to left on Market Place (the Watermill Tea Shop is on the right), following signs for *Wellow*. Pass the church on the left and leave the village uphill on Wellow Road, then take the first (very sharp) right turn into Bescar Lane. This road is blocked off at the end. Wheel your bike between the bollards, cross Kingston Drive/Hardwick Drive and go straight on, still on Bescar Lane, to pass under a railway bridge. Continue on Bescar Lane for about 1 mile to a T-junction, at which you turn right (no sign).

Go down the hill to **Rufford**, through the ford (the 'rough ford' that gives the place its name – there is an alternative

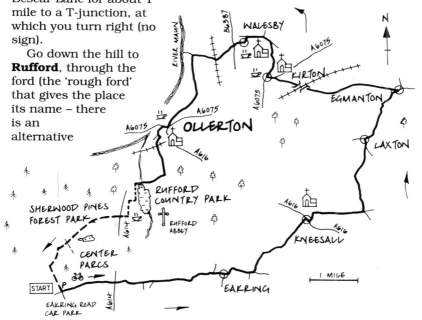

25

continued

footbridge), then after about 200yds turn left, signed *Rufford Mill and Country Park*, into the car park area. Keep round to the left of the car park to join a path by the **Rufford Country Park** noticeboard. Cycling isn't permitted in the Park, so it is necessary to **walk** for **the next section of about 800yds** as far as the Old Coach House. Bear right on the lakeside path, keeping the lake on the left and at a junction of paths, bear right, signed *Rufford Abbey*. The path follows the Mouflon Sheep enclosure on the left; just opposite the information board on these sheep, turn right up a path between lines of trained trees, then follow this path round to the left (ramp beside steps) towards Rufford Abbey. Continue between shaped yew trees onto the tarred path. The second building on the left is the Old Coach House craft centre and tearooms.

To leave Rufford Park continue straight on across the access road to a small wooden gate in the brick wall. Go through the gate onto a gravel road (you can start riding again though the loose gravel makes it tricky!), bear right at the end of this on a concrete-surfaced road, then take the first left opposite Rufford Parish Council noticeboard for about 200yds. Shortly after a tennis court on the right, turn right and follow the road, signed *Robin Hood Way*, past a metal barrier, to the T-junction with the A614.

Go straight over on the old road (now bridleway, signed *Road closed*) for about 300yds to a set

---

Distance: 26 miles

Terrain: Except for the finish section on **forest tracks** through Clipstone Forest and a short section which has to be walked through Rufford Country Park, entirely **on-road** through rolling countryside.

Refreshment opportunities: There are pubs serving food in several of the villages (the Dovecote Inn in Laxton is highly recommended), and teashops in Kirton, Walesby, Ollerton and Rufford Park.

Start: As described, the route starts at the Sherwood Pines Eakring Road car park (GR 620 616). It would also be possible to start from either of the Rufford Abbey car parks (GR 643 647 or 646 656) or, if you are on holiday there, the Center Parcs' Sherwood Holiday Village (GR 637 640).

Ordnance Survey maps: Landranger sheet **120** Mansfield and Worksop

Public transport links: by rail to Mansfield Woodhouse (Robin Hood Line), then follow route **23** (either outward or return legs as described) as far as *Old Clipstone*, follow B6030 east for ½ or ¾ mile to the Sherwood Pines Visitor Centre, then follow link **L7** to the cross-tracks west of Center Parcs' Sherwood Holiday Village to join this route.

Other routes: Route **18** is a shorter (13-mile) version of this one; link **L7** leads from Center Parcs Sherwood Holiday Village to Edwinstowe and Sherwood Forest, giving another link to route **23**. Route **28**, Southwell Trail and the Dumbles, overlaps this one through Eakring and Kneesall, and route **34**, the northern Trent valley, touches this one at Egmanton and Laxton.

of metal gates. Pass through the gap to the right of the gates to cross a tarred road, which leads to Center Parcs Sherwood Holiday Village, onto a firm-surfaced but untarred track – concessionary cycle way, signed *Robin Hood Way* – keeping Center Parcs' perimeter fence on the left.

After about 1^1/$_4$ miles, at the cross tracks with the information board marked 'Start of cycle route', go straight on, past the green metal barrier, for about 1 mile, then left up a slight hill. (This is part of the waymarked cycle route in reverse: you can check that you're on the right track by means of the red cycle route signs, which are mounted on short wooden posts, also painted red.) Follow this track to the green metal barrier at T-junction of tracks at the **Eakring Road car park**.

25
continued

---

26 miles • on-road • almost flat • Newark-on-Trent

26

South from Newark

This circular route from Newark meanders gently through the villages and quiet landscape of the Trent valley south of Newark-on-Trent. It's another of our routes to venture outside Nottinghamshire: Newark lies very close to the Lincolnshire boundary, and about seven miles of the route lie in that county. Although the route is broadly in the Trent valley, it in fact crosses the watershed to drop to the River Witham near Claypole and Long Bennington. Instead of joining the Trent and eventually the Humber to reach the sea at Hull, the Witham makes its way to Lincoln and then by Boston to the Wash.

While not as sparsely populated as other parts of Lincolnshire, the roads on this route in both counties are remarkably quiet, passing through pleasant and sleepy, if unspectacular, villages and hamlets. One notable feature on the way is the 'Leaning Tower of Doddington' – Dry Doddington's church tower leans out at an angle of several degrees from the rest of the building.

Another building of note beside the route is Sibthorpe dovecote, a large circular building prominent in a field beside the track as you

26 continued

approach the hamlet. It is the only remnant of a mediaeval religious foundation that once stood here. The 60ft-high building had nesting places for 1260 birds: the pigeons were used for winter food and their droppings much prized as a fertiliser.

From **Newark Castle** go south-west along Castlegate, follow this round to the left into Lombard Street, then at the traffic lights by the Robin Hood Hotel, go right and left into London Road, B6326, signed *Balderton*. After 3 miles, at a roundabout just after **Balderton**, turn right on B6326 signed *Grantham and Claypole* to pass over the A1. Continue for about 1 mile, then turn left, signed *Claypole*. In **Claypole**, just after a phone box on the right, turn right into Doddington Lane, signed *Dry Doddington*. On the outskirts of **Dry Doddington**, turn right on Main Street, signed *Grantham*. After passing the church with the leaning tower on the right

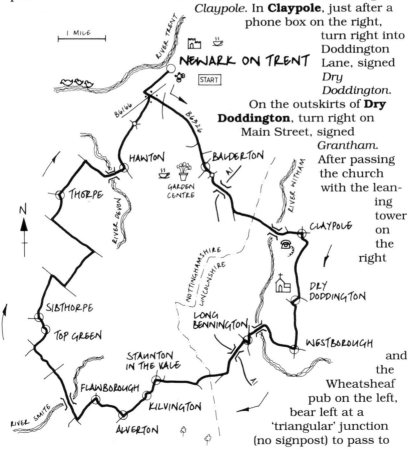

and the Wheatsheaf pub on the left, bear left at a 'triangular' junction (no signpost) to pass to the left of the new village hall. After $1^1/2$ miles at the staggered crossroads at **Westborough**, turn right, signed *Long Bennington*.

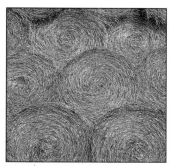

26

continued

At the T-junction on the outskirts of **Long Bennington**, turn left signed *Newark*. After 300yds, turn right into Valley Lane (just before Burton's Newsagents) signed *Newark*, and almost immediately left again, signed *Staunton*. Pass over the A1, then at a fork just before power lines cross the road, bear right, signed *Staunton*. At

Harvest-time near Newark

the T-junction after $^3/_4$ mile, turn right, again signed *Staunton*. Pass by the end of the hamlet of **Staunton in the Vale** to a T-junction; turn left, signed *Kilvington*. Go through **Kilvington** (which hardly appears on the map although it's quite evident on the ground) to **Alverton**, then take the first right, signed *Flawborough*.

Go through **Flawborough**, following the road round to the left through the village, then after about $^3/_4$ mile follow the sharp bend round to the right to cross the River Smite. At the first minor crossroads after the river bridge, go straight on, signed *Flintham*. After about another $^1/_2$ mile, at a minor crossroads, turn right (signpost missing, but Flintham is signed as straight on) on an open unfenced road through **Top Green** to **Sibthorpe**. Keep right (effectively straight on) at the end of the hamlet, signed *Elston*.

Distance: 26 miles

Terrain: entirely **on-road**, very gentle hills for the first part, almost flat for the second

Refreshment opportunities: there are several cafés in Newark, and a coffee shop at the garden centre at Balderton. There are pubs (which may or may not supply meals) in Claypole, Dry Doddington, Long Bennington, Staunton in the Vale, and just off the route in Orston and Elston.

Start: Castlegate, Newark-on-Trent (GR 795 540)

Ordnance Survey maps: sorry, Newark lies at the corner of several maps and if you want to cover the whole route it takes no less than *four* Landranger sheets – **120** Mansfield and Worksop (only about a mile lies on this sheet), **121** Lincoln, **129** Nottingham and Loughborough, and **130** Grantham!

Public transport links: East Coast Main Line services serve Newark Northgate. Local services on Nottingham line to Newark Castle, less frequently extending to Newark Northgate as well. At its nearest point (just after Flawborough) the route is only 1½ miles from Elton and Orston station on the Nottingham–Grantham line (however, not many trains stop there – and don't confuse Elton and Elston!)

Other routes: The Newark to Nottingham linear route, **40**, starts from Newark. Link route **L11** joins Newark north of the River Trent to Fiskerton and so to route **30**, while link route **L12** joins Newark to routes **28** and **34** at Norwell.

26
continued

About 1 mile further on at a T-junction, turn right, signed *Shelton*, then after a further 700yds, take the first left, signed *Thorpe*. After about 2 miles, take the first right, again signed *Thorpe*. The road winds through **Thorpe**, then continues, straight on, as a very straight road after the village; about 1 mile beyond the village, at a T-junction, turn right, signed *Hawton*. Cross the bridge over the River Devon (which the River Smite has mysteriously become), then at the T-junction in **Hawton**, bear left, signed *Newark*. You soon reach the built-up area; at a small (but not mini) five-way roundabout, continue straight on to the oblique T-junction with the B6166. Go right to the traffic lights, then either left at lights on the B6166 to **Newark Castle** or straight on (cycle bypass at 'No entry' sign) to the town centre.

27

27 miles • mostly on-road • gentle • Church Warsop

Clumber Park and Meden Vale

Note: do not confuse Clumber Park South Lodge (this route) with Worksop Manor South Lodge (route 14 and link L4)

This route starts by picking its way through what was part of the Nottinghamshire coalfield, with efforts now obviously being made to restore the landscape and attract visitors to local attractions and curiosities. The outward route follows the valley of the Millwood Brook, which is dammed to form the Great Lake of the Welbeck estate, emerging as the River Poulter. The highlight of the route, though, is a circuit of Clumber Park with its attractive double central avenue of lime trees – but watch out while crossing the slippery ford south of Hardwick village! (Don't be alarmed – there's a footbridge close by.)

Clumber Park was the domain of the Dukes of Newcastle but, unlike the other large estates which form the Dukeries, the great house has now gone, demolished in 1938 with only its foundations now traceable. Other estate features, such as parts of the formal garden and vineries and the prominent Victorian Gothic Revival chapel, remain, while the clock tower now

houses a welcome cafeteria and restaurant. There is also a
cycle hire centre. The real attraction though is the 3800 acres
of parkland – a mixture of woodland, open space and heathland
surrounding an 80-acre lake. There is a network of 13 miles of
tarred roads plus many other tracks and bridleways, with
cyclists able to make use of most of them. Clumber Park is now
in the care of the National Trust, who charge motorists for
access to the central area while sensibly letting people on
bicycles in free.

> **27**
> *continued*

The route returns to Church Warsop by the valley of the
River Meden. The name of the last village on the route, Meden
Vale, is very recent: for half a century after it was built to
service the colliery the settlement was known as Welbeck
Colliery Village – it was officially changed to Meden Vale only in
1975 but many local people still use the old name.

Link route **L10** has been specially devised to allow you to
join this route and so reach Clumber Park from Mansfield
Woodhouse station on the Robin Hood Line from Nottingham,
Bulwell, Hucknall, Sutton and Mansfield. Bikes go free on these
trains, so you can leave the car at home!

The church which gives **Church Warsop** its name lies at the
junction of Bishops Walk, B6031, and Church Road, A60: head
west along Bishops Walk, signed *Shirebrook*. After about ¹/₂ mile
turn right into Wood Lane for *Nether Langwith*, and after 1¹/₂ miles,
at the T-junction with the main road (A632 but unsigned), turn
left. Follow the A632 (a relatively quiet road, despite its A-road
status) into **Nether Langwith** and just before the traffic signals
controlling traffic through the tall railway bridge, turn right for
Whaley. This is a delightful little road which follows a tributary of
the River Poulter.

Just before the village of **Whaley**, where the road bears round
to the left, take the first turning to the right. At the T-junction
about 300yds later turn right, and right again at the next T-
junction a further 400yds on: these junctions are not
signposted. Cross the railway line at the gated level
crossing, and bear left (effectively straight on) at the
next junction 500yds later, again unsigned, to reach
the A616. Go straight over the main road for *Holbeck*,
and bear right on passing the **Holbeck** village sign,
for *Norton*. Take care as you meet an unexpected
minor cross roads – no signs or indications of priority
– continuing straight ahead until you reach the A60

27
continued

after about 1 mile. Cross the main road into Norton Lane, and after 1 mile go left at the T-junction in **Norton** village for *Carburton*. This road skirts the southern edge of the Great Lake of Welbeck Park,

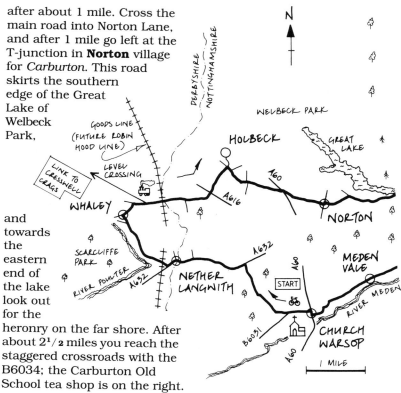

and towards the eastern end of the lake look out for the heronry on the far shore. After about 2 1/2 miles you reach the staggered crossroads with the B6034; the Carburton Old School tea shop is on the right.

Go right and left across the B-road to follow signs for *Clumber Park*, passing through the hamlet of **Carburton** before reaching the entrance to the park. Stay on the wide tree-lined avenue for 2 1/2 miles, then turn right at the minor crossroads signed for *Hardwick Village*. Go through **Hardwick**, and through the ford across the weir over the River Poulter – there is a footbridge if you don't want to tempt fate! Where the road bears round to the left at the top of the slope, continue straight ahead round a low wooden barrier onto a bridleway. After about 300yds the track emerges onto a tarred minor road; turn right and follow this road westwards for about 1 1/2 miles.

Just before the road passes over the handsome arched bridge at the western end of **Clumber Lake**, turn left onto a 'No-through road' signed for *South Lodge*. As soon as you can see the large iron gates of South Lodge barring further passage, look for a forest track which crosses the road about 100yds before the gates. Turn right onto the track, round a low wooden barrier and along a pine-tree-bordered path for approximately 1/2 mile. Turn left at the first

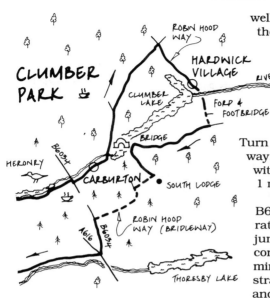

well-defined track to cross the one you are on, and follow this until it emerges onto a bridleway – blue arrows – which is signed as part of the *Robin Hood Way*. Turn right onto the bridleway, fairly bumpy in places with tree roots, for nearly 1 mile to the B6034.

Turn left on the B6034, down the hill to a rather convoluted junction with the A616, controlled by a couple of mini-roundabouts: go straight on at the first one and right at the second, then immediately left signed *Meden Vale*. This road follows the line of the River Meden, passes just south of the village of **Meden Vale** and then on into **Church Warsop**. At the junction with the A60, turn right back to the start of the route. 🚲

Distance: 27 miles (38 miles including link route **L10** going out-and-home from Mansfield Woodhouse station)

Terrain: Mostly on quiet **road**s, but includes a couple of stretches of **bridleway** in Clumber Country Park (and nearly 1½ miles of firm-surfaced **track** on the link to Mansfield Woodhouse station). There are also several main road crossings, and a mile or so of A-road, but these don't seem particularly busy at weekends. While undulating in places there are no hills to speak of.

Refreshment opportunities: There is a tea shop near Carburton – about half-way round, and another a little further on in Clumber Park (slightly off the actual route). This ride does not otherwise pass through many villages, nor by many pubs.

Start: Church Warsop, Parish Church of St Peter and St Paul (GR 568 688) (Link **L10** to Robin Hood Line starts at Mansfield Woodhouse station, GR 534 634)

Ordnance Survey maps: Landranger sheet **120** Mansfield and Worksop

Public transport links: Robin Hood rail line to Mansfield Woodhouse and Mansfield (no Sunday service). At the time of writing it was also intended that the Robin Hood Line should be extended to Worksop by 1998, with a proposed station at Langwith.

Other routes: Route **17** meets this one at Clumber, and route **39** gives a largely off-road link from Hardwick village to route **25** at Ollerton. Link route **L8** is an on-road link from Clumber to route **25** at Walesby; link route **L10** leads from Mansfield Woodhouse station to join this route at Langwith.

28

28 miles • on- and off-road • undulating • Southwell

The Southwell Trail and the Dumbles

The first few miles of this route make use of part of the
Southwell Trail – a disused rail line converted to a shared-use
path for walkers, cyclists and horse riders. This is flat, and
while the hedges on both sides obscure distant views, they also
offer shelter from the prevailing westerly winds and contribute
to the trail's attraction as a wildlife corridor. The route then
follows the very attractive leafy lanes of Hexgreave Park,
through one of Nottinghamshire's few remaining working
mining villages, Bilsthorpe, and out into rolling farmland
crisscrossed by minor rivers and streams and their valleys
('dumbles').

Head north-west from the start at the **Southwell**
Trail car park along the Trail towards Farnsfield.
Here the route leaves the Trail – after about 5 miles
(or possibly half an hour's riding or more: trail riding
of this sort isn't particularly fast). While there are no
signs, the point where you leave the Trail is where it
crosses its second minor road (as opposed to going
under or over them at bridges), at GR 648 572. This
means negotiating two wooden 'squeeze gates' in
quick succession and going down a ramp to the minor road (the
continuation of the trail goes up a similar ramp on the other side).
Turn right on the minor road, which is soon signed as a private
road – it nevertheless incorporates a bridleway. At the T-junction,
turn right where *Cockett Barn Farm* is signed off to the left, then
first left after about 200yds along a tree-lined avenue. This lovely
lane winds through **Hexgreave Park**, and eventually, after
descending gently through a second, more shady, avenue, the
official bridleway passes through the wicket gate beside a white
gate and a lodge to meet the A617. (Occasionally you may find the
main gate open, too.)

Turn left on the A617 and first right after about 150yds, then
after about 500yds turn left at the T-junction into **Bilsthorpe**. At
the T-junction with Kirklington Road, turn right through the

mining village (past a warning sign that ducks are crossing!), and soon after the entrance to Bilsthorpe Colliery turn right. Turn right again at the next T-junction after about 400yds, and follow this road for about $1^1/2$ miles to **Eakring**.

This road becomes Bilsthorpe

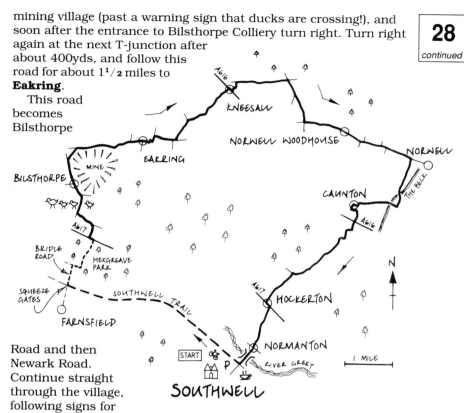

Road and then Newark Road. Continue straight through the village, following signs for *Kneesall*. After about $^3/4$ mile, take the first left, signed *Kneesall*, for about 2 miles to the T-junction with the A616 in **Kneesall**; turn right, signposted *Newark*. After about 150yds, turn first left just after the church into School Lane. Follow School Lane to the T-junction just after the school. Turn right, follow the road gently downhill for about $1^1/2$ miles to a crossroads; turn right, signed for *Kersall*. Take the first left turn (unsigned) after $^1/2$ mile, then left again at the next crossroads, just over $^1/2$ mile further on and through the rather straggling hamlet of **Norwell Woodhouse**.

Shortly before the village of Norwell, with a prominent plantation of willows on the left, take the right turn signed for *Caunton*. Turn right at the T-junction after about 1 mile, immediately crossing a stream known as 'The Beck'. Follow this road as it winds through **Caunton**, taking the left turn – Main Street, signed for *Hockerton* – just after a public telephone. At the southern edge of Caunton, go straight over the A616, again signed *Hockerton*, which you reach after 3 miles. In **Hockerton**, turn left at the junction with the

28
continued

A617, and shortly right for *Southwell*: this road will bring you to where the route started, just past the converted mill buildings on the outskirts of the Minster town of **Southwell**. 🚲

Distance: 28 miles

Terrain: Predominantly **on** quiet country **roads**, with a five-mile section of the *Southwell Trail*. In this area of rolling farmland there are inevitably one or two slopes, although these are generally fairly short and ridable with low gears.

Refreshment opportunities: Most of the villages en route have pubs serving food, many also have a number of shops. Southwell, where the ride starts and finishes, has several tea shops.

Start: Southwell Trail car park, Station Road, Southwell (GR 706 545)

Ordnance Survey maps: Landranger sheet **120** Mansfield and Worksop

Public transport links: The nearest rail station to Southwell is Fiskerton on the Nottingham to Newark Castle line, about 2½ miles south-east of Southwell. Fiskerton is a request stop: trains stop there if you tell the conductor when you get on, or give a hand signal as the train approaches. Not all trains on this route will stop at Fiskerton.

Other routes: Route **18** joins this one briefly between Bilsthorpe and Eakring; route **22** uses the same section of the B6386 over Oxton Bank to Oxton; route **25** overlaps it through Eakring and Kneesall. Route **30** comes out from Nottingham to Southwell. The very short link route **L1** joins this route to route **34** at Norwell.

29

29 miles • on- and off-road • mostly flat • Retford

Retford and Harworth

This circuit north and west of Retford is in a way a cycling pilgrimage. The mining village of Harworth has a claim to cycling fame as, sadly, the burial place of Tom Simpson, who grew up here. The first British rider to wear the coveted 'yellow

jersey' in the Tour de France, he collapsed and died on the baking slopes of Mont Ventoux in Provence in the 1967 event. He was only 29. His grave is a few yards in front and to the right of the entrance to Harworth cemetery, which is signposted from the centre of the village.

The route passes not only close to the Sutton-cum-Lound Wetlands Waterfowl Reserve (see route **16**) but also by the Daneshill Lakes Local Nature Reserve and Wildlife Sanctuary – 120 acres of woodland and lakes with public access. Admission is free.

About three miles farther on the route follows a fine bridleway above the valley of the

IN LOVING MEMORY OF
TOM SIMPSON,
THE DEAR HUSBAND OF HELEN
AND LOVING FATHER OF JANE & JOANNE,
WHO DIED ON MONT VENTOUX, FRANCE
13TH JULY 1967 – AGED 29 YEARS,
WHILST COMPETING WITH THE GREAT BRITAIN TEAM
IN THE TOUR DE FRANCE CYCLE RACE.
HIS BODY ACHED, HIS LEGS GREW TIRED
BUT STILL HE WOULD NOT GIVE IN.

29 continued

Tom Simpson's grave at Harworth

River Ryton, through open woodland which is a riot of bluebells in late spring before crossing the river just beyond Serlby. The return route from Harworth passes through Scrooby village with its Pilgrim Fathers associations (see route **37**), and then offers the option of an off-route section through to the pleasant village of Mattersey. From here the route back to Retford follows the same roads as route **24**.

Leave **Retford** Market Square at the northern end, turning left at the mini-roundabout by the White Hart into Bridgegate to cross the River Idle. At the next roundabout take the second exit, signed *Bawtry A638* and *Ranskill*; this is the old Great North Road, the original coaching route from London to York and Edinburgh. After about $1^1/2$ miles, just before the main road begins to climb to a railway bridge, fork right at an oblique cross-roads onto a minor road, Sutton Lane, signed *Sutton* and *Wetlands Wildfowl Reserve*. Follow the road round through **Sutton**, continuing on Mattersey Road. After about 1 mile, turn left into Daneshill Road, signed *Torworth*. Some 2 miles further on, go over the level crossing, then just before the junction with the A638, turn right by a house called The Briars into **Torworth** by an unnamed lane which runs parallel to the main road. Take the third left into the narrow Blacksmith Lane (the sign is behind you as you turn) to cross the main A638 just south of the Huntsman Inn, onto a minor road, signed *Blyth*. After about 1 mile, just over the brow of a gentle climb and where the road you are on bears left, fork right (unsigned) onto a very minor road. This joins the B6045 at a T-junction after about $3/4$ mile.

Turn right on the B6045 (unsigned) for about 200yds. Turn left into what appears at first to be *signed as the driveway of Blyth Cottage*. Keep to the right of Blyth Cottage, following the obvious

29

continued

bridleway which is however unsigned. After about 1 mile the bridleway crosses a private tarred access road. Continue straight on on the (still unsigned) bridleway for about $1/2$ mile past a golf course to the left, passing to the left of a metal gate to reach a tarred road.

Turn left (unsigned) between two white posts through **Serlby** to cross the River Ryton, following the road round to the left to the A614. Go straight over the main road, signed *Harworth*, past the glassworks and colliery. At the next T-junction, turn right, signed *Harworth* and *Tickhill*, to pass the colliery entrance. At the first mini-roundabout on the outskirts of Harworth, turn right into Scrooby Road, signed *Bircotes*. (Go straight ahead if you wish to visit **Harworth** village, then retrace to this roundabout.) Some 2 miles later this road reaches the A614 (unsigned), again at a T-junction.

Turn left on the A614 for about 500yds uphill, then take the first minor road turning on the right into Gibbet Lane, signed *Scrooby*. In about 300yds this road reaches the old Great North Road, A638 (also unsigned at this point). Go straight across on a minor road, Mill Lane, and cross two streams into **Scrooby**, where Mill Lane becomes Low Road. At the crossroads by the church, *if you do not want to negotiate stiles*, go straight on to rejoin the A638 to the outskirts of **Ranskill**, turning left about 500yds after passing the very decayed-looking Scrooby Top House on the right, into Folly Nook Lane. At the T-junction at the end, turn left on the B6045 over the level crossing to the centre of **Mattersey** village.

The *alternative off-road route* from Scrooby to Mattersey turns left into Station Road to the level crossing. There are two stiles to negotiate to go over the crossing when the gates are locked. Beyond the crossing follow the well-defined track that runs parallel to the railway, then just before a metal gate, turn left over a very narrow bridge (or follow the path across the field to a third stile). Bear

round to the right at the corner of the field, then almost immediately left over another footbridge over a second stream. Continue on this path beside a wetland area to the right, then across an open field. After some 400yds the path joins a firm-surfaced track. Bear right down this track, which is bordered on both sides by a tall hedge, then 200yds later left, following this track for about 1 mile until it becomes a tarred road. After about $1/2$ mile there is a T-junction; this is **Mattersey Thorpe**. Turn left, signed *Mattersey*, and then follow the

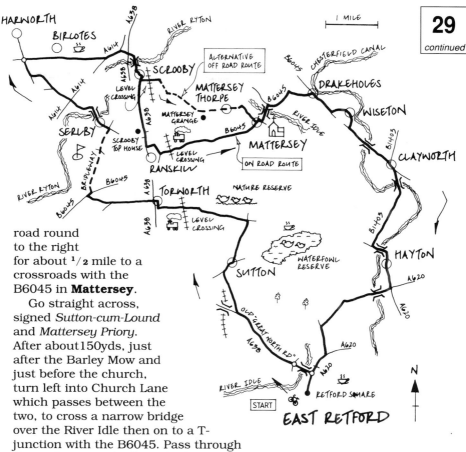

road round
to the right
for about ¹/₂ mile to a
crossroads with the
B6045 in **Mattersey**.

Go straight across,
signed *Sutton-cum-Lound*
and *Mattersey Priory*.
After about150yds, just
after the Barley Mow and
just before the church,
turn left into Church Lane
which passes between the
two, to cross a narrow bridge
over the River Idle then on to a T-
junction with the B6045. Pass through
the cycle gap in the fence and turn right on the B6045 (unsigned)
to **Drakeholes**. Just before the Griff Inn on the left, turn right,
signed *Wiseton, Clayworth* and *Hayton*, leaving the canal basin and
the entrance to Drakeholes canal tunnel on the left.

After just over ¹/₂ mile, turn left, signed *Wiseton*. Just past the
entrance to Wiseton Hall, follow the road round to the right, with
the Chesterfield Canal to the left, to rejoin the original road at a T-
junction. Turn left (unsigned) to the outskirts of Clayworth, then
over the canal bridge into the centre of **Clayworth** on Town Street.
In the centre of the village, the B1043 comes in from the left but
Town Street has priority. At the far end of the village follow the
B1043 over the canal bridge, following signs for *Hayton*. After
about 2 miles, this road bears sharp left on a very open and
windswept corner. From this point, you can **either** turn right onto

29
continued

Chain Bridge Road (unsigned and unsurfaced) and follow the bank of the River Idle (*see route 16*) **or** continue on the B1043 over the canal bridge by the Boat Inn, then round to the right through the long village of **Hayton**. Just before the give way sign at the approach to the A620 crossroads, opposite Corner Farm, turn right into Smeath Lane (the road is named but there's no signpost).

Distance: 29 miles

Terrain: mostly flat on quiet **roads** with some **bridleway** sections; optional section of gravel track along Chain Bridge Road.

Refreshment opportunities: there are tea shops in Retford, a tea shop/café in Harworth, and a café at the Waterfowl Reserve at Sutton-cum-Lound, just off the route. Most of the villages also have pubs.

Start: Market Square, Retford (GR 704 811)

Ordnance Survey maps: sorry, you'll need three Landranger sheets – **111** Sheffield and Doncaster, **112** Scunthorpe and **120** Mansfield and Worksop

Public transport links: East Coast Main Line trains (well, some of them) stop at Retford, and the Regional Railways service from Sheffield to Lincoln via Worksop and Gainsborough calls at the lower station at Retford.

Other routes: Routes **16** and **24**, and the longest one in the book, **37**, also start from Retford and use some of the same roads into and out of the town.

At the junction with the lane from Tiln, turn left, signed *Retford Market Place 1*. This soon enters the built-up outskirts of Retford and after about ³/₄ mile joins the A620, Moorgate. Turn right downhill, turn left at the traffic lights at the foot of the hill onto Arlington Way, then right at the next set of lights into Chapelgate to return via the short pedestrianised section to **Retford Market Place**. 🚴

30

30 miles • on-road • some hills • Daybrook

Daybrook Square to Southwell

This route starts in a north-east suburb of Nottingham but, once you are over the considerable lump of the misleadingly-named Mapperley 'Plains', is soon out into gently rolling countryside, passing through some of the most attractive of Nottinghamshire's villages. Just over half way, the route passes through Southwell, with its impressive Minster and numerous refreshment places. Heading back towards Nottingham, the route climbs up onto a ridge – Oxton Bank – which affords grand views over the surrounding valleys, which have been shaped by numerous small rivers or 'dumbles'. The route finally takes in Calverton, a large mining village whose colliery was a victim of the coalfield closure programme in the early 1990s, but soon reopened under private ownership.

Once across the main A6097, the route passes through the long attractive village of Epperstone, then down a delightful open lane to Gonalston, another pretty village. Gonalston is one of several Nottingham villages to have an elaborate forge with a large horseshoe-shaped entrance of black brick.

The next two villages, Hoveringham and Thurgarton, lie on the flat flood plain of the now-tamed River Trent. Although Thurgarton lies astride the busy main Nottingham to Southwell road, several of the little side roads are quiet attractive backwaters. One of them, Beck Lane, leading from Hoveringham up to the main road, runs beside the small and surprisingly clear stream that gives it its name, the houses that line it being approached by a series of small bridges. And if you need to know the time, the village clock on the main road appears – at least when we've passed by – to be a model of accuracy. It was originally above Platform 4 at Nottingham station and was installed here by a lifelong railwayman when he retired.

The route reaches the River Trent at Fiskerton, at one time quite an important inland port – the name is a Danish version of an Anglo-Saxon one meaning 'the settlement of the fishermen'. In the early days of the Industrial Revolution roads were very poor, railways had not been invented and most goods traffic was by water. Convenient deep-water riversides such as Fiskerton were valuable for exporting Nottinghamshire's mineral wealth, and bringing in other goods in exchange. The river frontage still has substantial piling and wharfage.

It's only two or three miles from here to the pleasing little town of Southwell which figures on several of our routes. (There's more on Southwell in the description of route **8**.)

After Oxton and its cobbled ford, the last village on the route before the built-up area of Nottingham is Calverton. Expanded from its former modest size – around a thousand inhabitants at the turn of the century – when mining came here as late as

30
continued

1952, it nevertheless has an earlier industrial history. In 1589 William Lee of Calverton invented the stocking-knitters' frame, later to become the nucleus of a cottage industry throughout the county. The operators of these frames needed good light to work by and several of the old cottages have the characteristic long windows of frame-knitters' homes. One fine example in Calverton is Windles Square, almost opposite the foot of Bonner Hill from Lambley, where the run of brick cottages has recently been expertly restored. It was the threatened displacement of these village hand industries by mechanised factories in the towns that sparked off the Luddite riots of the early 19th century.

With the Grove in **Daybrook Square** behind you, cross over the main – A60 – road into Nottingham Road. After about $^1/_2$ mile, at the first set of traffic lights, turn right into Arnot Hill Road, then very soon left at the mini-roundabout into Hallam's Lane. Continue along this road, which becomes Gedling Road, then Brookfield Road. At the T-junction at the end of Brookfield Road, turn left opposite a parade of shops – this is Rolleston Drive. After 600yds, at the signal-controlled crossroads, turn right up the hill – this is Coppice Road. There is a mini-roundabout at the end of Coppice Road where you turn left onto **Mapperley Plains**, B684, signed to *Woodborough*. When the road bears round to the left after about 1 mile, turn right, again signed *Woodborough*. This attractive descent brings you to the western end of **Woodborough**; turn right at the T-junction and continue to the eastern end of the village, and where the road bears to the right, turn left up Shelt Hill – opposite the Nags Head. Follow this road for about $^3/_4$ mile until it reaches the A6097, where you turn right and immediately left for *Epperstone*. Keep on this road for some $2^1/_2$ miles, through **Epperstone** to Gonalston. Passing through **Gonalston** look out for the old forge on the left, then cross straight over the A612 and on over a railway level crossing into **Hoveringham**. Just beyond St Michael's church, turn left at the T-junction signed *Thurgarton*. Cross back over the railway at a level crossing by Thurgarton station, then, where the road bears left, turn right into **Thurgarton**.

At the junction with the main road, A612, turn right and right again after about 150yds – just past the Coach and Horses – into Bleasby Road. A mile or so further on the road swings round to the right and there is a short descent into **Bleasby** village: look out for the Manor Farm tea rooms on the left (summer only). The Wagon and Horses in Bleasby dates back to the 17th century, and just beyond the sign for this, turn left at a minor crossroads into Gypsy Lane. This lane meanders between hedged fields; at the far end turn left, signed to *Fiskerton*. Just past the Bromley Arms in **Fiskerton**, turn left into Station Road. Go over the level crossing at Fiskerton Station, through **Brinkley**, past Southwell Garden Centre (which has a tea shop). This road emerges – after some $2^1/2$ miles – on the outskirts of **Southwell**. Turn left at the T-junction opposite the White Lion Inn, along Easthorpe. **Southwell Minste**r soon looms up on the left (tea shop open week-ends); at the end of this road,

turn left at the mini-roundabout, opposite the Saracen's Head, signed *A612 Nottingham*. Continue on this road (ignoring the turn where the A612 is routed off to the left) as it becomes Oxton Lane (B6386), and leaves Southwell. Climbing gradually over about 4 miles, the road comes out at the top of a fairly steep descent, known as Oxton Bank. Swoop down and continue along the valley bottom, taking the second turning on the right – Sandy Lane – into **Oxton** to go through a little ford (there is a footbridge you can wheel your bike over if you prefer). Just beyond the ford, turn left along the

123

30
continued

aptly named Water Lane, a narrow and quite pretty little road beside a stream which emerges opposite the Bridge Inn. Turn left into Main Street and immediately right into Nottingham Road, B6386 (effectively straight on from Water Lane). Go straight over at the roundabout, across the A6097, and along the B6386 signed to *Nottingham.* Continue on for about 1 mile, and at the minor crossroads, turn left for *Calverton*, past a Scout camp site. After about 300yds, turn right into Flatts Lane, by the blue 'Borough of Gedling/Calverton' sign on the right-hand side of the road. After about 400yds Flatts Lane crosses Park Road in a dog-leg, right-and-left crossing. Continue on Flatts Lane for another 400yds to a T-junction with Collyers Road (not signed at this point) by the Co-op Late Shop. Turn right, then almost immediately left into Mews Lane, in front of the Cherry Tree, a large roadhouse-style pub.

Where Mews Lane meets Main Street, **Calverton**, opposite Main Street Stores, turn right and in about 30yds, opposite Martin's Garage, turn left into George's Lane, signed *Arnold 3*, to go up George's Hill. This is quite a tough climb, but with fine views to the left. At **Dorket Head** crossroads at the top of the climb go straight on over the B684 into Calverton Road (not named at this point), signed *Arnold*, to go down a quite steep hill. Just after the Longbow Inn on the right towards the foot of the hill there is a 'speed table' – a long brick-paved road hump to slow traffic outside the school –

Distance: 30 miles

Terrain: Entirely **on-road**, mainly quiet country lanes except for the first and last couple of miles which are urban. For the most part gradients are fairly gentle, although the ridge of Mapperley 'Plains' presents quite a stiff climb both at the start and towards the finish of the route

Refreshment opportunities:Tea shops at Brookfields Garden Centre, Mapperley Plains; Manor Farm, Bleasby; Southwell Garden Centre; and Southwell Minster Refectory. There are other places in Southwell but just off the route. Most of the villages en route have at least one pub and a shop.

Start: Daybrook Square, north-east Nottingham (GR 579 446)

Ordnance Survey maps: Landranger sheets **120** Mansfield and Worksop, and **129** Nottingham and Loughborough.

Public transport links: The nearest rail station to Southwell is Fiskerton on the Nottingham to Newark Castle line, about 2½ miles south-east of Southwell. Fiskerton, and Thurgarton and Bleasby on the same line and also on the route, are request stops: trains stop there if you tell the conductor when you get on, or give a hand signal as the train approaches. Not all trains on this route will stop at Thurgarton, Bleasby or Fiskerton.

Other routes: Route **20**, Lambley and Lowdham, overlaps this one between Epperstone and Hoveringham, and route **22**, Blidworth and Halam, crosses at Westhorpe and in the centre of Southwell. Route **28**, Southwell Trail and the Dumbles, starts and finishes at Southwell. Link route **L11** joins this route, from Fiskerton, to Newark-on-Trent.

so take it steady! Calverton Road becomes Church Street shortly after this. At the end of Church Street, by the Robin Hood and Little John and facing the County Library, turn right at the mini-roundabout into Cross Street (not signed at this point), then after about 100yds at the traffic lights by Arnold Leisure Centre take the filter lane to turn left and bypass the lights into High Street, **Arnold**, signed *Nottingham (A60)*. Continue along High Street then, at the traffic lights by the Greyhound Inn and Sainsbury's, go straight on on Nottingham Road to complete the circuit at the Grove, **Daybrook Square.** 🚲

30
continued

---

31 miles • on-road • gently rolling • Bingham

31

Bingham and the Vale

This route shares for its first few miles the sometimes surprising delights of the shorter circuit from Bingham, route **13**. The charming little hamlet of Tithby, approached through wide open fields, seems very remote. The road through the next village, Cropwell Butler, leads eventually out out onto a tiny open hedgeless road crossing corn-covered open wolds, and then crests the brow to reveal one of the most attractive views in south Nottinghamshire, across the village of Shelford, nestled in a bend of the Trent.

From here the route follows for a few miles the top of the 'cliff' marking the south-eastern limit of the Trent's floodplain, through East Bridgford. The next hamlet of Kneeton, just off the route, seems peaceful enough now but was the scene of a vicious engagement in the English Civil War of the 1640s when no more than a handful of the losing side managed to reach the opposite bank and safety.

About four miles later the route crosses the Hawksworth to Scarrington road on its way to Thoroton. A two-mile detour from the described route at this point leads to the village of Scarrington. One of the most striking features here is a 17ft-high column of some 50 000 used horseshoes, beside the road that leads to Aslockton. For all its historic look, the stack is in fact very recent,

31
continued

having been accumulated by the local smith in the twenty years leading up to his retirement in 1965. At one time at risk of being sold to America, this curiosity now belongs to Nottinghamshire County Council.

After Thoroton the route crosses the River Smite to reach Orston. This village had, surprisingly, an illustrious industrial past going back to the Middle Ages as a source of gypsum for plaster. At one time the Royal Plaster Works in the middle of the village were described as the best in the land. The pits were worked up to 1873; all that is now left are undulations in the ground.

It seems strange to think in quiet Granby, one of the last villages on the route, that this village is honoured up and down the whole of England in a common pub name – the Marquis of Granby. The wide spread of the pub name is attributed to the large number of soldiers who had served under the Marquis in battle in the Seven Years War in the 1750s and 60s. In the days before there were pensions for common soldiers it was the practice for commanders to buy inns for men who had served them well, to give them a continuing income. The Marquis of Granby was one of the most generous in rewarding his troops. The name was further spread by his grandson who was a rather eccentric enthusiast for pubs.

From **Bingham** station go south on Station Street, then right along the edge of Market Place to Market Street. This becomes Fisher Lane and continues to a T-junction with The Banks. Turn right to the T-junction with Tithby Road, then left to the A52. Cross the A52 at a staggered crossroads, right and left, still on Tithby Road.

Head southwards and after about 1¹/₂ miles take the first right, signed *Tithby*. The road bears round to the left into the hamlet of **Tithby**. At a minor crossroads by the church, turn right, signed *Cropwell Butler* . After 1 mile at a T-junction, turn right. (The sign at this junction, for *Radcliffe*, is rather hidden, on the right-hand side of the road after you've gone round the corner.) The road bears right through the centre of **Cropwell Butler**: follow signs for *Bingham*. At the staggered crossroads over the A46 go right then left – effectively straight on – on an unsigned, unnamed minor road. After about 1 mile at the junction with the A52, go left, then almost immediately right, signposted *Shelford*. Follow this open unfenced road with its fine views over the Trent valley for about 1 mile to a crossroads. Turn right, signposted *Newton*, and after about 1¹/₂ miles on the outskirts of **Newton**, turn left, signed *East*

Bridgford, to the junction with the A6097. Go straight over the main road, signposted *East Bridgford*.

At the crossroads by the church in **East Bridgford** go straight on on Kneeton Road past a former windmill for about $2^1/2$ miles to a junction, where the road to Kneeton goes straight on. Turn right, signed *Screveton*, for about 1 mile to a T-junction with the A46. Turn right (care!) on the A46, signed *Leicester*, then after about 200yds turn left just after the Red Lodge, signed *Screveton 1*. Continue for about 1 mile to a T-junction in **Screveton** opposite a telephone box and bus shelter; turn left (*no signpost*). After about 200yds, take the first right, signed *Hawksworth*. About $1^1/2$ miles later, at a T-junction, turn right, then first left – in effect a stag- gered crossroads, with the signpost, to *Thoroton*, somewhere in the middle. After about 1 mile at a further T-junction, turn right, signposted *Thoroton*. Continue through **Thoroton** for about 1 mile to a crossroads, then turn left, signposted *Orston*. Cross the River Smite into **Orston**. At a T-junction after the church, turn right on Mill Lane, signed *Elton*. Mill Lane becomes Hill Road and bears left, signed *Elton and Elton Station*. Follow this road up a slight climb and keep right at both junctions at the top by the triangular green to

31
continued

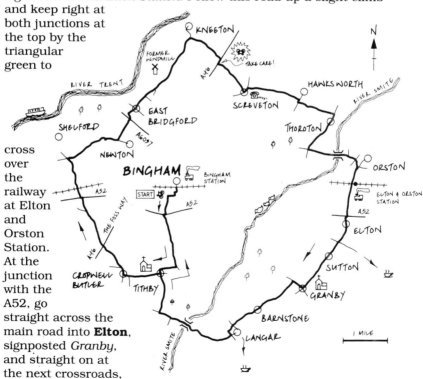

cross over the railway at Elton and Orston Station. At the junction with the A52, go straight across the main road into **Elton**, signposted *Granby*, and straight on at the next crossroads,

31
continued

about 1 mile after Elton, signed *Sutton and Granby*.

Continue through **Sutton** to **Granby**, then at the crossroads by the church, turn right into Main Street, signed *Barnstone*. Just after leaving the village, at the foot of a small hill, turn left, again signed *Barnstone*. Continue through **Barnstone**, a long straggling settlement, to a crossroads about $^1/_2$ mile past the village. Go straight on on Musters Road into **Langar** village. The road bears round to the left through the village, past the Post Office to a T-junction by the Unicorn's Head.

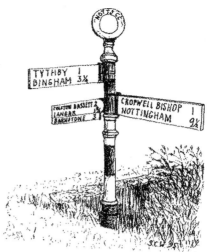

Turn right, signed *Colston Bassett*. After about 2 miles take the first right turn, signed *Tythby* (this is the spelling on the signpost).

In **Tithby**, go straight on by the church, signed *Bingham*. The road bears round to the right to a T-junction after about $^1/_2$ mile. Turn left, signed *Bingham*, for about $1^1/_2$ miles to a T-junction with the A52. Turn right, then left into **Bingham**. The road you are on is Tithby Road, which becomes Fairfield Street. Turn right into Newgate Street, signed *library and health centre*. Just after road bears round to the right, turn left along the edge of Market Square, then first left by two telephone boxes into Station Street; sure enough the station is at the end of this road. 🚲

Distance: 31 miles

Terrain: entirely **on-road**, gently rolling

Refreshment opportunities: Old Hill Farm, Redmile, and the parachute club tea room at Langar Airfield both lie about 1½ miles south-east of the route

Start: Bingham station (GR 705 401)

Ordnance Survey maps: Landranger sheet **129** Nottingham and Loughborough

Public transport links: Regional Railways services to Bingham and Elton & Orston on the Nottingham–Grantham line (not all services on this line stop at Bingham and only 2–3 per day stop at Elton & Orston)

Other routes: Route **13** is a shorter (11-mile) version of this one, also starting and finishing in Bingham. Route **35** uses a stretch of the same roads as this one between Cropwell Bishop and Elton, while route **36** also briefly overlaps south of Tithby. Route **40**, the linear route from Newark to Nottingham, crosses this one at Screveton and East Bridgford.

The calm waters of the Rivers Meden and Maun where they run together briefly, to the west of Bothamsall (see route 38).

Crisp winter days can be really wonderful for cycling – and some of the off-road routes are a good deal firmer under-wheel when they're frozen hard. Just remember to wrap up warm and wear windproof gloves. Hands and feet can get colder cycling than when you're walking. If your feet get cold, the trick is to walk or even trot for a short distance to warm them up again.

Right: The Lake in Wollaton Park (see route 10).

Below: Bestwood Mill Lakes (see routes 2 and 39)

32 miles · on-road · gently rolling · Nottingham

32

Sutton Bonnington and the Soar valley

Although quite long, this is an easy-going route, fairly flat with only the occasional incline. It goes right down to the south-western corner of Nottinghamshire, making use of the good network of cycle routes in the south-west sector of Nottingham to leave and re-enter the city, where this route starts and finishes. One of the features which struck us as we rode round this route was the very large number of roadside seats, many with pleasing views of the countryside or river – ideal for picnic stops.

Once it leaves the built-up area the route crosses a remarkable piece of open landscape – Clifton Pasture and Barton Moor – on its way to Gotham. Famed in a nursery rhyme, the Three Wise Men of Gotham may not have been as dotty as they seemed as they tried to fence in a cuckoo to ensure perpetual spring. One explanation has it that their foolery was part of an ingenious plot to hoodwink the authorities responsible for taxation, conscription, paying for compulsory roadbuilding and other such unpleasantnesses into giving their apparently sadly afflicted village a wide berth.

The route first meets the valley of the River Soar which it is to follow for some way at the pretty hamlet of Kingston on Soar, though the water which passes under the hamlet's picturesque bridge is not the Soar itself but the Kingston Brook. The River Soar marks the very edge of Nottinghamshire. The next valley village, Sutton Bonnington, is a long, straggling place – its length partly the result of its combining the once separate villages of Sutton and Bonnington. In the nineteenth century a thriving centre of the local hosiery industry, it is now largely a residential and commuter village, which also houses the School of Agriculture of Nottingham University, the latest name for this agricultural college which began life a century ago as the Midland Dairy Institute.

Normanton on Soar also straggles along the

129

32
continued

bank of the River Soar. There are several pathways cutting between the houses to the river – and several of those roadside seats offering pleasant picnic spots.

Eventually the route climbs away from the Soar. Its final return towards Nottingham follows an old trackway from Plumtree through the lost village of Flawford or Flawforth, now commemorated only in the names of a couple of farms. Where this track meets a tarred road again, about two miles east of Ruddington, is the site of Flawforth church. Now all that remains are a few gravestones set in a grassy lawn. A variety of finds from archaeological digs here are housed in an old house now a museum – The Hermitage in Ruddington village. This is one of many villages – now grown into a small town – around Nottingham to have

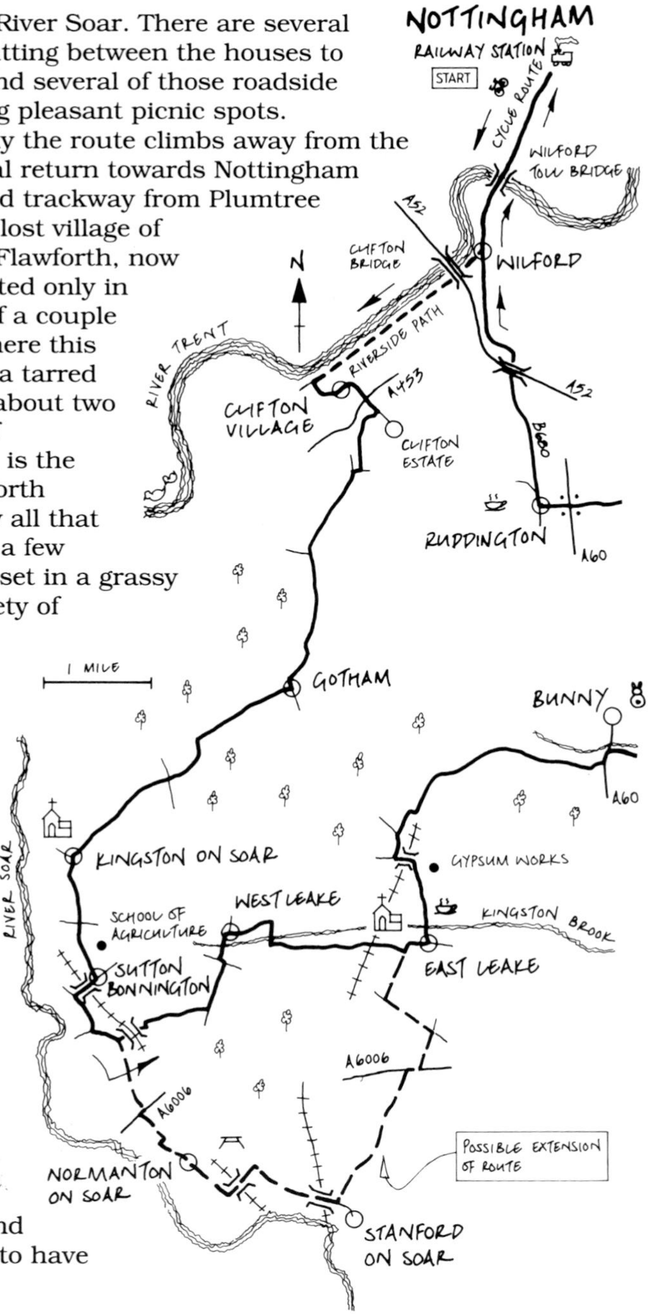

130

once been very much a centre of the hosiery trade. Here as elsewhere the long windows on many of the houses show their origins as the homes of frame-knitters, and one of the village's no less than three museums depicts a hosiery complex.

Cross over the dual carriageway outside **Nottingham Midland Station**, bearing left to join the cycle route on Queens Bridge Road, signed *Wilford*. After a short distance, use the double set of cyclists' traffic lights to cross Waterway Street and Meadows Way, and continue along the tree-lined Queens Walk cycle track. At the far end go straight on at the roundabout, over Wilford Toll Bridge – spanning the River Trent – following the cycle route signs for *Wilford*. Continue ahead at the far side of the bridge along Main Road through **Wilford** village, and at the signalled crossroads bear right onto the cycle track signed *Clifton Village*.

Soon after passing under the A52 Clifton road bridge, just beyond a signalled cycle crossing, turn right down a short slope into a 'river users' car park'. Pass round a metal barrier to join a firm-surfaced path which bears round to the left to follow the southern bank of the River Trent. Continue on this path, keeping more-or-less to the waterside for some 2 miles as far as another metal barrier – adjoining a wooden gate – just past which the route turns left, away from the river, up a wide but fairly steep track. At the top this emerges onto a minor road by Clifton Hall; bear left and follow this road (Village Road) as it winds through **Clifton** village to join the main road, A453.

Cross straight over the A453 dual carriageway (there is a signal-controlled pedestrian crossing which can be helpful), bearing slightly right, into Green Lane, signed *Ruddington*. Take the second turning on the right, Waterdown Road, go up a slight rise and second right again into Bransdale Road. Turn right at the mini roundabout at the far end of Bransdale Road, into Farnborough Road, and left at the T-junction signed *Gotham*. This road sweeps down across the broad open spaces of Clifton Pasture, Barton Moor and Gotham Moor and into **Gotham** village. Turn right just before the centre of the village into Kegworth Road, signed *Kingston*. In **Kingston on Soar**, after about 3 miles, turn left opposite the church into Station Road, past Nottingham University's School of Agriculture to bear right over the railway bridge and down Marlepit

32
continued

In Normanton on Soar

Hill into **Sutton Bonnington**.

You pass through this straggling village along Main Street. About two-thirds of the way along, bear left opposite the Old Plough, still on Main Street (the straight-on road now becomes Park Lane). The turning is marked as *Main Street leading to Hungary Lane* and shortly passes under a railway bridge and climbs gently for about 1 mile to a T-junction with Trowell Lane. Turn left, signed *West Leake* and *Nottingham*, gently downhill towards a prominent line of willows. At the foot of the slope take the second turn right, just after the left bend in the road and just before the Star pub, signed *West Leake, East Leake* and *Nottingham*. In **West Leake** the road bears round to the right, signed *East Leake* and *Costock*. This road follows the pleasant shallow valley of the Kingston Brook and after about 2 miles comes into **East Leake** by the church at a T-junction opposite the Three Horseshoes. Turn left on Brookside, signed *Costock* and *Gotham*.

Just beyond the village hall, turn left into Gotham Lane, signed *Gotham*. (Just after this turn there are public toilets and a tea shop-cum-bakery (not Sundays) on the right.) Continue along Gotham Lane out of East Leake, passing the British Gypsum works and, after crossing the disused rail line, take the first turning on the right, signed for *Bunny*. After about 2 miles the route comes into the outskirts of **Bunny** and meets the A60: turn left, signposted *Nottingham*, and first right after about 150yds into a very minor, unsigned, lane which it is quite easy to miss.

Follow this lane, which runs along the banks of a stream, for about a mile and then turn left at the T-junction, signed *Bradmore*. After $^3/_4$ mile, turn right at the minor staggered crossroads, into Bunny Lane for *Keyworth*. Left at the T-junction in **Keyworth**, signed *Plumtree* (although if you want a break, a right turn leads into the centre of the village where, just beyond the church, there is The Coffee Shop on the right). The road winds through Keyworth for about 1 mile and soon after leaving the village the route passes under a high railway bridge to come into **Plumtree**; continue straight on through the village, signed *Tollerton*.

On leaving Plumtree, just before a wooden bus shelter on the left, turn left up a signposted stony but firm-surfaced bridleway – which passes back under the railway and becomes grassy to follow the edge of a hedged field before emerging, after $1^1/_2$ miles, onto a minor road near the site of Flawford church (there are a few gravestones on a preserved turfed area on the right). Turn left (effectively still following the direction you have been following on the track), then – after a mile or so – continue straight on at the signalled crossroads with the A60 into Kirk Lane, B680, signed *Ruddington*. At the T-junction in **Ruddington**, turn right onto High Street, still B680, signposted *Wilford* (the Village Coffee Shop is on the left soon after this turn).

32
continued

Follow the B680 out of Ruddington and, after about 2 miles, pass under the A52 for a further mile into **Wilford**. On reaching the signalled cross roads – which you should recognise from earlier on in the route – go straight over from Ruddington Lane into Main Road, following cycle route signs for the *city centre*. Cross Wilford Toll Bridge, and retrace the outgoing route along Queens Walk back to **Nottingham Midland station**.

It is possible to **lengthen the route** by a little over 3 miles to take in the attractive village of Normanton on Soar and the little hamlet of Stanford on Soar by continuing straight ahead at the Old Plough in **Sutton Bonnington** along Park Lane where the main route goes left. At the T-junction with the A6006, turn right, signposted *Ashby*, and first left after a short distance into Moor Lane, signed for *Normanton*. Continue through **Normanton on Soar**, following signs for *Stanford on Soar*. Pass over the Midland Main Line railway and then over a disused line, before turning left at the T-junction – just before **Stanford** village – for *East Leake*. Go up the steady climb of Firdeal Hill for about 2 miles to join the A6006, turn right then first left after about 150yds, signed *East Leake*. Turn left at the first minor crossroads, again signed for *East Leake* and first right after ¹/₂ mile down the hill into **East Leake**. Turn right at the T-junction into the village centre. (The map shows other possible alternatives from the Soar valley to East Leake.)

Distance: 32 miles (increased to 35 with the Normanton and Stanford extension)

Terrain: Predominantly **on-road**, but using several **off-road links** – including a **Trent-side cycle path** and a **bridleway**.

Refreshment opportunities:There is a a good variety of pubs serving food en route, together with a number of village shops. The large villages of East Leake, Keyworth and Ruddington also boast tea shops – although none of these is open on Sundays. The Cosy Teapot Café is close to the station in Nottingham.

Start: Nottingham Midland Station (GR 574 393)

Ordnance Survey maps: Landranger sheet **129** Nottingham and Loughborough

Public transport links: Midland Main Line, Robin Hood Line and Regional Railways services go to Nottingham Midland Station.

Other routes: City routes **6** and **10**, and longer routes **33** and **36** also start and finish at Nottingham station. Route **40**, the linear route from Newark, finishes here. Link route **L5** joins Nottingham station to the short route round the Attenborough Nature Reserve, route **1**.

33

35 miles • on-road • undulating • Nottingham

Villages beginning with 'W'

Although it starts near the centre of Nottingham, this route takes you very quickly into open rolling country south of the city. It passes through a variety of villages, of which more than what seems a fair share start with the letter 'W': Wysall, Wymeswold, Willoughby-on-the-Wolds (two 'W's for the price of one there!) and Widmerpool. Most of the villages are worth a stop to look round the church and fine old buildings, the names of cottages – 'The Old Post Office', 'The Old Forge', 'Bakehouse Cottage' – often testimony to the once self-sufficient nature of these settlements. The route dips into Leicestershire to take in the tea shops at Six Hills – the home-made cakes at the golf clubhouse make it worth breaching the frontier!

The first settlement on the route, Ruddington – now grown into a small town, is one of many villages around Nottingham which was once very much a centre of the hosiery trade and the village houses a knitting museum. Ruddington is another village where the long windows on many of the houses show their origins as the homes of frame-knitters.

The route soon enters rolling countryside, the foothills of the higher wolds of south Nottinghamshire and Leicestershire. Many of the names of villages in this area betray their Danish origins: this was towards the edge of the Danelaw – the area of England ruled by the Danes at the end of the 9th century. A village sign without a village on the next stretch of road proclaims 'Thorpe in the Glebe', a now-lost village, its name derived from the old Danish word *thorp*, a farmstead, often one

dependent on a nearby larger village. Many villages in the Vale of Belvoir and on the surrounding wolds, end in *-by*, meaning a hamlet or homestead. Our W-rich Willoughby, which welcomes you back to Nottinghamshire after a ten-mile foray into Leicestershire, was the 'hamlet or homestead among the willows'.

Sometimes the place-names seem to have got a bit mixed up: the first part of Widmerpool means the 'wide or willow-fringed mere or lake'. The added 'pool' isn't really needed. Widmerpool has been an 'estate' village since the thirteenth century, giving rise to a Widmerpool family, although the name is a good deal older. Nowadays the pool is much smaller and the quiet village nestles in a hollow between rolling hills.

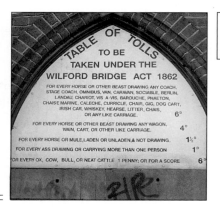

33

continued

TABLE OF TOLLS
TO BE
TAKEN UNDER THE
WILFORD BRIDGE ACT 1862

FOR EVERY HORSE OR OTHER BEAST DRAWING ANY COACH, STAGE COACH, OMNIBUS, VAN, CARAVAN, SOCIABLE, BERLIN, LANDAU, CHARIOT, VIS A-VIS, BAROUCHE, PHAETON, CHAISE MARINE, CALECHE, CURRICLE, CHAIR, GIG, DOG CART, IRISH CAR, WHISKEY, HEARSE, LITTER, CHAIS, OR ANY LIKE CARRIAGE, 6°

FOR EVERY HORSE OR OTHER BEAST DRAWING ANY WAGON, WAIN, CART, OR OTHER LIKE CARRIAGE, 4°

FOR EVERY HORSE OR MULE,LADEN OR UNLADEN,& NOT DRAWING, 1½°

FOR EVERY ASS DRAWING OR CARRYING MORE THAN ONE PERSON 1°

FOR EVERY OX, COW, BULL, OR NEAT CATTLE 1 PENNY; OR FOR A SCORE 6°

Cross over the main road outside **Midland Station**, turning left to join the cycle route on Queen's Bridge Road signed to *Meadows, Wilford and Clifton*. Use the two parallel sets of cyclists' traffic lights to cross Waterway Street and Meadows Way, and continue on the segregated cycle path down Queen's Walk. Straight on at the roundabout at the far end, to cross the River Trent by Wilford Toll Bridge – which is closed to all traffic except those on foot and bike, and whose toll charges disappeared long ago, although there's reminder on a board at the old toll-house.

After the river, straight on following the cycle route signs towards *Clifton*. After about 1 mile cross Wilford Lane using the traffic lights at the staggered crossroads, into Ruddington Lane. Follow this road as it leaves the outskirts of Nottingham, for some 2 miles to **Ruddington** village. Along the High Street, turn left just after the Bricklayers Arms into Kirk Lane; continue to the traffic lights and right onto the A60 – signed *Bunny*. Continue on this main road – which does not carry too much traffic outside peak periods – for about 1¹/₂ miles; just beyond **Bradmore**, take the second left turning, Pendock Lane, towards *Keyworth* and *Wysall*. Stay on this road, following signs to *Wysall*, which you will reach after about 2¹/₂ miles – and a climb up Windmill Hill!

At the T-junction as you reach the outskirts of Wysall,turn right for *Widmerpool* and *Wymeswold*. Through **Wysall** village turn left opposite the church, signposted *Wymeswold*. As you reach **Wymeswold** after some 2 miles, turn right at the T-junction along East Road, then almost immediately left down Church Street. At the next T-junction, turn left along Brook Street, which is bordered by a willow-lined stream on the right. After about 2¹/₂ miles following a winding country lane, turn left at the end onto the B676, for *Six Hills*. This road soon passes under the A46 and past **'Six Hills** Leisure' – which boasts tea shops at its golf course and jet-ski club houses. Some $^3/_4$ mile past this refreshment stop, the route crosses the A6006 at a staggered crossroads, following signs for *Old Dalby*. After a further mile, take the first turning on the left, again towards *Old Dalby*. In fact, the route does not go into Old Dalby village, but skirts it to the west, following signs for *Willoughby* along Nottingham Lane. A further $2^1/_4$ miles brings you to a T-junction; turn left for *Foss Road and Leicester;* cross over the A46 again, using the overpass, and take the first right after $^1/_2$ mile for *Willoughby.*

At the crossroads in the centre of **Willoughby-on-the-Wolds**, go right for *Widmerpool* for about $1^1/_2$ miles. In **Widmerpool**, turn right at the T-junction signed for *Keyworth and Nottingham.* Go up the hill out of Widmerpool, and follow this road for about $1^1/_2$ miles. Just as you enter **Keyworth** turn right into Willow Brook, signed for *Stanton and Plumtree.* At the end of Willow Brook, go left onto Nicker Hill. Go down the hill, past the British Geological Survey, then right at the T-junction for *Plumtree and Nottingham.* Follow this road for about 1 mile, through **Plumtree**, and when it meets the A606, turn left and first right after a short distance at the traffic signals, into Tollerton

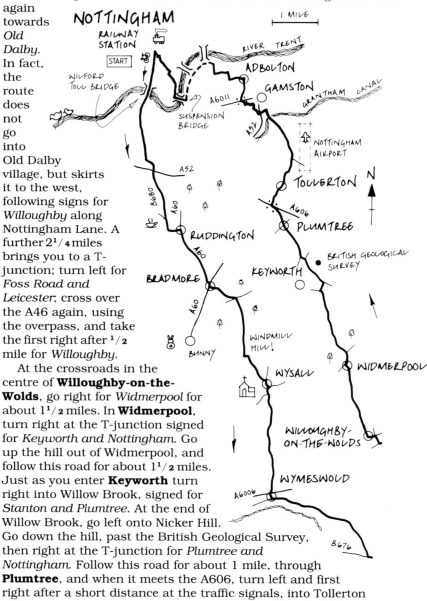

Lane. This lane skirts Tollerton to the east and Tollerton Airport to the west.

After about 2¹/₂ miles this road crosses the Grantham Canal; about 100yds further on turn right before you meet the busy A52, down a minor road signed to *Bassingfield*. As this bears round to the right after about 200yds, take the 'no-through' turning to the left between a pair of concrete bollards onto a tarred path, to cross the A52 using the designated path for

---

33
continued

Distance: 35 miles

Terrain: Entirely **on-road**, using quiet country lanes for the most part, with cycle routes to get in and out of the city of Nottingham. The countryside is generally gently rolling, with the occasional hill up to the Wolds.

Refreshment opportunities: Most of the many villages this route passes through have pubs and shops (the latter not usually open on Sunday). About halfway round there is a tea shop at the golf course (limited accommodation: not suitable for large groups) and another at the jet-ski centre which together comprise Six Hills Leisure Park.

Start: Nottingham Midland Station (GR 574 393)

Ordnance Survey maps: Landranger sheet **129** Nottingham and Loughborough

Public transport links: Midland Main Line and local services to Nottingham Station; Wymeswold, at the southern end of the route, is only 5 miles from Loughborough (Midland Main Line, local services (including Ivanhoe Line to Leicester)) and Barrow upon Soar (Ivanhoe Line) stations.

Other routes: City routes **6** and **10**, and longer routes **32** and **36** also start and finish at Nottingham station. Route **40**, the linear route from Newark, finishes here. Link route **L5** joins Nottingham station to the short route round the Attenborough Nature Reserve, route **1**.

---

walkers and cyclists (**care!** – make use of the waiting space on the central reservation if necessary). Go straight on at the other side, into the **Gamston** housing estate, where you join a minor residential road – Kirkstone Drive – which meanders through the housing development, to emerge eventually at an unsigned T-junction. Turn right, up to the traffic lights, left for a short distance along the A6011 dual carriageway, then right at the next set of traffic signals into Regatta Way, signed for *Holme Pierrepont*. Take the first left, after ¹/₂ mile, down Adbolton Lane, then first right – Adbolton Grove – as you enter the built-up housing area. Left at the bottom of Adbolton Grove, into Holme Road, and after about 600yds follow the cycle route signed for the *Meadows and City Centre*, which bears off to the right across open ground.

This cycle route meets the River Trent, where you turn left along the bank, and follow it under Lady Bay Bridge, past Nottingham Forest

33
continued

football ground, and under Trent Bridge. Cross the river using the cycle/pedestrian suspension bridge, just past County Hall. At the other side turn left on the road and then right, following cycle route signs for *City Centre via Arkwright Walk*: this route takes you along Bunbury Street, across Bathley Street, right into Radcliffe Street, left along Arkwright Walk, left and right through the Meadows shopping centre, under the subway below Meadows Way, and eventually back to **Midland Station**. 🚲

34

36 miles • on-road • almost flat • Tuxford

The northern Trent Valley

This ride follows the valley of the River Trent towards the northern end of the county. Starting and finishing at the small town of Tuxford, the route first heads south-east, then turns north – meandering through the minor lanes which link the numerous villages of this part of the Trent Valley. However, aside from a brief touch at Carlton-on-Trent, this is not a riverside route: the cooling towers of the power stations which are a feature of the waterway are kept at a comfortable distance – yet make an imposing skyline. The route eventually turns west and soon south, when the terrain becomes more undulating, yet the reward is some fine views over the county and its neighbours.

Now quiet and bypassed, Tuxford was once a bustling market town on the Great North Road from London to York and Edinburgh, boasting nine hotels, inns and taverns. There must

have been an unruly element among the travellers, since in 1823 a town lock-up was built to allow drunks and villains to cool off overnight. The building is still preserved, beside the Egmanton road by which the route leaves Tuxford.

In Carlton-on-Trent, just south of the route on the old Great North Road, lies Carlton's smithy, one of several to be marked with a giant

Carlton Smithy

34
continued

horseshoe emblem in black brick surrounding the entrance. There is another at Gonalston, on routes **20** and **30**. A footpath leads to the bank of the River Trent – a matter of yards – from the corner of Carlton Lane in Carlton-on-Trent. At this point the river is just below the lock which marks the upper limit of the tidal section.

Follow Newcastle Street, between the Newcastle Arms and the Sun Inn at the southern end of the town, out of **Tuxford**, signposted *Egmanton*. Go straight on in **Egmanton** after 1^1/$_2$ miles, signed for *Laxton*, which you reach about 1^1/$_2$ miles later. In **Laxton,** turn left at the T-junction by the Dovecote Inn. There is a visitor centre next to this pub, with an exhibition of the mediaeval strip cultivation that is still – uniquely in England – practised in the village. At the far end of Laxton at the foot of the slope, turn *left* – unsigned – where the road bears round to the right for Kneesall. Follow this pleasant little lane for about 2 miles to the hamlet of **Moorhouse**. At the T-junction, turn right, signed *Ossington*, and in **Ossington** turn left at the T-junction signed *Carlton-on-Trent*. After about ^{3}/$_4$ mile, turn right, signed *Norwell*, and on reaching **Norwell**, turn left at the T-junction for *Carlton-on-Trent.*.

Follow this pleasantly winding minor road for about 2^1/$_2$ miles to a T-junction. Turn right, signed *Carlton-on-Trent*, to cross the East Coast main railway line at a level crossing and the A1 via a bridge, then straight on at the cross-roads with the B1164, the old Great North Road, in **Carlton-on-Trent** into Ferry Lane. As the road bears right, turn left into an unnamed 'No-through road', signed *'No vehicular access to River Trent'*, then very shortly left again into Carlton Lane. This mile-long lane is impassable to motor vehicles as there is a narrow bridge over a stream about halfway along – but cyclists can go straight on into **Sutton on Trent**.

At the T-junction in Sutton, turn right (effectively straight on) and go through the village on Main Street, which becomes Church Street and, just beyond Sutton-on-Trent primary school, turn right

34
continued

Headon church

into Ingram Lane. Follow this little lane for nearly 2 miles until, about ¹/₂ mile beyond a sweeping left bend it reaches a T-junction in the hamlet of **Grassthorpe**, opposite Corner Farm. Turn right and then first left after a short distance for *Normanton*. Continue as the road meanders through **Normanton on Trent**, and turn left at the T-junction by the church, signed *Tuxford*. After approximately ¹/₂ mile, turn right for *Skegby* and, at the end of this mile-long road and just after passing through the hamlet of **Skegby**, go left and immediately right at an unsigned junction – effectively straight on.

Follow this open road as it winds through farmland for about 2¹/₂ miles then, at the junction with the main A57 in **Dalton**, turn left and in about 100yds first right for *East Drayton*. Go straight on at the cross-roads in **East Drayton**, signed *Stokeham*. After just over a mile, in **Stokeham**, go right at the unsigned T-junction, and left at the next – after about 100yds – for *Treswell*. After about a

---

Distance: 36 miles

Terrain: Entirely **on-road**, generally flat, save for a gently undulating section towards the end of the ride

Refreshment opportunities: Many of the villages this ride takes in have pubs serving food and small shops selling basic groceries. There is a tea shop at the Grove Garden Centre, three-quarters of the the way round.

Start: Newcastle Arms, Tuxford (GR 736 710)

Ordnance Survey maps: Landranger sheet **120** Mansfield and Worksop; in theory, you need sheet **121** Lincoln, too, to cover the 4 miles or so between Carlton-on-Trent and Grassthorpe, but we think the route description is clear enough that you can manage without the map.

Public transport links: although the East Coast main line passes through the outskirts of Tuxford there is no longer a station there. The nearest rail link to any part of the route is by way of route **L12** (below) from Norwell to Newark.

Other routes: Route 25 overlaps this one between Egmanton and Laxton. Link route **L1** is a very short link in the village of Norwell between this route and route **28**; link route **L3** joins this route to route **24**; link route **L12** is a route from this route to Newark.

further mile take the second turn on the left into **Treswell** and, at the T-junction in the village, turn left, signed *Grove*. There is a gentle 3-mile climb into **Grove**, but the reward is a tea-shop at the garden centre – on the right as you enter the village.

Carry straight on

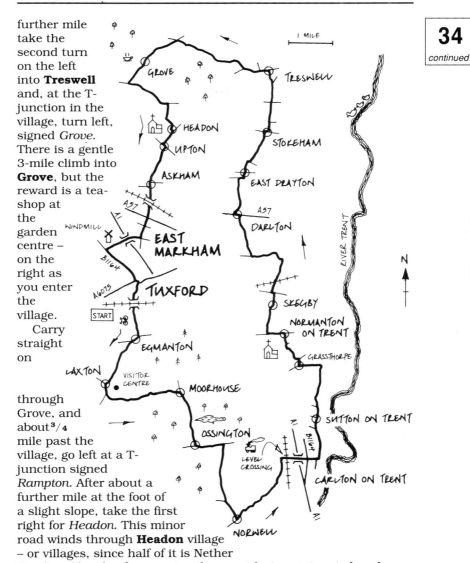

through Grove, and about 3/4 mile past the village, go left at a T-junction signed *Rampton*. After about a further mile at the foot of a slight slope, take the first right for *Headon*. This minor road winds through **Headon** village – or villages, since half of it is Nether Headon. Shortly after passing the squat but prominent church, turn right at the T-junction signed *Askham*. In the next village, **Upton**, turn left at the T-junction, signed *East Drayton*, then first right after about 100yds along an unsigned minor road – the building on the corner is named Trinity Farm. Continue straight through the attractive village of **Askham** and on following the sign to *East Markham*.

141

34
continued

On the approach to **East Markham** you cross directly over the A57, then go straight on at the first minor cross roads in the village – over High Street into Farm Lane – then at the next minor cross-roads, after a short climb, turn right into Priestgate, signed *West Markham*. This road climbs over a bridge to take you back over the A1 to join its predecessor, B1164, the old Great North Road. Turn left at the T-junction on the B1164 for *Tuxford*, on the approach to which you pass a working windmill which is sometimes open to the public (opening dates are given on a singboard by the entrance gate). Climb Eldon Street, **Tuxford**, which becomes Newark Road, then Market Place. On the right are the two pubs marking the start of the excursion. 🚲

35

---

38 miles • on-road • gentle • Nottingham, Trent Bridge

The Vale of Belvoir

This route, longish but across gentle countryside, travels almost the length of the Vale of Belvoir – dominated at its south-east end by Belvoir Castle itself. Part of the attraction of this end of the route is the chance to sample a real cyclists' refreshment stop – at Old Hill Farm. It's a traditional stopping place for many local cycling clubs, so the bikes parked outside offer a free show of the latest bike equipment and there's even the chance of spotting international riders, past and present.

The route begins by climbing up to the low ridge which separates the valley of the Trent from the broader Vale of Belvoir. We choose an off-road route for this, but one that can be tacked with any bike. Once at the top and across the old Roman Foss (or Fosse) Way, the road swoops down to a crossroads, the left-hand limb of which leads to the tiny hamlet

of Owthorpe up a dead-end road. Owthorpe has an attractive little church, set in the fields, and one other claim to fame: the village hall can seat 102 – nearly five times the hamlet's total population of 22!

Another couple of miles brings you to Colston Bassett, passing the impressive Colston Bassett Hall on the left before crossing the River Smite.

Colston Bassett Hall

The now-peaceful village has had a turbulent past, with a number of Civil War skirmishes and visitations of the plague. In mediaeval times, Colston Bassett was a large and prosperous wool village, but the trade declined and the village with its old church on the hill was abandoned. Later, the place's fortunes revived and the new village and eventually church grew on the present site.

Colston Bassett has another important role: as a producer of delicious Stilton cheese, which you can buy direct from the dairy (Mondays to Fridays 9am–12.30pm and 1.30–4pm; Saturdays 9–11.30am) or from the village shop. The famous blue cheese was never actually made at Stilton – which is just south-west of Peterborough – but in Vale of Belvoir villages like this. In fact, Stilton is the only British cheese which *has* to be made in a closely defined area to qualify for its name – like fine wines in wine-growing countries. It gained the Stilton name by being transported eastwards and then sold at the inn at Stilton to the many passing travellers on the Great North Road.

After Colston Bassett, villages turn up at two- or three-mile intervals for the rest of the route. If one of them, Granby, sounds familiar it could well be because this village is honoured up and down the whole of England in a common pub name – the Marquis of Granby. Presumably the village's own inn of this name in the middle of the village is the original. The wide spread of the pub name is attributed to the large number of soldiers who had served under the Marquis in battle and then retired to wayside inns provided for them by their generous comander! It's also believed to owe something to the

35
continued

promotional zeal of his grandson.

The final stretch of way back into Nottingham passes the impressive red brick Holme Pierrepont Hall and then skirts the National Water Sports Centre, with its long straight 2000-metre rowing course – a landmark that makes it instantly recognisable from the air, should you find yourself flying over the East Midlands on a clear day.

Leave **Trent Bridge, Nottingham** by the riverside cycle path on the south side of the river past Nottingham Forest FC ground, signed *Cycle Route Lady Bay*. Continue along the path to pass over the Grantham Canal and under Lady Bay road bridge, between concrete bollards, with playing fields on the right and river on the left. At the end of the playing-field fencing on the right, turn right on a path (no sign) leading to Holme Road (not named at this point); turn left signed *Cycle Route Lady Bay*. Follow the road round to the right, becoming Adbolton Road. At the T-junction at the end , turn left on Adbolton Lane, signed *Cycle Route Holme Pierrepont*. At the next T-junction, turn right onto Regatta Way to

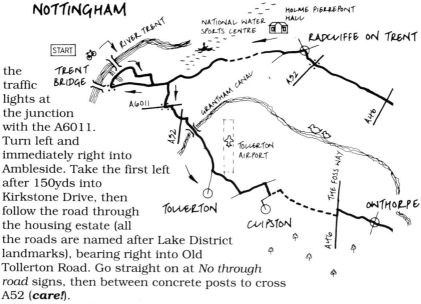

the traffic lights at the junction with the A6011. Turn left and immediately right into Ambleside. Take the first left after 150yds into Kirkstone Drive, then follow the road through the housing estate (all the roads are named after Lake District landmarks), bearing right into Old Tollerton Road. Go straight on at *No through road* signs, then between concrete posts to cross A52 (*care!*).

Once past the concrete posts on the far side, turn right onto a minor road. At the next T-junction, unsigned, turn left into

144

35
continued

Tollerton Lane, over the Grantham Canal. Continue to pass the airfield and after about 1 mile, in **Tollerton**, turn left on Cotgrave Lane, signed *Cotgrave*. Follow this road for about 1 mile to T-junction, then turn left, again signed *Cotgrave*. After about ³/4 mile, take the first right, signed *Clipstone on the Wolds*. Where the road bears right near the top of the hill, turn left on a track with a wooden *RUPP* signpost, round a metal gate, then go straight on. The track becomes a path with a hedge immediately on the right; follow the path

Barnstone church

round to the right up the slope. At the end of the hedge, turn left on a wide gravel track. After about 1 mile at a crossing of tracks, go straight on along a narrow track

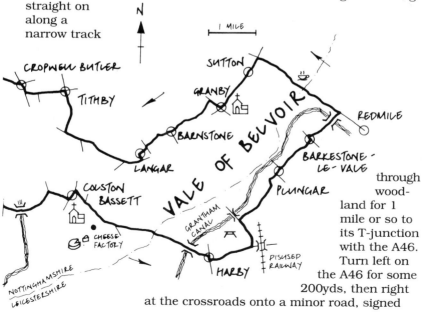

through woodland for 1 mile or so to its T-junction with the A46. Turn left on the A46 for some 200yds, then right at the crossroads onto a minor road, signed

145

35
continued

Owthorpe. Go down the hill past the end of the hamlet of **Owthorpe**, continue straight on signed *Colston Bassett*, then go straight on at the next crossroads, still signed *Colston Bassett*. After about 1 mile at a T-junction, turn right on Hall Lane, signed *Colston Bassett*. Follow the road as it winds through **Colston Bassett**, leaving the church on the right, then follow the road round to the right, Harby Lane, signed *Hose and Harby*. Go past the Stilton cheese 'factory' (Colston Bassett Dairy) and continue straight on for $3^1/2$ miles following signs for *Harby*. At the T-junction in **Harby** opposite the Nags Head, turn right, signed *Waltham*, then take the first left, Stathern Lane, signed *Stathern and Plungar*. Follow this road for about 1 mile then, just before railway bridge, turn left signed *Plungar*.

Just before the hump-backed bridge over the Grantham Canal, follow the road round to the right (picnic spot) and continue to follow it as it winds through **Plungar**, following signs for *Barkestone and Redmile* along Barkestone Lane. Go through

---

Distance: 38 miles

Terrain: apart from using the signed *Trentside cycle track* to begin with, entirely **on-road** (with a rough few hundred yards at Holme Pierrepont near the end). The countryside is never more than gently rolling, although there is a steepish little pitch up Clipston-on-the-Wolds.

Refreshment opportunities: the cyclists' halt at Old Hill Farm, Redmile, is about halfway round

Start: Trent Bridge, south side (GR 582 382) (This has been a starting-point for cycle outings for over a century: the *CTC Monthly Gazette* of 1894 mentions rides starting there!)

Ordnance Survey maps: Landranger sheet **129** Nottingham and Loughborough

Public transport links: Midland Main Line, Regional Railways and Robin Hood Line trains serve Nottingham station, just under 1 mile from Trent Bridge.

Other routes: This is the only route that starts and finishes at **Trent Bridge**. However, several start from **Nottingham Midland Station**, which is just under a mile away. The outward leg of route **6**, which starts and finishes at the station, crosses the A612 about 200yds north of Trent Bridge – just turn right to cross the bridge. Probably the most pleasant way to reach the station from Trent Bridge is to join the riverside path a short distance towards the boathouses (or continue on it at the end of this route), pass back under Trent Bridge and cross the suspension bridge to The Embankment. Turn left on the Embankment as far as the roundabout by the north side of Wilford Bridge. (This roundabout has unusual priorities: take care.) Take the fourth exit (including the bridge) into Queens Walk, a shared pedestrian and cycle route to the station. From the station entrance, turn left and follow the outward section of route **36** to the suspension bridge; cross the bridge and continue along the riverside path which is the outgoing leg of this route. City route **10**, and longer routes **32**, **33** and **36** also start and finish at Nottingham station. Route **40**, the linear route from Newark, finishes at Nottingham station. Link route **L5** joins Nottingham station to the short route round the Attenborough Nature Reserve, route **1**. Route **36** overlaps this one for part of the outgoing and return route near the start and for a mile or two near Colston Bassett.

Barkestone, then follow signs left and right to *Redmile*; the road becomes Redmile Lane. At the T-junction turn left, signed *Whatton*, past Old Hill Farm (the cyclists' tea-stop), then at the next crossroads after about 1 mile turn left signed *Sutton*. Go through **Sutton** and on to

35
continued

Primitive Methodist chapel at Sutton

Granby. At the crossroads in **Granby** by the church, turn right onto Main Street, signed *Barnstone*. Leave Granby down hill and at the foot of the hill, turn left, signed *Barnstone*. Follow the road through **Barnstone,** then at the crossroads, go straight on, signed *Langar village*, into **Langar**. Follow the road round to the left past the Post Office and shop, then at the T-junction at the Unicorn's Head, turn right signed *Colston Bassett*. After about 1^1/$_2$ miles, turn right, signed *Tythby* (but spelt Tithby on OS map). In **Tithby**, turn left at the minor crossroads just before the church, signed *Cropwell Butler*. At the T-junction on the outskirts of **Cropwell Butler**, turn right (signed *Radcliffe*, visible on the right only after you have turned). Follow the road round to the right past the Plough Inn, then at the minor crossroads in the village, turn left, signed *Radcliffe*. Go straight on at the crossing of the A46, into a minor road, signed *Radcliffe*.

On the outskirts of **Radcliffe-on-Trent**, go straight on on Cropwell Road at the traffic light-controlled crossing of the A52, then turn left at the crossroads in the centre of Radcliffe, signed *Nottingham*. After about 400yds, just after passing the Cliffe Inn on the left, turn right into The Green (marked as a 'No through road'); this bears round to the left and becomes Holme Lane. Continue straight on through **Holme Pierrepont** – the road is rough for a stretch before Holme Pierrepont Hall on the right, and there are some sharp traffic-calming humps on the tarmac section. Pass the National Water Sports Centre and camping site after about 1^1/$_2$ miles, then take the first turn right into Adbolton Lane, signed *Adbolton*. Continue along Adbolton Lane which becomes Trent Boulevard. At the traffic lights, go straight on on Radcliffe Road, signed *Trent Bridge* to return to **Trent Bridge, Nottingham**.

147

36

44 miles · mostly on-road · fairly flat · Nottingham

The Grantham Canal

The off-road section of this route follows part of the towpath of the Grantham Canal, while the road sections cross it from time to time. The Grantham Canal was opened just on 200 years ago, in spring 1797, and ran from the River Trent at Nottingham (soon after the start the route passes Trent Lock where it joins) to Grantham, bringing to that town a valuable connection to a major waterway and the sea at a time when land transport was slow and laborious. Despite the coming of the railways which killed off many canals this one carried commercial traffic for 132 years before being closed in 1929. Subsequently most of the humpback bridges were demolished and replaced by concrete culverts, effectively putting paid to continuous navigation. A restoration society has ambitious plans to re-open it as a navigable waterway but faces many difficulties since not only bridges but locks have been concreted in. Now the canal has become a wildlife haven, some of it even designated a Site of Special Scientific Interest, which could be endangered by re-opening. Parts of the towpath have been improved with a crushed stone surface making it eminently suitable for cycling, which is specifically permitted (with a free permit – see p18) over the whole length of the canal, though some sections are – to say the least – challenging. We don't include any of those!

The first part of the towpath from West Bridgford is fine but ends rather ignominiously in a supermarket car park, while the canal suffers the indignity of being in a pipe under the A52. Beyond the main road, there is a fine stretch of towpath, which

the route follows for just over five miles. Although it is all readily ridable, don't expect towpath riding to be particularly fast.

The route leaves the canal near the village of Cropwell Bishop, which, like Colston Bassett on the return leg of the route, is a producer of delicious Stilton cheese, which you can buy direct from the dairy. (There are others in the

Leicestershire villages of Harby on route **35** and Hose nearby.) The famous blue cheese was never actually made at Stilton – which is just south-west of Peterborough – but in Vale of Belvoir villages like this. In fact, Stilton *has* to be made in a closely defined area to be allowed to bear the Stilton name – like *appellation contrôlée* wines in France – and is the only British cheese to enjoy this status. It gained its name and fame by being transported eastwards and then sold at the inn at Stilton to the many passing travellers on the Great North Road.

36

continued

Poplars at Vimy Ridge Farm

The route next meets the canal again north of Kinoulton, where a section of path leads round a sharp bend somewhat imaginatively named the Devil's Elbow. It emerges onto a bridleway bordered by a striking avenue of poplars leading from Vimy Ridge Farm. Until the end of the first world war, the farm was known as Pasture Hill Farm, but was renamed by the owner in memory of his son, killed in action in 1916 during the fighting at Vimy Ridge in northern France. He also planted the avenue of some 188 poplars, supposed to be one for every officer killed in the same action.

In the next village but one, Hickling, the most prominent feature is the large basin of the Grantham Canal, recently cleared and restored. It now has 'resident' flocks of ducks and swans and makes a fine summer picnic spot.

Shortly after this the route leaves the flat country (and – for about ten miles – Nottinghamshire) to climb up to the Belvoir ridge. Apart from passing a useful tea stop, the ridge gives commanding views. Before taking up the reward for your earlier efforts by swooping down the open hill to Long Clawson, pause to take in the stunning view out over the Vale of Belvoir – extending right across to Lincoln Cathedral on a clear day. From here, after crossing the Grantham Canal once again between Long Clawson and Colston Bassett, it's a mainly gentle run in through vale villages to return to Nottingham beside the Trent.

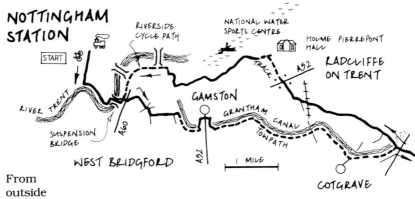

From outside **Nottingham Midland station**, cross the main road (left and then almost immediately bearing right) to join the signed cycle route on Queens Bridge Road. Use the double set of cyclists' traffic lights to cross Meadows Way and Water-way Street, then straight on along Queen's Walk cycle track. At the roundabout near Wilford Toll Bridge, take the second exit, passing through the gates and along The Embankment for about ³/₄ mile, or use the signed shared-use cycle and pedestrian path that runs parallel to it, between the road and the river. Keep the river on your right and then turn right to use the pedestrian and cyclists' suspension bridge to cross the River Trent, bearing very sharp left at the far side to continue along the river bank for a short distance. Go right, through the gap between houses marked by a cycle route sign for *West Bridgford Town Centre*, and use the cyclists' traffic-lights to cross the dual carriageway into Millicent Road. Go straight on at the crossroads, continuing along Millicent Road, then right at the T-junction with Bridgford Road – still following cycle route signs for *West Bridgford Town Centre*. Once in the town centre, Bridgford Road becomes Central Avenue and then Gordon Road as you continue straight ahead. Take the third turning on the left, Eltham Road, and at the end go straight on up Buckfast Way and where this bears right, go straight on to join the **Grantham Canal**.

Turn right along the towpath for a mile or so, until the path rises up to meet a road – the canal itself passes through a culvert under the A52. Turn left on the service road running parallel to the A52 and right after 400yds into Windermere Close, at the end of which a bridleway passes through a gap in a fence onto a tarred road: bear right on this road, between concrete bollards at the end of it to cross the A52 with the aid of the wide central reservation. Turn right twice in quick succession past the bollards on the far

150

36
continued

side of the main road, to a T-junction after about 300yds where you turn left onto Tollerton Lane. A short distance along this lane leave the road, bearing left to rejoin the **Grantham Canal** towpath. Follow the towpath for approximately 5 miles, crossing minor roads at Cotgrave Bridge and Hollygate Lane. The surface of the towpath varies from a well-drained stone-surfaced track to grassy, undulating sections – although none should present a particular problem to riders with reasonably sturdy tyres.

On reaching Mann's Bridge, turn right onto the road again, shortly to cross straight over the A46 (Fosse Way) for *Cropwell Bishop*. On entering **Cropwell Bishop** take a minor road to the right signed for *Colston Bassett*, go straight over at the crossroads by the Lime Kiln Inn, signed *Kinoulton*, and at the next crossroads after about a mile, right for *Owthorpe*. Skirting the village of **Owthorpe** to the south, turn first left, again signed for *Kinoulton*, and a mile or so along this country lane, where you cross the **Grantham Canal** once again, turn right through a gate onto the towpath. This final grassy stretch of towpath is fairly short, taking you round a bend in the canal known as the **Devil's Elbow.** At the first bridge you come to, turn left away from the canal, down a well-surfaced bridleway bordered by a striking avenue of poplar trees.

Map labels: A46 THE FOSS WAY; CROPWELL BISHOP; RIVER SMITE; OWTHORPE; COLSTON BASSETT; NOTTINGHAMSHIRE; LEICESTERSHIRE; CHEESE FACTORY; CANAL TOWPATH; "DEVIL'S ELBOW"; KINOULTON; BRIDLEWAY; GRANTHAM CANAL; HICKLING; N; LONG CLAWSON; LOVELY FREEWHEEL DOWN; A606; NETHER BROUGHTON; A606; OLD DALBY; STEEP HILL UP; WARTNABY; A606

36

continued

Grantham Canal mile marker

On reaching the road, turn right, through **Kinoulton** for *Hickling*, and go straight on through **Hickling,** signed *Nether Broughton*. At the top of the climb into Nether Broughton, turn right at the T-junction near the church, signed *Old Dalby*. Turn right again in the centre of **Nether Broughton**, up Chapel Lane – following signs for *Old Dalby*. Turn left at the T-junction with the A606 and, after a short distance where the main road bears round to the left, turn right (effectively straight on) for *Old Dalby*. Where this minor road bears right for Old Dalby, carry straight ahead on an even more minor road, signed as a left turn for *Saxelbye*. Climb the main hill of the route – quite a steep one – then turn left at the crossroads signed *Wartnaby*; $^1/_2$ mile or so along this ridge road is Stonepits Farm tea room. Continue along the ridge, to go straight across the A606, signed *Eastwell*, then bear left at the shallow T-junction for *Long Clawson*. **Do not take** the first turning on the left for Long Clawson, but the second one, after a further $1^1/_4$ miles, which is also signed for *Long Clawson*.

On reaching **Long Clawson** at the foot of this superb downhill swoop, turn right at the junction, onto Hose Lane, and first left after a short way (effectively straight on), signed *Colston Bassett*. Continue right to the end of this lane, some $2^1/_2$ miles, following any signs for *Colston Bassett*, then left at the T-junction and on into **Colston Bassett**. Go past the Stilton cheese creamery, turn right where the road bears left – there is a sign for *Tithby* high on the wall of the house on the right on the corner. Go down the hill and over the River Smite and up Spring Hill, then right at the T-junction signposted *Cropwell Bishop*, and left at the next T-junction, once more signed *Cropwell Bishop*.

Through the village of **Cropwell Bishop** you retrace a short section of outward route back over the A46 (Fosse Way) to where you left the Grantham Canal towpath at Mann's Bridge. Here continue straight on along the road, past the former Cotgrave Colliery, eventually to meet the A52 at a signalled junction. Use the lights to cross straight over the dual carriageway and onto an unsurfaced farm track, which is quite bumpy in places and brings you out near **Holme Pierrepont** Hall. Turn left opposite the gates to the Hall, past the National Water Sports Centre and campsite, then right after $1^1/_2$ miles into Adbolton Lane. Take the first right – Adbolton Grove – as you enter the built-up housing area. Turn left at the bottom of Adbolton Grove, into Holme Road, and after

600yds follow the cycle route signed for the *Meadows and City Centre*, which bears off to the right across open ground. This cycle route meets the River Trent, where you turn left along the bank, and follow it under Lady Bay Bridge, past Nottingham Forest football ground, and under Trent Bridge. Cross the river using the cycle/pedestrian suspension bridge, just past County Hall, and retrace your route to **Nottingham Midland station** via the Embarkment and Queen's Walk cycle track. 🚲

36

continued

Distance: 44 miles

Terrain: Fairly flat but with one significant hill, and mostly **on-road** but there is one fairly lengthy **off-road** section – on the **towpath** of the *Grantham Canal*

Refreshment opportunities: Tea shop at Stonepits Farm, about half way round; the route also passes through a number of villages with pubs and small grocery shops.

Start: Nottingham Midland station (GR 574393)

Ordnance Survey maps: Landranger sheet **129** Nottingham and Loughborough.

Public transport links: Midland Main Line, Robin Hood Line and Regional Railways services go to Nottingham Midland station

Other routes: City routes **6** and **10**, and longer routes **32** and **35** also start and finish at Nottingham station. Route **40**, the linear route from Newark, finishes here. Link route **L5** joins Nottingham station to the short route round the Attenborough Nature Reserve, route **1**. This route overlaps route **35** near the start and finish and also near Owthorpe and Colston Bassett.

---

45 miles • on-road • mostly flat • Retford

37

Retford and the far north

As we saw on route **24**, north of Retford, Nottinghamshire takes on quite a different character. This route probes further into the geometrical landscape of the drained marshland. Here the great square arable fields are separated by straight drains, while the dead flat straight roads turn apparently inexplicable right-angle bends: maybe they are tacking their way across the often

windy landscape, like a sailing boat beating into the breeze. That's not to say there aren't some slight rises on the route: at Gringley-on-the-Hill the route reaches a dizzy 70m – enough to give broad views over the flatter country to the north and west.

The early part of the route follows part of the former Great North Road, passing through several workmanlike but not really picturesque villages. One of these, Scrooby, has a claim to fame for its connection with William Brewster, one of the Pilgrim Fathers. Born in the village, he travelled first to Holland with other members of his Separatist church to escape religious persecution, and then on to America on the *Mayflower* in 1620, to found the state of New England. The connection is commemorated in the Pilgrim Fathers inn but there remain few other links with Brewster. Sturton le Steeple, which figures on route **24**, also has connections with early Separatist church members.

The route leaves Nottinghamshire for rather over two miles to pass through the little coaching town of Bawtry in South Yorkshire. Bawtry may no longer lie astride the artery to the north but there is a fine broad market square with some handsome buildings – and shops and places to eat.

From Bawtry, the route heads north-east – as far as the right-angle bends in the marshland road allow – and after about seven more miles, and the village of Misson, reaches the northernmost point of all our routes. The extreme northern pointed tip of the county lies about a mile from the junction after Beech Hill Farm, just to the left of the track straight ahead which becomes a bridleway. The 'hill' in Beech Hill must be pretty relative, since this is also about the lowest point on any of the routes, at a mere 2 metres above sea level.

The route continues on its geometrical way to the high levée bank of the River Trent at Heckdyke, then follows the river upstream through West Stockwith, where the River Idle joins the Trent, and on to the fringes of Misterton. Misterton provides a link with one of the great names in Fenland engineering – Cornelius Vermuyden, the Dutch engineer who was brought over in the mid-17th century to drain many of eastern England's marshland areas. The drained land proved immensely fertile and laid the base for the agricultural prosperity of settlements such as Misterton. Later its strategic position close to where the River Idle and the Chesterfield Canal meet the Trent made it a centre for local trade.

From the flatlands of Misterton the route actually does

climb, to Gringley on its hill, then runs down to Clayworth and over the Chesterfield Canal to follow the same roads as route **16** back to Retford.

From the Market Square in **Retford** go north-west along Bridgegate to a roundabout. Go straight ahead (second exit) into North Road, A638, for about 4 miles to **Barnby Moor**. Continue on A638 – the old Great North Road, relatively quiet now that it's bypassed by the new A1 – for another 6 miles through **Torworth**, **Ranskill** and **Scrooby**, then straight on at traffic lights to **Bawtry** town centre. At the north end of the Market Place, turn right in front of a prominent red-brick chapel on Station Road, A614, signed *Thorne*. On the outskirts of **Austerfield**, where the A614 bears left, go right, effectively straight on, on Newington Road through **Newington** to **Misson**.

At the crossroads in the village centre, turn left on Station Road, following the road for about 4 miles, first round a succession of right-angle bends and then over a level crossing, to join the B1396. Turn right on the B1396, signed *Westwoodside*. At the next crossroads after about $1^1/2$ miles turn right to pass the Park Drain Hotel, and recrossing the railway at another level crossing. Take the first turn on left after the railway by Fountain Farm for a little over 3 miles to a crossroads with the A161, go straight on over another level crossing. Continue for about 2 miles to a T-junction at the River Trent bank at **Heckdyke**.

Turn right through **West Stockwith** and over the River Idle and the Chesterfield Canal to a T-junction (almost a staggered crossroads) with the A161 again. Turn right on the A161, then immediately left into Fox Covert Lane. Follow the road round to the right past a school, then turn left into Gravelholes Lane to its T-junction with the B1403, Gringley Road. Turn left on the B1403, towards *Gringley on the Hill*. At the top of Beacon Hill after just under 3 miles, turn right on High Street into **Gringley on the Hill** village, then at the cross, Cross Hill, follow the road round to the left and then right to the dual

Not picturesque, perhaps – but much of Britain's power is generated under the broad skies of the Trent valley

155

37
continued

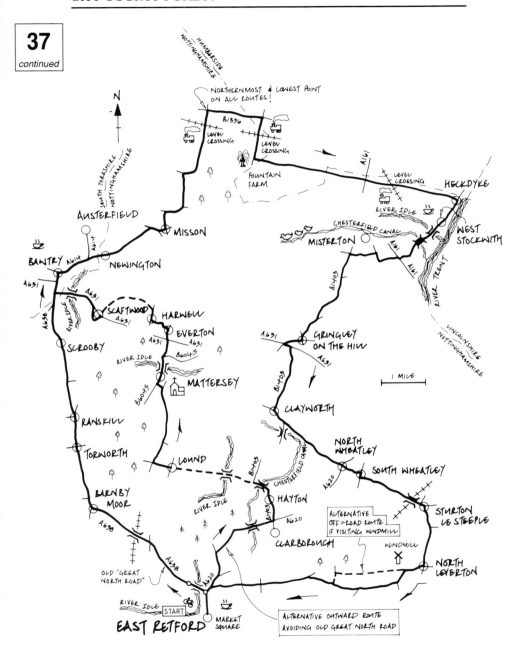

It is possible to avoid the 10 miles or so of the old Great North Road, A638, to Bawtry by the following **alternative**, which involves some **off-road** riding and adds about $5^1/2$ miles to the total distance:

37

continued

From Market Square, **Retford**, go into Cannon Square, then fork right into Chapelgate, then left into Arlington Way, A638. Turn right at the traffic lights, still on A638, to go up Moorgate. At the top of the hill bear left on a minor road, Tiln Lane, signed *Hayton*. After about $3/4$ mile this bears round to the right as Smeath Road, which becomes Smeath Lane to cross the Chesterfield Canal and reach a crossroads with the B1043 and the A620. Turn left on the B1043, Main Street, **Hayton**, and go through the village past the Boat Inn and over the Chesterfield Canal at the far end. After about 400yds, the B1043 turns sharp right; go straight ahead onto a track and follow this over the River Idle for about $2^1/2$ miles to **Lound**. In Lound, go straight over at the first crossroads (with Town Street) and at the second 700yds further on, turn right, signed *Mattersey*.

On the outskirts of **Mattersey**, turn first left, Job Lane, and then right on Main Street, B6045, through the village. After crossing the bridge over the River Idle, bear left where the B6045 goes right uphill, to *Everton*. Cross A631 onto High Street to the centre of **Everton**. Take the second left, Brewery Lane and follow this where it bears round to the right; this is Old Post Office Street. At the end, turn left into Ferry Lane, then in about 100yds, turn right into Chapel Lane. Follow this lane, which becomes Harwell Lane, round to the left to **Harwell**. Turn right, then after about 400yds where the road forks, bear left onto a track, Pasture Lane. Follow this track for about $1^1/2$ miles until it meets the A631. Cross the dual carriageway (**care!**) onto Theaker Lane into **Scaftworth**. At the end of the lane, turn right to rejoin the dual carriageway A631. Turn left on the A631 and follow it over the River Idle into **Bawtry**; turn right at traffic lights onto High Street, A638, to rejoin the main route.

carriageway A631. Turn left on the A631 and then right (**care!**) on the B1403 to **Clayworth**. Turn left on Town Street, still B1403, but after 300yds at a fork where the B1403 goes over a canal bridge, bear left on Wheatley Road, signed *North Wheatley*, which follows the canal for about $1/2$ mile. Just before North Wheatley cross the dual carriageway A620, signed *North and South Wheatley* and *Sturton le Steeple*, to **North Wheatley**. In North Wheatley, follow the road round, signed *Sturton, North Leverton* and *Littleborough* into **South Wheatley** and continue for about 2 miles, crossing over the railway, on to **Sturton le Steeple**.

37
continued

Turn right in Sturton on Cross Street, which becomes Leverton Road and continue to **North Leverton**. At the crossroads in the centre of the village, turn right on Main Street, which becomes Retford Road – leaving the working windmill on the right – and continue for about 6 miles to **Retford**. (An alternative for the first part of this, if you visit the windmill, is to continue on the road past the mill which becomes a broad grassy track, then at a T-junction of tracks by a wood, turn left to rejoin the road into Retford.) At the traffic lights go straight ahead to Cannon Square and subsequently into Market Square by way of the pedestrianised area. 🚲

Distance: 45 miles (nearly 53 using the alternative route to Bawtry)

Terrain: entirely **on road**, including some relatively quiet stretches of A-road, and almost flat, except for climbs to Gringley on the Hill and North Wheatley. (The alternative route to Bawtry involves quite a bit of **bridleway** riding.)

Refreshment opportunities: There are tea shops in Retford, Bawtry and at the Doll Museum in West Stockwith, while most of the villages have pubs – and some (we noted Ranskill and Misterton, which the route passes just south of, soon after West Stockwith) even boast chipshops.

Start: Market Square, Retford (GR 704 811)

Ordnance Survey maps: sorry, you'll need three Landranger sheets – **111** Sheffield and Doncaster, **112** Scunthorpe and **120** Mansfield and Worksop

Public transport links: East Coast Main Line trains (well, some of them) stop at Retford, and the Regional Railways service from Sheffield to Lincoln via Worksop and Gainsborough calls at the lower station at Retford.

Other routes: Routes **16**, **24** and **29** also start from Retford and use some of the same roads into and out of the town.

158

LINEAR ROUTES

9 miles · largely off-road · gentle · Hardwick or Ollerton

Linear route: Hardwick village and Ollerton by bridleways

Although essentially a link route – joining route **27**, Clumber Park and Meden Vale, with route **25**, Laxton, Ollerton and Rufford from Sherwood Pines – this largely off-road route is of interest in its own right. It is described in both directions.

Hardwick village to Ollerton: From the telephone box in the centre of **Hardwick** village go south, downhill, and at the end of the houses on the left of the road there is a gate with a *blue bridleway arrow* to the left. Go eastwards along this bridleway. The first section is a bit rough and rubbly but this lasts for no more than about 200yds. The path is well marked with *bridleway blue arrows* on a firm earth-based track. After a short section through a wood,  this emerges through a swing gate with a chain fixing onto the A614 at a layby. Cross the A614, still on the bridleway marked with a blue bridleway arrow. The route follows the river valley for about 1¹/₂ miles past **Crookford Farm** to reach a minor tarred road.

Turn right down a gentle hill for about 200yds and, where the tarred road bears sharply round to the left, continue straight ahead on a broad track with a 'Ford' road sign. There is a footbridge, which is as well since the ford – of the **River Poulter**, which has already formed the lakes in Welbeck and Clumber Parks – is quite deep. Continue along this track and after about 400yds the main track bears round to the left. A minor track, which you follow, bears round to the right towards a gate marked 'Private – keep out'. Just before the gate, a bridleway bears left following a line of telegraph poles along a firebreak, some of which have 'Robin Hood Way' signs. Where the path emerges from the woods it continues as a well-defined path across open fields, with occasional 'Robin

38
continued

Hood Way' signs. About 350yds after the end of the woods it reaches a minor road; continue straight across, signed *Public bridleway*. This is a well-defined compacted track which continues for a little over ¹/₂ mile to a point where two well-defined tracks diverge to right and left underneath some overhead power lines (the right-hand track leads to a small enclosure by the road with a 'nodding donkey' oil-well pump.) Follow a narrower path which goes straight ahead to the road, keeping a hedge to your right-hand side.

At the tarred road, turn left for about 300yds to a T-junction with another minor road. Turn right, signed *Thoresby* and *Warsop*. After about ³/₄ mile, the bridleway version of the Robin Hood Way crosses, about 400yds short of the main road which you can see in the distance. At the time we checked the route there was a standing bridleway sign to the right, but the left-pointing sign, marked *'Bridle road to Walesby and Ollerton'* was lying in the hedge. There are, however, *blue bridleway arrows* and *Robin Hood Way* signs on some fenceposts.Turn left here along the edge of a field, keeping the hedge to your right. At the far end of the field the path crosses the **Rivers Meden** and **Maun** by two wooden bridges, again following *blue bridleway arrows* and *Robin Hood Way* signs. At the far side of the second bridge, bear right and left, following *bridleway arrows* through a wood. There are occasional clearings to the left, then after about ¹/₂ mile the path emerges from the woods near a Scout camp, with the **River Whitewater** and a (very) miniature rocky gorge on the right. It is well marked throughout by *blue arrows*. Keep to the wide sandy track for 1 mile or so to reach a road at a small car park.

Turn left on the road and then almost immediately right onto an unsigned, unnamed road with woodland to your left. After about 1 mile, just after the start of the built-up area of Ollerton, fork right into Walesby Lane, over a rise and down hill to the junction with Forest Road, A6075. Turn right on Forest Road for a few yards to the roundabout junction with the A616. Bear right (second exit) on Ollerton Road, signed *Ollerton village*, then shortly first left onto Main Street, **Ollerton** (no road name sign, but there is a sign to the *Watermill Tea Shop*).

Ollerton to Hardwick village: From **Ollerton** Watermill turn left on Main Street up to Ollerton Road. Turn right for about 200yds to a roundabout junction, continuing straight on on Forest Road, A6075 for a few yards. Turn left into Walesby Lane and climb through the built-up area to an oblique T-junction. Bear left for about 1 mile to a further T-junction; turn left and then almost immediately right through a gap in the fence which is signed *Public*

160

Above: high summer on the Teversal Trail near Pleasley village (see route 11).

Left: on a track south of Hardwick village in Clumber Park (see route 27).

Off-road paths like the Pleasley, Southwell and Teversal Trails, and the largely traffic-free surfaced roads and paths in Clumber Park, make ideal places for young children to learn the techniques – and the enjoyment – of riding a bike.

A welcome lunch-time break in the sun at Edwinstowe (see route 23).

bridleway and **Walesby Scout Camp.** Follow the broad sandy track, keeping the **White-water** stream to the left. The path, clearly marked throughout by *blue bridleway arrows* and occasional *Robin Hood Way* signs, goes into a wood, with occasional clearings to the right. At the end of the wood bear right and left, then over two bridges over streams (the **Rivers Meden** and **Maun**), Follow the path round a field, keeping the hedge to your left and following *blue bridleway arrows.*

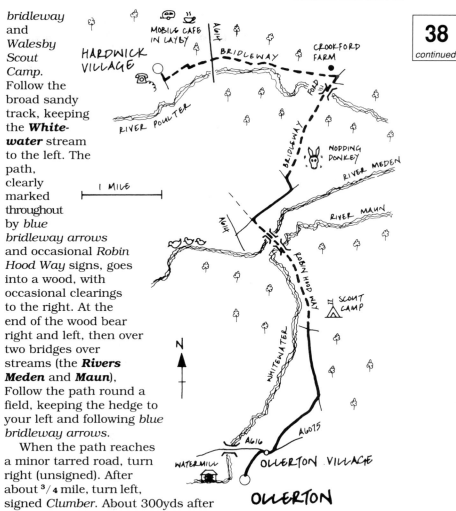

When the path reaches a minor tarred road, turn right (unsigned). After about ³/₄ mile, turn left, signed *Clumber*. About 300yds after the T-junction turn right at a *bridleway sign* onto a path through a gap in the hedge. Follow the path beside the field, keeping the hedge to your left, to a meeting of paths and tracks. Continue straight ahead on a now broader path, going slightly uphill still with a hedge on the left, towards some buildings. At a minor road, continue straight across, signed *Public bridleway*, and follow this across an open field towards some woods. In the woods, the path follows a line of telegraph poles along a firebreak, some of which have '*Robin Hood Way*' signs. At a gate on the left marked 'Private – keep out', bear right onto a path and after about 50yds you reach a

38
continued

more substantial path where you bear left to a ford. This is quite deep but there is a footbridge. Go uphill from the ford to reach a minor tarred road.

Go straight on up this road for about 200yds, then turn left onto a firm track signed *'Public bridleway West Bridge 1¹/₂ miles'*. Go past **Crookford Farm**, past a *'Private road'* sign, with occasional reassuring *blue bridleway arrows*. The path emerges after about 1¹/₂ miles onto the A614. At the A614 go straight over into the layby, then through a swing gate with a chain fixing, following *blue bridleway arrows*, through the woods to **Hardwick** village. 🚲

Distance: 9 miles

Terrain: mainly **off-road** and mostly easily ridable with any type of bike, although some short sections near the Walesby Scout Camp are very loose and sandy in dry weather.

Refreshment opportunities: Clumber Park, Ollerton and at the layby where the route crosses the A614. There is a mobile café in this layby (GR 648 759) every day except Monday. On weekdays it is open from about 7.30am to at least 5pm, later in the summer, and at weekends from 9am for as long as there is custom.

Start: either (Old) Ollerton (GR 653 674) or Hardwick village in Clumber Park (GR 638 756)

Ordnance Survey maps: Landranger sheet **120** Mansfield and Worksop

Public transport links:

Other routes: This route links routes **25** and **27**; link route **L8** is an on-road alternative. Route **17** also visits Clumber Park and passes about 400yds north of Hardwick village.

39

9 miles · mainly off-road · flat · Basford

Linear route: Leen Valley Path from Basford to Newstead

A great deal of work has been put in over the last few years to create 'green corridors' out of the city, following waterways. The River Leen rises just above Newstead Abbey and is dammed to form the lakes in the Abbey grounds. It then flows through Papplewick, Bulwell and Basford until, at Radford, it is ignominiously culverted for much of the remainder of its journey to the River Trent, about 300yds west of Wilford Bridge. At the Basford and Bulwell end a riverside path has been constructed. This route continues this path as far as Newstead Station.

39
continued

At the T-junction by Saint Leodegarius' church, **Basford**, turn north (right) into Church Street, and then first right again by the White Swan, still marked Church Street although it is a definite turn. Church Street becomes Lincoln Street. Shortly after the left turn of Cowley Street, opposite Lincoln Street children's playground and just before the Post Office, turn left round metal barriers into a gap signed as *cycle and pedestrian path*, uphill to emerge into Academy Close. Turn left and first right into Arkers Close, then at the end of the short close continue along a *cycle path marked on the ground* (but no blue sign), down a dropped kerb, then straight on across Bramble Close (not signed at this point). Bear round to the right towards the

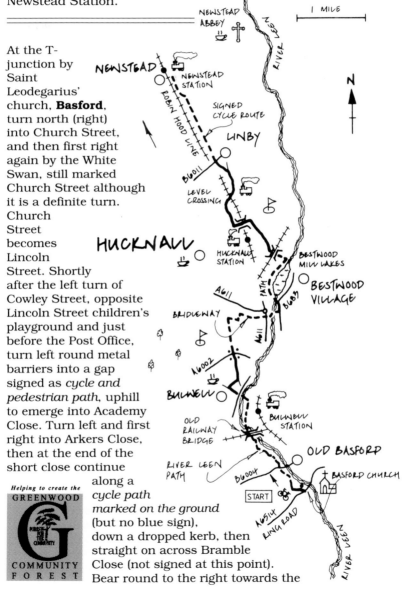

Helping to create the
GREENWOOD
G
COMMUNITY
FOREST

163

Bulls' head castings at Bulwell

back of the Horse and Jockey public house, then past a concrete bollard down a concrete path which runs between a brick wall and black metal railings towards the B6004. At the foot of the concrete path (another concrete bollard), keep left on the stone-surfaced path until you are opposite the start of the *Leen Valley path* and have a clear view of the crossing.

Cross the B6004, Mill Street (*care!*) just after you pass the Murco garage and go through the green railings, signed *Greenway to Bulwell* with cycle route sign *Bulwell Market Place*. Continue on this path, leaving a blue steel latticework bridge to the right, and ignore the next, green, bridge. Continue on the path which switches from the left-hand to the right-hand side of the River Leen and pass under a disused railway bridge, keeping the river on your right. The Leen Path emerges by Bulwell Station (Robin Hood Line) opposite the Horseshoe Inn in **Bulwell**, soon after having passed a children's playground with mini-Sheffield cycle stands.

From Bulwell Station pass the Horseshoe Inn, and bear left to cross the bridge over the River Leen, then bear right across the road into Bulwell Market Square. Cross the square diagonally and bear left up Marketside, leaving Boots to the left and Geo Akins to the right. Pass under Bulwell High Road at the underpass (with black cast-iron decorative bulls' head bollards) to join Commercial Road. Take the first right after about 200yds, Latham Street (the entrance is closed to cars but there is a cycle gap), then at the next T-junction turn left into Ravensworth Road which becomes Squires Avenue. Cross the A6002, Camberley Road/Sandhurst Road, at the traffic lights into Norwich Gardens, and go straight on into Bulwell Hall Park where Norwich Gardens bears left. At the car parking area on the left, where the tarred traffic-calmed road bears left to the golf course, bear right (effectively straight on) on a tarred path past some football pitches.

After Bulwell Hall Wildflower Meadows on the left, and the football pitches on the right, go over a tiny bridge across a minute but very clear stream, then, at the end of the tarred path, go right on a bridleway. Leave an open field to the left, trees to the right, then enter a stretch with trees on both sides. Where the trees on the left stop, bear left on a path to the easily visible gap in the old railway embankment, where you bear right onto a firm-surfaced track. When the bridleway meets Hucknall Lane, A611, turn left on the cycleway marked beside the road, then cross the A611 by the central island onto a path signed *To Bestwood* (**caution: cross railway with care at the swing gates**), then go straight on past a disused mill into Old Mill Close.

Turn left out of Old Mill Close at the T-junction with the B683, Bestwood Road (not signed). After about 200yds, on the outskirts of **Bestwood**, turn left off B683, at the brown *Mill Lakes* sign, wheeling your bike up the concrete channel beside steps (on the wrong side if you're right-handed!) onto a stone-surfaced path in the **Leen Valley Country Park** (although everybody calls it Bestwood Mill Lakes). Follow the path through the park, keeping Mill Lake to the right, then through two wooden chicane-style barriers either side of a surfaced path to carry straight on on a stone-surfaced path. At the top of a slight rise, turn left off the path to pass through a metal gate and under a railway bridge, then over a wooden bridge across a stream and along the path between wooden fences. Go down the kerb (no drop kerb!) into Wigwam Lane (not signed), leaving the golf course on the reclaimed pit spoil heap to your right.

At the top of Wigwam Lane, turn left at the mini-roundabout onto Station Road over the railway bridge, then first right into Linby Road.

(For **Hucknall Station** (Robin Hood Line), turn immediately right into Station Terrace in front of the Station Hotel. *From* Hucknall station platform turn left and follow the one-way route out via Baths Road and cross Station Road into Linby Road.)

After about $^1/_2$ mile Linby road passes over a level crossing, then after another 700yds, just after a turn (unsigned) for Linby village on the right, join the signed

Distance: nearly 9 miles in total; Basford–Bulwell, 2 miles; Bulwell station–Hucknall station, 3$^1/_2$ miles; Hucknall station–Newstead station, 3 miles

Terrain: the route follows a considerable distance of firm-surfaced **cycle track** and **bridleway**, with some **small urban roads**.

Refreshment opportunities: The route passes several pubs and shops. There are several weekday cafés in Bulwell and Hucknall and a teashop at Newstead Abbey, about 1$^1/_2$ miles east of Newstead station (see route **15**) (*there is a charge to enter the Abbey grounds*).

Start: St Leodegarius' church, Basford (GR 553 428). It would also be possible to start at Bulwell station (GR 540 449)

Ordnance Survey maps: Landranger sheets **120** Mansfield and Worksop, and **129** Nottingham and Loughborough.

Public transport links: Robin Hood Line from Nottingham, Sutton Parkway, Mansfield and Mansfield Woodhouse to Bulwell, Hucknall and Newstead (no Sunday service).

Other routes: The Hucknall–Newstead Abbey–Papplewick circuit, route **15**, follows the same line between Hucknall station and Newstead. Route **2**, Bestwood Park, overlaps for a short stretch at Bestwood Mill Lakes.

39
continued

cycle/pedestrian path on the right which brings you to the B6011, just to the right of a roundabout. Cross the B6011, onto the cycle path following blue cycle route signs to *Newstead*, passing a wooden barrier. Just beyond a second wooden access control barrier after about 1 mile bear left to a further wooden access control barrier by a metal gate. Continue straight ahead to pass **Newstead** station (Robin Hood Line) on the left. For access to the station, continue to the level crossing, turn left over the crossing, then left again to the station. 🚲

40

26 miles · on-road · almost flat · Newark-on-Trent

Linear route: Newark to Nottingham – south of the Trent

This linear route links Nottingham to Newark-on-Trent, travelling to the south of the River Trent by quiet minor roads and two short stretches of track. So that you can make a two-way trip, in one of the route information boxes we suggest four ways in which parts of other routes in the book can be combined to give a similarly quiet route *north* of the river.

Although it's never very far from the Fosse Way, the first part of this route passes through a surprisingly unpopulated countryside. Hamlets and villages are not infrequent but outside these and the isolated farms set in their broad fields there is little habitation.

After about five miles a mile of firm-surfaced track leads to the hamlet of Sibthorpe. Prominent in a field beside the track

as you approach is a large circular building. It is a dovecote, the only remnant of a mediaeval religious foundation on the site. The 60ft-high building had nesting places for 1260 birds: the pigeons were used for winter food and their droppings much prized as a fertiliser.

A further five miles on, Car Colston is notable for its two large open greens, the larger – not illogically called the Large Green – covering some

40
continued

16 acres. The greens were left open for villagers to graze their stock when the rest of the fields were enclosed around 1598, rights which are still exercised. The green also forms a fine setting for the village cricket club's matches on summer weekends. The 'Car' part of the name comes from the old Scandinavian word for 'church'.

The route now heads towards the Trent. One of the most attractive views in Nottinghamshire is to look down northwards from the Malkin Hills, the ridge road linking Radcliffe-on-Trent and East Bridgford, to see the village of Shelford with its prominent church tower nestling in its bend of the River Trent (see routes **13** and **31**). Like Rufford, Shelford is another of those almost unchanged place-names, relatively rare in England: it simply means the 'shallow ford' – though the now-managed Trent doesn't look particularly shallow today. Until relatively recently a ferry linked Shelford, where it's still signposted, to Stoke Bardolph on the opposite bank. The *Domesday Boke* records the village as having had 250 inhabitants in 1086. At a guess it's about the same today! The now-quiet village had, like many in this length of the Trent valley, its times of turbulence in the Civil War when over two hundred men were slaughtered following a siege of the church tower. The route's final run in to Nottingham is through Holme Pierrepont and then onto the cycle route along the south bank of the Trent.

From **Newark Castle** go south-west along Castlegate, follow this round to the left into Lombard Street, then at traffic lights by the Robin Hood Hotel, go right on the B6166, then fork left after about 150yds into Albert Street, signed *Hawton 1¹/₄*. At a small (but not mini) five-way roundabout, continue straight on, signed *Hawton*; this road is now Hawton Road. In **Hawton** go straight on at the church, signed *Cotham*. Continue for about 3 miles through **Cotham**, then at the far end of the village, turn right, signed *Shelton*. After just under 1 mile this road joins another at a right-angle bend. Turn right (effectively straight on), signed *Shelton*, then, after 1 further mile, just after crossing the bridge over the River Devon, turn right at a T-junction, signed *Elston*.

Continue for about ³/₄ mile, then, just after Elston Grange Farm on the right, turn left on an unsigned bridleway (tarred surface where it leaves the road) which follows a line of electricity poles. Continue past the farm buildings, where the track becomes stony-surfaced. On reaching the tarred road at **Top Green**, turn right for

40
continued

Nottingham to Newark
north of the River Trent

Option A: route **6** as far as Manvers Street, where turn right and follow the marked cycle route out to Netherfield. From Netherfield follow Chandos Street under the Colwick Loop Road (A612) and under the mineral railway line bridge. This road becomes Emerys Road. At the T-junction with the level crossing to the left, turn right through Stoke Bardolph to return to the A612 in Burton Joyce. Go straight across into Main Street, then take the third right, Meadow Lane to join route **20**. Follow this route in reverse past Gunthorpe Bridge to Hoveringham, then turn right to follow route **30** to Fiskerton. From here use link route **L11** to Newark.

Option B: route **20** as far as Fiskerton, then link route **L11**.

Option C: route **30** to Mapperley Plains, then right on route **5** (road version) to Lambley. Continue straight on on Main Street, Lambley to join route **20** to Fiskerton, then **L11**.

Option D: route **30** in reverse via Southwell to Fiskerton, then **L11**.

about ¹/₂ mile through **Sibthorpe** (mediaeval dovecote in field on right). At a right-hand bend in the road at the far end of Sibthorpe, fork left, signed *Flintham*. Shortly after a very sharp left-hand bend (a T-junction with a roughly tarred track) there is a further T-junction; turn right, signed *Flintham*.

In **Flintham**, just after the Boot and Shoe, turn left, signed *Screveton*. Continue straight on for about 1¹/₂ miles into **Screveton**, following the sign for *Car Colston*. At the T-junction in **Car Colston**, facing the wide village green and cricket pitch, turn right, signed *Fosse Way*. At the T-junction with the A46 (which is the Fosse Way), turn left, signed *Leicester*, then after about 300yds,

turn right, signed *East Bridgford*. (It is possible to avoid these 300yds of the A46 by going almost straight across at the main road on a bridleway into East Bridgford, but this track is inclined to be sticky in anything other than very dry weather.) At the crossroads in the centre of **East Bridgford** by the church, continue straight on down Trent Lane,

GUNTHORPE
(SEASONAL)
GUNTHORPE BRIDGE
RIVER TRENT
A6097
SHELFORD

NOTTINGHAM STATION
NATIONAL WATER SPORTS CENTRE
SIGNED CYCLE ROUTE
RIVER TRENT
HOLME PIERREPONT HALL
RADCLIFFE ON TRENT
SIGNED CYCLE ROUTE ON RIVER BANK
SUSPENSION BRIDGE

1 MILE

168

signed *Gunthorpe*. The road emerges by the south bank of the Trent, to meet the A6097 by Gunthorpe Bridge.

40
continued

Go straight across the A6097, signed *Shelford*, still on the south side of the river. Continue through **Shelford**, then uphill to a crossroads. Turn right, signed *Radcliffe*. After about 2 miles, at a T-junction in **Radcliffe on Trent**, turn right, signed *Nottingham*, for about 400yds, leaving the church on the left. Just after passing the Cliffe Inn on the left, turn right into The Green, signed as *no through road*. The Green becomes Holme Lane which continues to **Holme Pierrepont** Hall, where there is a short section of unsurfaced road. About ¹/₂ mile past the exit from the

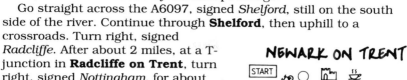

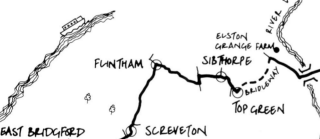

Water Sports Centre on the right and the campsite on the left, turn right into Adbolton Lane. Take the first right – Adbolton Grove – as you enter the built-up area. Turn left at the bottom of Adbolton Grove, into Holme Road, and after 600yds follow the cycle route signed for the *Meadows and City Centre*, which bears off to the right across open ground. This cycle route meets the River Trent, where you turn left along the bank, and follow it under Lady Bay Bridge, past Nottingham Forest football ground, and under ***Trent Bridge***. Cross the river using the cycle/pedestrian suspension bridge, just past County Hall. At the road, The Embankment, on the north side of the bridge, turn left to the small roundabout by the entrance to Wilford cycle-and-pedestrian bridge. Go round the

169

40
continued

Holme Pierrepont Hall

roundabout (care! – *not* the usual priorities) and take the third exit into Queen's Walk cycle track. Continue straight on, crossing two sets of cycle traffic lights to **Nottingham Midland Station**. 🚲

Distance: 26 miles

Terrain: nearly all flat, except for the unexpectedly sharp climb up from Shelford, between Gunthorpe Bridge and Radcliffe on Trent, and almost entirely **on-road.**

Refreshment opportunities: teas are available on summer Sundays at St John the Baptist, Gunthorpe, and also morning coffee on certain Saturdays. There is usually some sort of refreshment available on the north side of the river at Gunthorpe Bridge, while most of the villages have pubs, some of which serve food. There are several cafés in Newark.

Start: Newark Castle (GR 796 540)

Ordnance Survey maps: Landranger sheets **120** Mansfield and Worksop, and **129** Nottingham and Loughborough.

Public transport links: East Coast Main Line from London Kings Cross and Doncaster to Newark Northgate, Regional Railways services from Nottingham to Newark Castle, calling also at Carlton, Burton Joyce and Lowdham (not all services on this line call at these smaller stations, and on some services they are 'request' stops – you ask the conductor when you get one or make a hand signal to the driver if you are waiting at the small station).

Other routes: Route **26** explores some of the villages south-east and south-west of Newark. Routes **13** and **31**, the Bingham circuits, join this route at Shelford crossroads; route **20**, the half off-road route from Lambley and Burton Joyce, virtually joins this one at Gunthorpe Bridge and offers an alternative route back to the eastern suburbs of Nottingham. Link route **L11** joins Newark north of the River Trent to Fiskerton and so to route **30**, while link route **L12** joins Newark to routes **28** and **34** at Norwell.

LINK ROUTES

Link: Norwell village

This very short link joins together two circular routes, **28** Southwell Trail and the Dumbles, and **34** North Trent Valley, so that they can be combined to make a larger circuit or part of a linear route from north to south of the county. It is described in both directions.

East to west: from the junction by the Wesleyan Chapel in **Norwell**, turn right, signed *Caunton* and *Ollerton*. Continue through the village, sweeping round to the right, signed *N (for Norwell) Woodhouse* and *Kneesall*. After about 500yds, turn left to rejoin the Southwell Trail route, signed *Caunton* and *Southwell*.

Start: in Norwell village, either at GR 773 618 or GR 765 618
Ordnance Survey maps: 120 Mansfield and Worksop
Other routes: **28** Southwell Trail and the Dumbles, and **34** Northern Trent Valley. Link route **L12** joins Norwell, and hence both these routes, to Newark.

West to east: from the T-junction about 2 miles after Caunton, where the road from Caunton joins the Norwell to Kneesall road, turn right, signed *Norwell* and *Cromwell*. Bear round to the left in **Norwell**, signed *Cromwell* and *Newark*. At the junction just past the Wesleyan Chapel on the left, turn left, signed *Ossington* and *Carlton on Trent*. 🚲

Link: Mansfield Woodhouse to Pleasley Vale

From **Mansfield Woodhouse station**, walk down the ramp and turn left through the pedestrian exit beside steel gate at the north end of the station car park into Oxclose Lane (unsurfaced and

L2
continued

unnamed at this point). Turn right on Oxclose Lane, then at diagonal crossroads where the road bears round to the right, sharp left and left again into Thoresby Road (sign on wall on left by pillar box). At the end of the houses, just before the railway embankment, turn right into Manor Road. At T-junction, turn left into Vale Road (not signed). Where Vale Road bears round to the right as Brown Avenue, continue straight on under low railway bridge on Common Lane (not signed). Follow this road for about 1¹/₂ miles to join *Pleasley Trails route 11*.

Distance: about 1¹/₂ miles
Terrain: flat, **on-road**
Start: Mansfield Woodhouse station (GR 534 633).
Ordnance Survey maps: Landranger sheet **120** Mansfield and Worksop
Public transport links: by rail to Mansfield Woodhouse (Robin Hood Line)
Other routes: Route **11**. Routes **19** and **23** also start at Mansfield Woodhouse station and link route **L10** joins Mansfield Woodhouse station to route **27**

L3

2 miles • on-road • flat • North Leverton or Treswell

Link: North Leverton and Treswell

This short route provides a link between routes **24**, Retford round, and **34**, Northern Trent Valley, so that they may be combined or used to form part of a linear route from north to south of the county – or vice versa. It is described in both directions.

From North Leverton to Treswell: Leave **North Leverton** south on Southgore Lane, signed *Rampton, Newark* and *Cottam*; this becomes Station Road. In **South Leverton**, follow the road as it bears round to the right, becoming Church Street, then round to the left past the church. Continue straight on on this road, ignoring all minor road crossings, to **Treswell**.

Distance: 2 miles
Terrain: **on-road**, flat
Start: either Treswell (GR 782 792) or North Leverton (GR 785 822)
Ordnance Survey maps: Landranger sheet **120**, Mansfield and Worksop

From Treswell to North Leverton: In **Treswell**, turn right just after the Red Lion hotel on the left, signed *South Leverton* and *Gainsboro'*. Follow this road into **South Leverton**, where it becomes Church Street. Follow this where it bears round to the right after the church, then round to the left, becoming Station Road into **North Leverton**.

2½ miles • mostly off-road • gentle • Worksop Manor South Lodge or Creswell Crags

Link: Workspop Manor South Lodge and Creswell Crags

Note: do not confuse Worksop Manor South Lodge (this link and route 14) with Clumber Park South Lodge (route 27)

This route is a spur off route **14** allowing a visit to the Creswell Crags archaeological site. It is described in both directions.

The route follows a public bridleway which skirts the well-kept grounds of Welbeck Abbey. Welbeck is one of the places which earned the area the title of the Dukeries: it is the country seat of the Dukes of Portland, whose influence in north Nottinghamshire in particular is shown by the frequency with which Portland Roads and pubs named The Portland Arms crop up in the nearby towns and villages. Most of the current building dates from the middle of the last century and is set in a vast park.

Distance: 2½ miles

Terrain: almost entirely **off-road**, some up-and-down

Refreshment opportunities: light refreshments at the Creswell Crags Visitor Centre

Start: either Worksop South Lodge (GR 568 754) or Creswell Crags Visitor Centre (GR 537 744)

Ordnance Survey maps: Landranger sheet **120**, Mansfield and Worksop

Public transport links: only as below

Other routes: Link route **L9** joins Creswell Crags to route **27** at Whaley, and so could be used in conjunction with link route **L10** to reach Mansfield Woodhouse station on the Robin Hood Line.

L4

continued

Creswell Crags lie half in Nottinghamshire and half in Derbyshire, on either side of a small lake. In the caves and rock shelters beside the lake have been found remains indicating that they were lived in at least as early as late Palaeolithic times – some 10 000 years ago. The caves are not generally open to the public but there is an extensive display in the nearby visitor centre. The opening times of the Creswell Crags Visitor Centre – which has a display and tea room as well as offering occasional led walks and organised tours of the prehistoric caves – are February to October, daily, 10.30am to 4.30pm; November to January, Sundays only, 10.30am to 4.30pm. In summer, the lake shore by the crags makes a very pleasant picnic spot.

From the Worksop Manor South Lodge to Creswell Crags:

From the **Lodge** follow the bridleway signed *Public Bridleway, Welbeck Abbey*. Pass through two wooden gates, then follow the grassy bridleway downhill across a broad field. (There are occasional *Robin Hood Way bow-and-arrow signs*.) At the foot of the slope go through the broad opening in the wooden fence to cross a broad bridge between two lakes to emerge on a tarred road by **Welbeck Abbey**. Turn right, following *bridleway signs*. After about 250yds, at the end of the woodland on the left, turn left on a wide grassy track following the wooden *bridleway fingerpost*. This track follows the edge of a wood and past a playing field, emerging after about 500yds onto a concrete road. Turn right, still following *bridleway fingerpost*, across a cattle grid, first down a sweeping open concrete road, then along a tree-lined access road for ³/₄ mile to emerge at the A60. Go straight across on a compacted but untarred track signed as *bridleway and Robin Hood Way*. At a gate

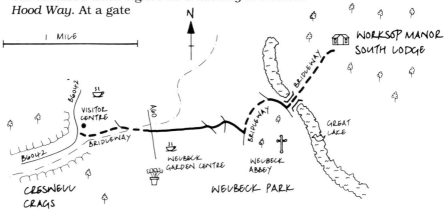

across the path, the official bridleway bears off to the right. Go straight ahead through the side swing gate beside a cream-coloured barrier: this is now a footpath, leading to the **Creswell Crags Visitor Centre**, which is about 200yds down the path.

From Creswell Crags to Worksop Manor South Lodge: From the **Visitor Centre** head east from the far end of the car park to the vehicular access on a footpath for 200yds, passing through a swing gate beside a cream-coloured barrier onto a bridleway. Continue straight on to the A60. Go straight across onto a minor concrete road signed as a bridleway, following *bridleway blue arrow signs and fingerposts*. This climbs at first gently, then more steeply, for ³/₄ mile; at the top of the incline cross a cattle grid and turn left off the concrete road onto a grassy track, still following *bridleway signs* for about 500yds, past playing fields onthe right. At a tarred road on the edge of the wood, turn right and follow *blue bridleway arrows* along the left fork in the road for about 250yds. Where the road ahead is marked as a private entrance to **Welbeck Abbey,** turn left following the *blue bridleway arrows and Robin Hood Way bow-and-arrow signs* across a broad bridge between two lakes. Go through the opening in the wooden fence at the far side and up a grassy track across an open field. At the top of the incline at the edge of the wood go through a wooden swing gate, then follow the path to the right parallel to the fence to a second swing gate to emerge at **Worksop Manor South Lodge**. 🚲

---

4 miles · on- or off-road cycle route · flat · Beeston

L5

Link: Beeston and Nottingham

This route provides a link between the centre of Nottingham and route **1** to the Attenborough Nature Reserve. Link route **L6** continues from Beeston to join route **4**

From **Beeston** Square, follow *cycle route signs* to *University and Nottingham*, across Wollaton Road/Station Road at traffic lights into Beeston High Road, signed *'Cyclists dismount for Beeston High Road'*. (Cycling is not permitted from 10am to 4pm, Monday–Saturday.) At the far end of pedestrianised section of the High Road, turn right into City Road, with *cycle route sign* to *Highfields, Lenton, City Centre*. Halfway along City Road pass through the cycle gap in the road closure. At the foot of City Road, turn left

L5
continued

following *cycle route signs* to *Highfields, Lenton, City Centre* along the contraflow cycle lane on Middle Street. At the end of Middle Street, at the junction with Humber Road, cross by the central island to go straight on into Fletcher Road, still following *cycle route signs* to *Highfields, Lenton, City Centre*. Towards the end of Fletcher Road, bear right on a segregated shared-use cycle track with the blue pedestrian-plus-cyclist sign but no direction sign. This runs between fences and winds round gardens to emerge on a road (Lower Road but not signed at this point). Go straight on and, just before this road joins the main road, turn right, following the *cycle route signs* to a toucan pedestrian-plus-cycle light-controlled crossing over the A6005, Queens Road East, just south of a roundabout.

Beyond the crossing, turn left onto an unsegregated shared-use cycle track along the south side of University Boulevard, with occasional *cycle route signs* now reading *University, Lenton, City Centre*. Follow the cycle track as far as the entrance to Highfields Science Park, then follow the cycle route directions, which are to join the traffic stream leaving the Science Park to cross the dual carriageway of University Boulevard at the traffic lights. At the University South Entrance, bear right on a segregated cycle track now along the north side of University Boulevard. Take the first left into Greenfield Street, with *cycle route sign* now reading *QMC, Lenton, City Centre*, then first right into City Road, still following *cycle route signs*. At the end of this road use the double set of cycle/pedestrian traffic lights to pass under the Dunkirk flyover, and at the far side turn right on the shared-use segregated path, which bears round to the left into Abbey Street.

Follow the cycle path over the bridge over the River Leen past the Texaco garage, then use the pedestrian/cycle lights to cross Abbey Street. At the far side, go left and right into Priory Street, with the *cycle route signs* now reading, *City Centre, Meadows, West Bridgford*. Just before the dead end of Priory Street, bear left, still following the cycle route signs to *City Centre, Meadows, West Bridgford*, through a gap between fenced gardens, then straight on to a T-junction. Turn right following the *cycle route signs* onto a segregated shared-use footpath, then after 200yds, again follow cycle route signs to cross by an advisory crossing, signed *Castle Boulevard, City Centre*. Continue straight on between the BT depot on the right and iron railings on the left, under a low railway bridge and between bollards to emerge onto a minor road, with more *cycle route signs* to *Castle Boulevard and City Centre*. Continue straight on along Grove Road, taking the second on the right, Alderney

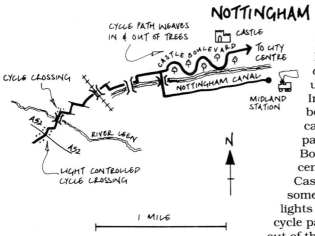

Street, following *cycle signs*. At the end of Alderney Street, turn left alongside the Beeston Canal (more *cycle route signs*) to go under a road bridge. Immediately after this bear left away from the canal along the cycle path to join Castle Boulevard. For the city centre, bear right along Castle Boulevard and after some 400yds cross by the lights and follow the famous cycle path that weaves in and out of the trees, and then follow *cycle route signs* to the *Castle and City Centre*.

For the station, turn right along the shared-use path on the south side of Castle Boulevard, then just beyond the HSS Hire Shop take the footbridge on the right over the canal. Follow the curve of the footbridge round to the right, then turn right on reaching the canal towpath and continue along it, keeping the canal on your left, for about ¹/₂ mile, leaving at the ramp just after the new Magistrates' Court building up to Carrington Street, almost opposite **Nottingham Midland Station**.

Terrain: Mostly on signed cycle route, a **mix of on-road and** tarred **off-road** paths, plus a length of improved canal towpath; flat

Refreshment opportunities: Nottingham, Beeston

Start: Beeston town centre (GR 528 369)

Ordnance Survey maps: Landranger sheet **129** Nottingham and Loughborough, or Pathfinder sheet **833**, Nottingham (South) and Long Eaton. The whole route is also on the *AZ Premier Street Map of Nottingham* and on the cycle route map produced by Nottinghamshire County Council.

Public transport links: Midland Main Line, Robin Hood Line and Regional Railways services go to Nottingham Midland station. Regional railways services and a few Midland Main Line InterCity services call at Beeston.

Other routes: City routes **6** and **10**, and longer routes **32**, **35** and **36** start and finish at Nottingham station. Route **40**, the linear route from Newark, finishes there. Link route **L6** joins Beeston to the short, largely off-road, route **4**.

L6

3¹/₂ miles • on- and off-road • gentle • Beeston or Strelley

Link: Beeston and Strelley village

This route is a link between Beeston town centre and the short off-road route **4** to Strelley and Cossall.

Beeston to Strelley: From **Beeston** Town Centre, head south-west on Chilwell Road following blue *cycle route sign* for *Bramcote*. Just before its junction with B6464, Middle Street, and opposite the church, turn right on Devonshire Avenue, passing Broxtowe Borough Council offices on the right. At the head of Devonshire Avenue turn right on Glebe Street and then left to climb Bramcote Road. At the top of Bramcote Road, which is quite uphill, go

diagonally across Bramcote Drive following the blue *cycle route sign* for *Bramcote* (and a green *Public Bridleway* sign) to join a walled path which becomes a well-surfaced fenced bridleway between trees across a golf course.

At the far side of the golf course, follow the *cycle route signs* for *Bramcote* to turn onto a tarred cut-through between houses with a bollard at the end, then turn right, still following *cycle route signs* for *Bramcote*, on Claremont Avenue (not named at this point). Claremont Avenue curves round to the left to come to a T-junction; turn right and almost immediately left into Beeston Fields Drive, marked with blue *cycle route sign* to *Bramcote*. After about 100yds, go straight across Cow Lane into Bridle Road and continue on this road until it meets the A52.

The route goes, or would go, straight ahead but there is no gap in the central reservation of the A52, so turn left for a short distance to a light-controlled pedestrian crossing and cross the A52 on foot, then turn right back to the junction with Moor Lane opposite Bridle Road, and turn left into Moor Lane. Continue on Moor Lane leaving schools to the left. Go straight on at the sign *'Unsuitable for motor vehicles'* onto a well-surfaced bridleway which goes through a cutting, then through a wooded area. Shortly after crossing a humpbacked railway bridge, turn right between bollards in a metal rail fence into Beverley Close (not signed at this point). At the T-junction at the end of this short close, turn left up Teesdale Drive (not signed at this point), then right at the end of Teesdale Drive into Farndale Drive. Ignore the first left turn

(Monmouth Close) and then follow Farndale Road round to the left to its junction with Wollaton Vale (not signed at this point).

Turn left on Wollaton Vale, passing the Gondola pub on the left, then bear left across traffic lights onto Nottingham Road, A609. Immediately after the traffic lights, turn right (care!) into a minor road, The Moor, signed *Bridleway to Cossall and public footpath to Strelley*. At the entry to Moor Farm on the left, continue straight on, passing to the right of metal barrier onto a well-surfaced track. After about 300yds you reach a junction of bridleways at GR 501 409 (*Route 4: Strelley and Cossall, joins here*). Turn right, signed *Bridleway* to pass a small wood on the left and go through several gates. After about ¹/₂ mile at a T-junction of tracks, turn left and follow this bridleway between hedges until it bears round to the right and reaches a tarred road. Turn left for about 300yds to **Strelley** church.

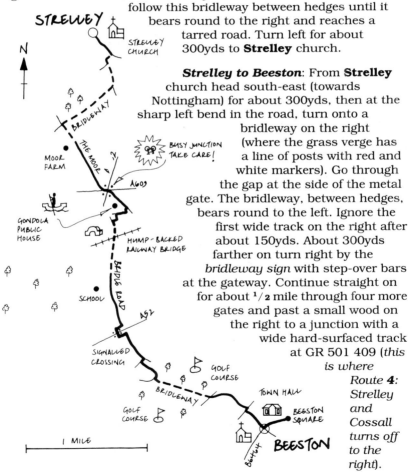

Strelley to Beeston: From **Strelley** church head south-east (towards Nottingham) for about 300yds, then at the sharp left bend in the road, turn onto a bridleway on the right (where the grass verge has a line of posts with red and white markers). Go through the gap at the side of the metal gate. The bridleway, between hedges, bears round to the left. Ignore the first wide track on the right after about 150yds. About 300yds farther on turn right by the *bridleway sign* with step-over bars at the gateway. Continue straight on for about ¹/₂ mile through four more gates and past a small wood on the right to a junction with a wide hard-surfaced track at GR 501 409 (*this is where Route 4: Strelley and Cossall turns off to the right*).

L6
continued

A plaque on the wall of Thomas Humber's original bicycle factory in Humber Road, Beeston

For this link route, turn *left* to head south-east on a firm well-surfaced track, passing to the left of a metal barrier where the track from Moor Farm comes in from the right. Continue straight on to join a tarred road by the entrance to Spring Farm on the left. Follow this road, Moor Road, to its oblique T-junction with the A609, Nottingham Road. Turn left on A609 to the traffic lights where the outer ring road, A6002, crosses. Bear right at about 45° at the lights into the fifth arm of the junction, Wollaton Vale, to pass the Gondola pub, then take the first right, signed as *Farndale Drive leading to Wheeldale Close etc*, then go left into Dentdale Drive which runs parallel to Wollaton Vale, then immediately first right into Farndale Drive. Take the second left into Teesbrook Drive, then first right into Beverley Close, signed as *No through road*. At the end of this short close, pass between some bollards to join a bridleway. Turn left on the bridleway over the railway bridge, and continue straight on at all crossing tracks. Go through a set of barriers at the end of the wooded section and continue straight on on this well-surfaced track until it becomes a tarred road, Moor Lane (not signed at this point), which passes some schools on the right.

At its junction with the A52 the route goes straight on but as there is no gap in the central reservation, go right to a light-controlled pedestrian crossing, cross the road on foot, and then come back to turn right into Bridle Road, which is signed as *No entry* with an exemption for cycles. At the end of Bridle Road, go straight across Cow Lane into Beeston Fields Drive, signed as *cycle route* to *Beeston Town Centre*. After about 100yds, turn right and almost immediately left, following *cycle*

> **Distance**: 3¹/₂ miles
>
> **Terrain**: fairly gentle, with a mixture of **bridleway and minor roads**
>
> **Refreshment opportunities**: Beeston; the Broad Oak inn, about ¹/₂ mile on the Nottingham side of Strelley church also serves food.
>
> **Start**: junction of bridleways at GR 501 409 (on Route **4**: Strelley and Cossall) or Beeston town centre(GR 528 369).
>
> **Ordnance Survey maps**: Landranger sheet **129** Nottingham and Loughborough. The whole route is also on the *AZ Premier Street Map of Nottingham*
>
> **Public transport links**: Regional Railways services (and a few Midland Main Line trains) call at Beeston station, about ¹/₂ mile south-east of Beeston town centre.
>
> **Other routes**: Route **1**, Attenborough Nature Reserve, starts and finished at Beeston. Link route **L5** gives a route from Beeston to Nottingham city centre.

L6
continued

route signs into Claremont Avenue, which curves round to the right. At the apex of the bend, turn left, still following blue *cycle route signs* to *Beeston* past a bollard onto a tarred cut-through between houses, then onto a fenced well-surfaced path between trees across a golf course.

At the end of the path go diagonally across Bramcote Drive into Bramcote Road, still following blue *cycle route signs* for *Beeston*. Follow Bramcote Road downhill, still following occasional blue *signs*, cross Park Street (give way), then continue on Bramcote Road to its junction with Glebe Street. Turn right, then first left into Devonshire Avenue past Broxtowe Borough Council offices to the junction with Chilwell Road, just before that road meets the B6464, Middle Street. Turn left, following the *cycle route sign* for *Beeston Town Centre*. The **town centre** is about 300yds along this road. 🚲

L7

2¹/₂ or 5 miles • on- and off-road • gentle • Sherwood Pines

Link: Sherwood Pines and Edwinstowe

This route links Sherwood Pines Forest Park to route **23** at Edwinstowe, with an extension to or from Center Parcs' Sherwood Holiday Village, hence giving a fairly traffic-free route from there to Sherwood Forest. By combining this link route with either outward or homeward legs of route **23** it is possible to follow a largely traffic-free route to Mansfield Woodhouse station; the route is described in both directions.

Sherwood Pines to Edwinstowe: From **Sherwood Pines Visitor Centre** car park ignore cycle way-marking and follow *Exit* signs until you reach a tarred road, where *Exit* is signed to the right. Turn right down the slope for about 400yds to the B6030. Turn left on the B6030 and then after about 100yds turn right onto a minor road, signed *Edwinstowe*. After about 1¹/₂ miles at a T-junction on the outskirts of Edwinstowe, turn left (red stop sign but no direction  sign) over the river bridge to the foot of the High Street. Follow the one-way system round to the left up West Lane, signed *Sherwood Forest Visitor Centre*. At the traffic light-controlled junction with

L7
continued

Mansfield Road, A6075, turn right, signed *Ollerton* and *Budby* and still signed for the *Visitor Centre*. After about 150yds at the next set of traffic lights **either** turn right for **Edwinstowe** High Street **or** left on Church Street, B6034, to follow signs for *Sherwood Forest Visitor Centre*.

Edwinstowe to Sherwood Pines: At the foot of the High Street in **Edwinstowe**, head straight on over the river, then take the first turning on the right, Mill Lane, signed *Clipstone*. Follow this road for about 1¹/₂ miles to a T-junction with the B6030. Turn left, then after about 100yds take the first right, signed *Sherwood Pines Forest Park*. Follow the road steadily uphill for about 400yds to a point where the road divides, the right-hand turning being signed *Forest Office*. Go straight on, following the pictorial signs for *Toilets, Picnic area, Information*, past a green barrier used to close the car park at night. Follow this road down to the car park and **Sherwood Pines** Forest Park **visitor centre** (toilets, drinking water tap; cycle hire and light refreshments at weekends).

Center Parcs to Sherwood Pines: Leave Center Parcs **Sherwood Holiday Village**, and at the S-bend at the foot of a slight slope bear left on a firm-surfaced but untarred track – concessionary cycle way, signed *Robin Hood Way* – keeping Center Parcs perimeter fence on the left. After 1¹/₄ miles, at a cross tracks with an information board marked 'Start of cycle route', turn right on a broad forest road, passing beside a red-oxide painted barrier and follow the red *cycle route waymark signs* on red posts to the **Sherwood Pines** Forest Park **visitor centre** area.

Sherwood Pines to Center Parcs: From the **Visitor Centre**, follow the waymarked cycle route in reverse to pass between two green posts with small 'no entry' symbols on them (these apply to cars). Continue on this path which runs almost parallel to the road on which you came in for about 250yds to a T-junction of tracks. Turn right, following the obviously more used track (there is a *red cycle-route marker* at the junction). Follow this track for about 400yds down a slight slope between tall pines to a crossroads of tracks. (*If you are returning from Edwinstowe to Center Parcs* and *don't* want to call in at the Visitor Centre, turn left before the Visitor Centre/Forest Office junction, just after the 20mph speed restriction sign, across a short stretch of grass to pass between some boulders placed to stop car traffic onto a gravel path. Continue on this path for about 200yds to join the waymarked cycle route in reverse. Continue straight on for about 400yds down a slight slope between tall pines to a crossroads of tracks.) From either route, turn left on a sandy but firm-surfaced broad track (there is a *red cycle-route* marker just to the left of the junction on the far side of the track). After about 300yds, at the top of a slope at a T-junction of tracks, turn right (there is a *red cycle-route marker* immediately to the right, and there are plenty of red cycle-route repeater signs later). Follow this track for about 500yds down a slight slope and pass to the left of a red-oxide painted barrier. Almost immediately after the barrier, turn left at a crossroads of tracks (by the cycle

Distance: 2¹/₂5 miles

Terrain: a mix of forest track and minor road; gently rolling

Refreshment opportunities: Sherwood Pines (limited) and Edwinstowe

Start: Sherwood Pines Forest Park Visitor Centre (GR 612 642) (extension to/from Center Parcs' Sherwood Holiday Village (GR 637 640))

Ordnance Survey maps: Landranger sheet **120** Mansfield and Worksop

Public transport links: by rail to Mansfield Woodhouse (Robin Hood Line), then follow route **23** (either outward or return legs as described) as far as *Old Clipstone*, follow B6030 east for ¹/₂ or ³/₄ mile to join this link route, **L7**, to the *Sherwood Pines Visitor Centre*.

Other routes: Route **7** is a short off-road forest circuit and routes **18** and **25** are mainly on-road circuits, all from the Eakring Road car park and using some of the same forest roads. Route **23** is joined by this link at Edwinstowe.

route information board) along the concessionary route. This reaches a tarred road after about 1¹/₄ miles. Turn right up the slope to Center Parcs **Sherwood Holiday Village**. 🚲

---

4 miles • on-road • flat • Hardwick or Walesby

L8

Link: Clumber Park and Walesby

This link joins route **27**, Clumber Park and Meden Vale, with route **25**, Laxton, Ollerton and Rufford from Sherwood Pines Forest Park. It is described in both directions.

From Walesby to Clumber Park: From the Carpenter's Arms in **Walesby**, head north on the B6387, signed *Bothamsall* and *Retford*, then straight on at the next crossroads, signed *Gamston* and *Retford*. After about 1¹/₂ miles, shortly after a double bend by the railway and bridges over the Rivers Maun and Meden, where the B6387 goes right, turn left on a minor road signed *Bothamsall* and *Thoresby*.

In **Bothamsall**, by the church, follow the road round to the left,

L8 *continued*

signed *Thoresby* and *Warsop*. About 3/4 mile after the village, and about 1/2 mile after climbing past a prominent mound on the left (marked on the map as 'Motte' – the mound on which a castle was built) and then going down a gentle slope, turn right onto a minor road, signed *Clumber*. After about 1 1/2 miles this meets the A614 at a T-junction; go straight across the A624 to a layby on the west side of the road. At the south end of the layby there is a wooden fingerpost, signed *bridleway*. Follow this path for a short distance as far as a picnic area, with wooden benches and tables. Turn right, along an unsigned but very well-defined broad path, which runs parallel to the main road for about 200yds. (Ignore other paths signed Clumber Park which veer off to the left.)

The path emerges onto a minor tarred Park entrance road just before two gateway portals. Turn left between the portals and past the barrier into **Clumber Park**. After about 600yds there is a substantial low timber pole barrier on the right. Turn right to pass by the barrier and between two five-barred gates onto a firm track

HARDWICK VILLAGE — RIVER POULTER — CLUMBER PARK — ENTRANCE TO CLUMBER PARK — CLUMBER LAKE — N — BOTHAMSALL — B6387 — RIVER MEDEN — RIVER MAUN — "MOTTE" — B6387 — 1 MILE — WALESBY

Distance: 4 miles

Terrain: almost entirely **on-road**; flat except for the up-and-down just south of Hardwick village

Refreshment opportunities: Clumber Park, Walesby **Start**: Hardwick village in Clumber Park (GR 638 756) or the Carpenter's Arms crossroads, Walesby (GR 680 705)

Ordnance Survey maps: Landranger sheet 120, Mansfield and Worksop

Public transport links:

Other routes: This route links routes **25** and **27**; route **38** is an off-road alternative. Route **17** also visits Clumber Park and passes about 400yds north of Hardwick village.

flanked by fences. Continue along this track for about 350yds, passing another low wooden barrier about halfway along, to emerge on a minor tarred road at a bend. Go straight ahead on

L8
continued

this road, downhill, passing a metal barrier that closes access to the Park from 9pm to 8.30am. At the bottom of the hill there is a ford – with a footbridge for the wary. Cross this and climb gently to **Hardwick** village.

From Clumber Park to Walesby: Go south from **Hardwick** village, gently downhill to a ford – which has an alternative footbridge if you don't want to ride through. At the top of the rise from the ford on the other side, pass a metal barrier, and where the road bends left, go straight ahead on a firm-surfaced but untarred track for about 350yds, passing a low timber barrier about halfway along. The track reaches a tarred minor road at another low timber barrier. Pass round the barrier and turn left on the road to one of the gateways to the Park. Pass between the gateway portals and immediately after, and before reaching the main road, turn right onto a well-defined but *unsigned* path which runs through the woods parallel to the main road. After about 200yds this reaches a picnic area with wooden benches and tables. Turn left onto a bridleway path which emerges onto a layby on the west side of the A614 (unsigned).

Go almost straight across the main road onto a minor road with 7.5T limit sign, signed *Bothamsall 2*. After about 1^1/$_2$ miles, at a T-junction, turn left, signed *Bothamsall*. In **Bothamsall** follow the road round to the right, signed *Gamston* and *Retford*. After about ^{1}/$_2$ mile this road meets the B6387 at a bend on the B-road. Turn right on the B6387, signed *Walesby* and *Ollerton* to the Carpenter's Arms at **Walesby**.

---

4 miles • on- and off-road • flat • Whaley Common or Creswell Crags

L9

Link: Whaley Common and Creswell Crags

This link is a spur from route **27** Clumber Park and Meden Vale at Whaley Common to the Creswell Crags Visitor Centre. Combined with route **L4** Worksop Manor South Lodge to Creswell Crags, it provides a route into Worksop and an

185

L9

continued

alternative route to and from Clumber Park. The route is described in both directions.

For details of the Creswell Crags archaeological site, see the description for route **L4**.

Whaley Common to Creswell Crags: About 150yds east of the T-junction at **Whaley Common**, turn north (that is, left if you are following the instructions for route **27**, Clumber Park and Meden Vale) along a well-defined firm-surfaced track that runs between hedges. (There is no bridleway sign at the junction but there is a wooden post with one of the metallic yellow arrowed plaques of the Archaeological Trail.) After a little over $^1/_2$ mile the track joins a minor tarred road (Frithwood Road, but unsigned at this point), at a minute triangular grass green, near a farm (Frithwood Farm). Turn left on the road (effectively straight on) for about $^3/_4$ mile to a T-junction. Turn right (no sign) gently downhill into **Creswell**, and just after the Black Diamond pub on the left, turn right into Model Village, just before a village shop. Go straight across the grassy oval centre of the Model Village to the large Clubhouse, now sadly derelict. At the T-junction go right and immediately left to pass by the side of the Clubhouse on a little unsigned road. Immediately behind the building turn left along a path that skirts two sides of a playing field (keeping the field on your right) to reach a railway footbridge at the opposite corner of the field. Go over the footbridge and then down a residential street (Morven Street – not named at this point – which becomes Duchess Street) gently downhill to a T-junction with the A616 (not signed at this point). Turn left and almost immediately right on the B6042, signed *Creswell Crags Visitor Centre*. Continue on the B6042 for about $^1/_2$ mile to **Creswell Crags** Visitor Centre.

Creswell Crags to Whaley Common: Turn left from **Creswell Crags** Visitor Centre on the B6042 for about $^1/_2$ mile to a T-junction with the A616. Turn left, signed *Newark*, then after about 50yds, turn right into Duchess Street, and continue uphill, continuing ahead where the road bears round to the right, to a railway footbridge. Cross the bridge, and then follow a path that skirts two sides of a playing field, keeping the field to your left, to reach the opposite corner of the field. The path emerges beside the derelict Clubhouse of **Creswell** Model Village. Turn right along the side of the building, and then right and immediately left to cross the central grass oval of the Model Village to reach the main street at a

T-junction. Turn left (unsigned), passing the Black Diamond pub on your right, and go gently uphill. About 400yds after the end of the built-up area, turn left into Frithwood Road (otherwise unsigned) and follow this road for about ³/₄ mile until it reaches a minute triangular grass green, just before some farm buildings (Frithwood Farm). Turn right on a firm-surfaced but untarred track (there is a bridleway sign a

L9

continued

Distance: 4 miles

Terrain: a mix of **on-** and **off-road**, the latter firm-surfaced track and path

Refreshment opportunities: Creswell Crags Visitor Centre (light refreshments)

Start: either Whaley Common (GR 520 720) or Creswell Crags Visitor Centre (GR 537 744)

Ordnance Survey maps: Landranger sheet **120**, Mansfield and Worksop

Public transport links: only as below

Other routes: Route **27**. Link route **L4** also goes to Creswell Crags, while link route **L10** offers a route from route **27** to Mansfield Woodhouse station on the Robin Hood Line.

few yards further along it) for about ¹/₂ mile. At the end of the track, at a T-junction with a tarred minor road about 150yds east of **Whaley Common**, turn left towards the level crossing visible about 600yds away to continue on route **27**. 🚲

5¹/₂ miles · on- and off-road · flat · Mansfield Woodhouse

L10

Link: Mansfield Woodhouse to Langwith

This 5¹/₂-mile link, involving some off-road riding, is a route from Mansfield Woodhouse Station on the Robin Hood Line to join the Clumber and Meden Vale route **27** at Langwith. Together, these can also serve as a link route from Mansfield Woodhouse station to Clumber Park.

From **Mansfield Woodhouse station**, walk down the ramp and turn left through the pedestrian exit beside a steel gate at the north end of the station car park into Oxclose Lane (unsurfaced and unnamed at this point). Turn right on Oxclose Lane, then at the diagonal crossroads where the road bears round to the right, sharp left and left again into Thoresby Road (sign on wall on left by pillar box). At the end of

the houses, just before the railway embankment, turn right into Manor Road. At the T-junction, turn left into Vale Road (not signed). Just before the railway arch, follow the road round to the right; this is Brown Avenue. Go straight on at a small roundabout, still on Brown Avenue, to a second small roundabout. Turn sharp left into Cox's Lane, then first right into Hazel Grove, and first left into Charnwood Grove which becomes Littlewood Lane. At the T-junction at the end of the surfaced road, turn right on the gravel road and then almost immediately left just after a bungalow named Rivendell along a signed *bridleway* between wooden fences. Follow the bridleway past the quarry on the left, then down to a sharp left turn to pass under a railway bridge. Pass to the left of the steel gate, cross the bridge over the **River Meden**, bear round to the right up a slope and then left past abandoned Littlewood farm and continue to a second steel gate at the T-junction with the tarred road, Wood Lane (not signed).

Go through the gap by the steel gate and turn left on Wood Lane, then after about 300yds, turn right into Field Drive (not named but signed *'Model Village Traffic Calming'*); this becomes Central Drive. A little way before the T-junction with the B6031, turn right just before a garage named Clements Quality Cars into Long Lane (signed, but with the sign broken when we checked the route), then after about 150yds at a T-junction, turn left opposite a Chinese fish-and-chip shop on Church Drive, **Shirebrook**. Go straight on over the B6031 at the next crossroads by two churches on the right into Byron Street. After about 200yds at a T-junction, turn right for about 200yds, then first left into Park Road. Follow this residential road past two schools and a park for about $^1/_2$ mile to a T-junction with Recreation Road

TO CLUMBER PARK & MEDEN VALE

A632

NETHER LANGWITH

LANGWITH

LANGWITH JUNCTION

B6031

SHIREBROOK

DERBYSHIRE / NOTTINGHAMSHIRE

ABANDONED LITTLEWOOD FARM

RIVER MEDEN

BRIDLEWAY

QUARRY

N

1 MILE

RAILWAY STATION

MANSFIELD WOODHOUSE

START

(not named at this point). Turn right – and slightly uphill – for about 500yds until you reach a junction at which you have to give way. Go left, which is effectively straight ahead and not into Albine Road, following the road (still Recreation Road but not named at this point) which bears right to join the A632 to **Langwith**. Just after the railway bridge controlled by traffic lights, turn left to join route **27** Clumber Park and Meden Vale.

L10
continued

Distance: 5½ miles

Terrain: Mostly **on** quiet **roads**, but includes nearly 1½ miles of firm-surfaced **track** with no hills to speak of.

Refreshment opportunities: there are pubs and shops in Shirebrook and Langwith.

Start: Mansfield Woodhouse station (GR 534 634)

Ordnance Survey maps: Landranger sheet **120** Mansfield and Worksop

Public transport links: Robin Hood rail line to Mansfield Woodhouse. At the time of writing it was intended to extend the Robin Hood Line to Worksop by 1998, with proposed stations at both Shirebrook and Langwith.

Other routes: Routes **19** and **23** also start at Mansfield Woodhouse station and link route **L2** joins Mansfield Woodhouse station to route **11**.

L11

6 miles • on-road • flat • Newark or Fiskerton

Link: Newark and Fiskerton

This link joins Newark to route **30** Daybrook to Southwell, which makes possible a north-of-the-Trent route from Nottingham to Newark or vice versa. Other Nottingham to Newark suggestions are give with route **40**. The route description of this link is given in both directions.

From Newark to Fiskerton: Leave **Newark** northwards on the

B6326 over the level crossing by Newark Castle station. This road reaches a large and rather unpleasant roundabout junction with the A46, A616 and A617. Unfortunately there is no alternative, but there are shared-use cycle and pedestrian paths which cross each arm of the roundabout individually. Take the second exit from the roundabout, A617, signed *Kelham* and *Mansfield*. The A617 is quite a busy road but – once again –

189

there is really no alternative. Cross the western arm of the River Trent and continue through **Kelham** on the winding A617. After about 1 mile, fork left onto a minor road, Staythorpe Road, signed with a brown *Robin Hood Theatre* sign, into **Averham**. At the next T-junction, after a short distance, turn left, still on Staythorpe Road, signed *Staythorpe, Rolleston* and *Fiskerton*. Ignore the turning to the Robin Hood Theatre and continue through the hamlet of **Staythorpe** over the level crossing and past the now-closed power station to Rolleston. In **Rolleston** bear round to the left, signed *Fiskerton*. After about a mile the road

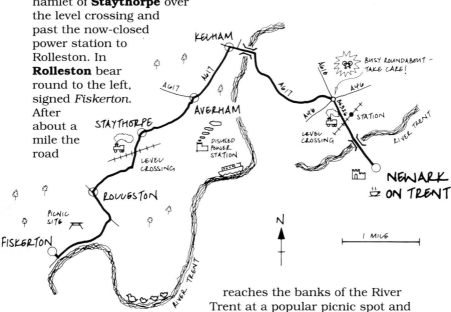

reaches the banks of the River Trent at a popular picnic spot and joins route **30**, Daybrook to Southwell, which comes in from the right on a road signed *Railway station* and *Southwell*, in **Fiskerton**.

From Fiskerton to Newark: From Southwell on route **30** at the T-junction in **Fiskerton**, turn left, signed *Rolleston*. The road shortly reaches the bank of the Trent on the right, a popular picnic spot. After $1^1/2$ miles, in **Rolleston**, bear right, signed *Staythorpe* and *Newark*. Go past the now-closed power station, over the level crossing and through the hamlet of **Staythorpe** into **Averham**. At the T-junction turn right, signed *Kelham* and *Newark* to join the A617 at a second T-junction. Turn right on the A617, signed *Newark A617*, to pass through **Kelham** and over the western arm of the River Trent. This fairly busy main road is, unfortunately, really the only way into Newark. After about $1^1/2$ miles there is a large roundabout at the junction with the A46 and A616. If you are

190

not confident about negotiating this admittedly quite unpleasant junction, there are shared-use cycle and pedestrian paths which cross each arm of the roundabout in turn to join the B6326 and over the level crossing by Newark Castle station into **Newark**. 🚲

L11

continued

Distance: 6 miles

Terrain: entirely **on-road**; flat.

Refreshment opportunities: Newark, pubs in the villages

Start:Newark Castle (GR 796 540) or Fiskerton (GR 737 513)

Ordnance Survey maps: Landranger sheet **120** Mansfield and Worksop

Public transport links: East Coast Main Line from London Kings Cross and Doncaster to Newark Northgate, Regional Railways services from Nottingham to Newark Castle, calling also at Fiskerton and Rolleston (not all services on this line call at these smaller stations, and these are in any case request stops: inform the conductor when you get on or give a hand signal to the driver of the approaching train).

Other routes: Route **26** explores some of the villages south-east and south-west of Newark. Route **40** is a linear route linking Newark with Nottingham, south of the River Trent. Link route **L12** joins Newark to routes **28** and **34** at Norwell.

---

7 miles • on-road • almost flat • Norwell or Newark

L12

Link: Norwell and Newark

This link route joins routes **28** Southwell Trail and the Dumbles, and **36** North Trent Valley, to Newark and the Newark-based routes, and also provides a link in a possible linear route between Newark and the north of the county.

From Norwell to Newark: Leave the centre of **Norwell** southwards on a minor road, signed *Bathley*. A short distance after rounding a left-hand bend over a stream the road climbs through a wood and then goes gently downhill again. About 1^1/$_2$ miles from Norwell, opposite the entrance to Foxholes Farm, turn right, signed *Bathley* and *Newark*. Go straight on at a minor crossroads after about 400yds where you have to give way, still signed *Bathley* and *Newark*. In **Bathley**, keep round to the right on what is marked on the ground as the through route, passing to the right of the Crown.

191

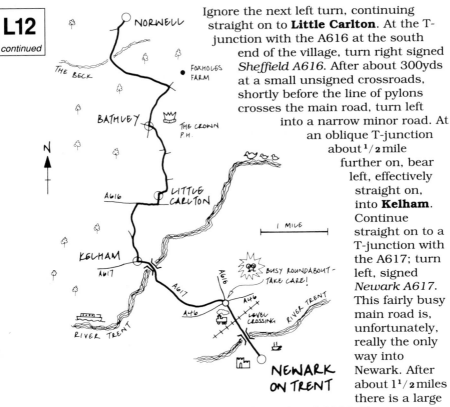

L12
continued

NORWELL

THE BECK

FOXHOLES
FARM

BATHLEY

THE CROWN
P.H.

N

A616

LITTLE
CARLTON

1 MILE

KELHAM

A617

A617

BUSY ROUNDABOUT -
TAKE CARE!

A616

A46

LEVEL
CROSSING

RIVER TRENT

RIVER TRENT

NEWARK
ON TRENT

Ignore the next left turn, continuing straight on to **Little Carlton**. At the T-junction with the A616 at the south end of the village, turn right signed *Sheffield A616*. After about 300yds at a small unsigned crossroads, shortly before the line of pylons crosses the main road, turn left into a narrow minor road. At an oblique T-junction about $1/2$ mile further on, bear left, effectively straight on, into **Kelham**. Continue straight on to a T-junction with the A617; turn left, signed *Newark A617*. This fairly busy main road is, unfortunately, really the only way into Newark. After about $1^1/2$ miles there is a large roundabout at the junction with the A46 and A616. If you are not confident about negotiating this admittedly quite unpleasant junction, there are shared-use cycle and pedestrian paths which cross each arm of the roundabout individually to join the B6326 and over the level crossing by Newark Castle station into **Newark**.

From Newark to Norwell: Leave **Newark** northwards on the B6326 over the level crossing by Newark Castle station. This road reaches a large and rather unpleasant roundabout junction with the A46, A616 and A617. Unfortunately there is no alternative, but there are shared-use cycle and pedestrian paths which cross each arm of the roundabout individually. Take the second exit from the roundabout, A617, signed *Kelham* and *Mansfield*. The A617 is quite a busy road but – once again – there is really no alternative. After about $1^1/2$ miles, just after crossing the western arm of the River Trent, in **Kelham**, turn right on a minor road, signed *South Muskham* and *Ollerton*, and then at the next junction continue

straight on, signed *Ollerton*. Take the first fork on the right after Kelham, about 300yds after the speed derestriction sign. It is completely unsigned. At the T-junction with the A616 (unsigned at this point), with an unmarked entrance to a farm opposite, turn right past the village sign for **Little Carlton**, then after about 300yds, turn left, signed *Bathley*. At the north end of Little Carlton follow the road round to the left to Bathley. In

In Norwell

Bathley, follow the road through the village, passing the Crown on the right. Soon after leaving the village go straight on at a minor crossroads where you have to give way, signed *Norwell*, then after about 400yds at a T-junction, opposite the entrance to Foxholes Farm, turn left, signed *Norwell* and *Ossington*. The road climbs steadily through a wood, then drops to an attractive bridge and old watermill, swinging right for Norwell. At the T-junction in the centre of **Norwell** village, turn left, signed *N* (for Norwell) *Woodhouse* and *Kneesall* to follow route **28** Southwell Trail and the Dumbles, or right, signed *Cromwell* and *Carlton on Trent* for route **36** North Trent Valley.

Distance: 7 miles

Terrain: all **on-road**, almost flat with one hill.

Refreshment opportunities: Newark and pubs in one or two of the villages

Start: either Newark on Trent (GR 797 541) or Norwell (GR 769 616)

Ordnance Survey maps: Landranger sheet **120** Mansfield and Worksop

Public transport links: East Coast Main Line from London Kings Cross and Doncaster to Newark Northgate, Regional Railways services from Nottingham to Newark Castle.

Other routes: Route **28**, Southwell Trail and the Dumbles, and route **34**, Northern Trent Valley are linked to Newark by this route. Route **26** explores some of the villages south-east and south-west of Newark. Route **40** is a linear route linking Newark with Nottingham, south of the River Trent, while link route **L11** joins Newark to route **30** at Fiskerton.

TEA STOPS

While we have indicated as far as possible in the listing below opening days and hours, it is advisable to check ahead by phone if you are relying on a particular stop, especially outside the summer months and, in the case of tearooms attached to shops, bakeries etc, at weekends. Map grid references are given only for tea stops outside towns or large villages, or if the address might otherwise be misleading. The listings for Nottingham and the larger towns are not claimed to be complete but give a selection of refreshment places on or near the routes.

Balderton
The Coffee Shop
Danny-Lyp Garden
Centre
41 Sibcy Lane
NG24 3LR
(at junction with London
Road, B6326)
Tel (01636) 74840
Open daily except Tues,
9am to 5pm
*(OS map 121; grid ref
819 511)*

Bawtry
(South Yorkshire)
Maxwells Restaurant
(Bawtry Lodge Hotel)
Market Place
Open daily except Wed,
10am to 4pm

The Town House Tea
Rooms
21 Market Place
Tel (01302) 719397
Open Mon–Sat, 9am to
5.30pm, Sun 9am to
5pm

Bestwood Park
Bestwood Lodge
Bestwood Lodge Drive,
Bestwood Country Park,
Arnold
Tel (0115) 920 3011
Open daily
*(OS map 129; grid ref
569 466)*

Bingham
Bitz and Pizzas
Union Street
Tel (01949) 836969
Open Mon–Thurs
10.30am to 10pm; Fri–
Sat 10.30am to
10.30pm.

Bleasby
Manor Farm Tea
Shoppe
Tel (01636) 830241
Open March–mid-
December 10.30am to
6pm; closed Mon –
except Bank Holidays
*(OS map 129; grid ref
707 499)*

Bothamsall
Haughton Park Farm
Tearooms
nr Bothamsall
Tel (01623) 860320
Open April–end
September, daily 10am
to 6pm; October–March,
Wed—Sun, 10am to
5.30pm
*(OS map 120; grid ref
683 740)*

Burton Joyce
Mulberries Coffee Shop
Tall Trees Garden
Centre
Lowdham Road
Bulcote
Tel (0115) 931 2356
Open Mon–Sat 9am to
6pm, Sun 10am to 6pm
*(Bulcote – on A612 , 1
mile east of Burton
Joyce. OS map 129; grid
ref 661 452)*

Calverton
Patchings Farm
Oxton Road
Tel (0115) 965 3479
Open daily 9am to 10pm
*(OS map 129; grid ref
597 499)*

Carburton
Olde School Tearoom
Ollerton Road
Tel (01909) 483517
Open Tues—Sun 10am
to 5pm
*(OS map120; grid ref 606
727)*

Clumber Park
Clumber Park Restaurant
Cafeteria
Tel (01909) 484122
Open daily 10.30am to
6pm during British
Summer Time; 10.30am
to 5pm during Greenwich
Mean Time (winter)

There is an admission charge to Clumber Park for cars, while cyclists and National Trust members get in free (OS map 120; grid ref 626 746)

On the west side of A614, where the bridleway from Hardwick to Crookford Farm (Route 38) crosses, there is usually a mobile transport café in the layby on weekdays. *(OS map 120; grid ref 648 759)*

Creswell Crags

(Derbyshire – by about 100yds!)
Creswell Crags Visitor Centre, Creswell
Open February–October, daily, 10.30am to 4.30pm; November–January, Sundays only, same times.
(Approximately 1 mile east of Creswell village, 4 miles south-west of Worksop. OS map 120; grid ref 537 744)

East Leake

S and R Coombs
Gotham Lane
Tel (01509) 852811
Open Mon, Tues, Thurs, Fri 9am to 5pm, Wed 9am to 4pm, Sat 9am to 4.30pm

Eastwood

The White Peacock Teashop
Scargill Walk
Tel (01773) 765237
Open November–March 10am to 4pm; April–October 10am to 5pm

Edwinstowe

Bentley's Bakery
High Street
Tel (01623) 822667
Open Mon–Fri 9am to 5pm, Sat 8am to 2pm, closed Sun

Church Farm Tea Rooms
Mansfield Road,
Tel (01623) 824033
Open Thurs–Sun and Bank Holidays 10am to 5pm

Lime Tree Pantry
High Street
Tel (01623) 824790
Open daily 9am to 5pm

Gamston

(near Nottingham)
Safeway Store
Gamston
West Bridgford
Nottingham

Grove

Grove Garden Centre
Tel (01777) 703182
Open Mon–Fri 11am to 5pm; Sat–Sun 11am to 4.30pm
(OS map 120; grid ref 740 798)

Gunthorpe

St John's Church
Main Street
Teas served 3 to 5pm, Sun only, Easter to Harvest Festival (usually last Sunday in September)
(OS map 129; grid ref 680 444)

Hardstoft

(Derbyshire)
The Herb Garden
Hall View Cottage,
Hardstoft, Pilsley

Tel (01246) 854268
Open daily March–September 10am to 6pm daily
(OS map 120; grid ref 436 633)

Hardwick Hall

(Derbyshire)
National Trust Shop and Restaurant
Hardwick Hall, Doe Lea, Chesterfield, S44 5QJ
Tel (01246) 850430
Open April–October, Wed, Thur, Sat, Sun and Bank Holiday Mons, 12 noon to 5pm
There is an admission charge to the gardens in which the restaurant is situated (OS map 120; grid ref 463 637)

Harworth

Tasty Dish Café
75 Scrooby Road
Tel (01302) 746691
Open Mon–Sat 7.30am to 10pm, Sun 10am to 10pm

Hucknall

Butlers Hill Café, Portland Road
Tel (0115) 963 9018
Open Mon–Fri 7am to 2,45pm; Sat 7am to 2pm

Market Fish Shop and Café, West Street (just off Market Place, next to Library)
Tel (0115) 953 2206
Open Mon–Thur 11.15am to 1.15pm and 4.30pm to 8.30pm; Fri 10.30am to 9.30pm; Sat ⁻1.15am to 7pm

Tasty Bites, Watnall Road
Tel (0115) 952 2100

195

Open Mon–Fri, 8.30am to 2.30pm; Sat 9am to 12.30pm

Three Cooks, 68 High Street (opposite main Post Office)
Tel (0115) 963 0213
Open Mon–Sat 8.30am to 4.30pm

Keyworth
The Coffee Shop
Main Street
Open Mon, Tues and Fri 8.30am to 3.30pm, Thurs 8.30am to 3pm, Wed and Sat 8.30am to 2pm, closed Sun

Kirkby-in-Ashfield
Portland Park Visitor Centre
Lindleys Lane, off Station Street
Tel (01623) 721617
Open Mon–Fri 9am to 5pm, Sat–Sun 8am to 5pm

Kirton
Pasture Farm Tea Room, Main Street
Tel (01623) 836291
Open daily 9am to 5pm
(OS map 120; grid ref 690 690)

Langar
Langar Parachute Clubhouse
Langar Airfield

Naturescape Wild Flower Farm Tearooms
nr Langar Airfield

Mansfield
Harold's Bistro Coffee Shop,Old Market Place
Tel (01623) 472030
Open Mon–Sat, 9am to 4pm

Greenwood Craft Centre
Nottingham Road, nr Mansfield
Tel (01623) 792141
Open daily 10.30am to 4.30pm
(approximately 3 miles south of town: OS map 120; grid ref 552 568)

Mapperley
Brookfields Garden Centre
Mapperley Plains,
Tel (0115) 926 8200
(OS map 129; grid ref 604 454)

Newark on Trent
Baker's Oven
Stodman Street
(just off Market Square)
Mon–Sat 8am to 5pm
(Plaque over shop reads: 'Prince Rupert stayed here after his quarrel with the King, 19 October 1645')

The Coffee Stop
33 Castlegate
Open Mon–Fri 7am to 4.30pm, Sat 8am to 4.30pm, Sun 8.30am to 4.30pm

Gannets Cafe
35 Castlegate
Tel (01636) 702066
Open Mon–Fri 9.30am to 4pm, Sat 9am to 5pm, Sun 9.30am to 5pm

Lord Byron's Coffee Lounge
27/28 Market Place
(01636) 613390
Open Mon–Sat 8.30am to 4pm

Oscar's
25 Castlegate
(01636) 610661
Open Tues–Sun,

10.30am to 2pm (plus evenings from 7pm)

Queen's Head Pantry
Market Square
All-day opening (children admitted)

Newstead Abbey
Newstead Abbey Tea Rooms
Newstead Abbey, Mansfield Road, Ravenshead
Tel (0115) 9797392
Open November–March 10am to 4pm; April to October 10am to 6pm
There is an admission charge to Newstead Abbey grounds
(OS map 120; grid ref 542 538)

Nottingham
The Castle Buttery
Castle Road
Tel (0115) 9483504
Open October–March 10am to 4.30pm; April–September 10am to 5.30pm
There is an admission charge on Saturdays, Sundays and Bank Holidays to the Castle grounds, where the Buttery is situated.

Café Lautrec
The Djanogly Art Gallery, University Boulevard
Tel (0115) 9513192
Open Mon–Fri 10am to 7pm, Saturday 11am to 5pm

The Lakeside Café
Wollaton Park
Open daily 10.30am to 5.30pm (earlier closing in winter)

196

Cosy Teapot Café
Carrington Street
*(about 50yds north of
Nottingham Midland
Station)*
Tel (0115) 950 1194
Open Mon–Sat 8am to
6pm; Sun 9am to 5pm

Ollerton

Ollerton Water Mill Tea
Shop, Market Place
*Tel (01623) 824094 or
822469*
Open April to October:
Wed–Sun, 10.30am to
5pm; March and
November: Sat and Sun
only, 10.30pm to
4.30pm; Bank Holiday
Mondays, 10.30am to
5pm
*(OS map 120; grid ref
653 674)*

Ranby

From Blyth Road in
Ranby there is access to
a mobile snack bar in a
layby on the east side of
the A1. This appears to
be open for much of the
day on weekdays.
*(OS map 120; grid ref
650 815)*

Ravenshead

Longdale Craft Centre
Longdale Lane
Tel (01623) 796952
Open daily 10am to 6pm
*(In Long Dale, about 2
miles south-east of
Ravenshead. OS map
120; grid ref 575 528)*

Redmile

(Leicestershire)
Old Hill Farm
Tel (01949) 842336
Usually open Mon, Tue
10.30am to 5.30pm,
Wed 10.30am to 5pm,

Thur–Sat 10.30am to
5.30pm, Sun 9am to
6pm. **Check weekday
opening times in
winter.**
*(About 1¹/₂ miles north-
west of Redmile village).
OS map 129; grid ref
780 367)*

Retford

Baker's Oven
33 Carolgate
Tel (01777) 708280

Boaters Restaurant
17 Grove Street
Tel (01777) 701818

Britalia Coffee Shop
Grove Street

Jane's Bakery and
Coffee Shop, 5 West
Street
Tel (01777) 702538

John Sinclair's Coffee
Shop
The Square
Tel (01777) 709670

Open Mon, Tue, Wed,
Fri 10am to 3.30 pm;
Thur and Sat 9.30am to
4pm

Tiffin Bar
Cannon Square

Ruddington

The Village Coffee Shop
14 High Street
Tel (0115) 940 5736
Open Mon–Sat 7.30am
to 5pm
*(OS map 129: grid ref
573 331)*

Rufford

The Coach House
Rufford Country Park,
Old Rufford Road
(A614), Nr Ollerton
Tel (01623) 824153
Open January and
February 11am to 4pm;
March–December
10.30am to 5pm
*(OS map 120; grid ref
645 647)*

197

Southwell

Gossips Coffee House
24/26 King Street
Tel (01636) 815816

The Minster Centre,
Southwell Minster,
Church Street
Tel (01636) 815691
Open Mon–Fri 10am to
5pm, Sat 10am to
5.30pm, Sun noon to
5.30pm (tends to close
around dusk in winter)

Merryweather's Garden
Centre
Halam Road
Tel (01636) 813204
Open daily 10.30am to
5pm
*(OS map 120; grid ref
696 541)*

Reg Taylor's Garden
Centre
Hill Farm Nurseries,
Normanton
Tel (01636) 813184
Open daily 10am to
5.30pm
*(OS map 120; grid ref
710 548)*

Southwell Garden
Centre
Fiskerton Road
Open daily 9am to 6pm
*(OS map 120; grid ref
710 535)*

Sutton-cum-Lound

Wetlands Waterfowl
Reserve
Tel (01777) 818099
Open daily 10am to 5pm
*There is an admission
charge to the Reserve
but you do not have to
pay to get to the
teashop.
(OS maps 111,120: grid
ref 693 851)*

Teversal

Teversal Trail Visitor
Centre
Carnarvon Street, off
Fackley Road
Tel (01623) 442021
Open April–September
Tues 11am to 3pm, other
days 11am to 4pm;
October–March 11am to
3pm
*(About 3/4 mile south-
south west of village
centre. OS map 120; grid
ref 480 613)*

Thoresby

The Gallery Tea Rooms
Thoresby Park, nr
Ollerton
Tel (01623) 822365
Open April to October
Fri–Mon 2pm to 5pm
*(OS map 120; grid ref
639 712)*

Walesby

Walesby Garden Centre
Tearooms (Sandhurst
Nurseries), Brake Road
Tel (01623) 860382
Open daily
*(OS map 120; grid ref
677 704)*

Wartnaby

(Leicestershire)
Stonepits Farm Tea
Room
The Salt Way
Tel (01664) 822293
Open: November–Easter
Fri–Mon 11am to 6pm;
Easter to October Thur–
Sun 11am to 6pm; Bank
Holiday Mondays 11am
to 6pm; closed Good
Friday
*(About 1/2 mile west-
north-west of Wartnaby
village. OS map 129;
grid ref 704 235)*

Welbeck

Dukeries Garden Centre,
Welbeck
Tel (01909) 476506
Open Mon–Sat, 10am to
6pm; Sun 10am to 5pm
*(OS map 120; grid ref
649 741)*

West Bridgford

ASDA Nottingham
Loughborough Road

Birds the Confectioners
Tea Room
Central Avenue

The Coffee Shop at
Corsons
Central Avenue

Worksop

The Coffee Bean
Watson Road
Open Mon–Wed, 9am to
4pm, Thur 9am to 2pm,
Fri, 9am to 4pm, Sat
9am to 4,30pm
Closed Sun

May's Café
Gateford Road
Open Mon–Sat, 9am to
3.30pm, Sun 10am to
3pm

Old Oak Café
Newgate Street
(south side of Market
Place)
Open Mon, Tue, Thur
11.30am to 2pm and
5pm to 6.45pm; Wed,
Fri, Sat 11am to 3pm
and 5pm to 8.45pm.
Closed Sun

Priory Gatehouse
Tearoom (Arts Alive
Gallery)
Cheapside
Tel (01909) 474173
Open November–March
Wed–Fri 10am to 5pm,

Sat 10am to 4pm, closed
Sun; April–October
Wed–Sat 10am to 5pm,
Sun 2pm to 5pm

Beeston
Sid Standard
35-37 Chilwell Road
Tel (0115) 925 6647

Chilwell
John Stafford
116 Bramcote Avenue
Tel (0115) 925 7558

Eastwood
The Bike Centre
233 Nottingham Road
Tel (01773) 719790

Mick Brown
233 Nottingham Road
Tel (01773) 719790

Hucknall
Frank Sisson
High Street
Tel (0115) 963 2011

Just Bikes
12 South Street
Tel (0115) 964 1489

Kimberley
The Bike Bank
26 Main Street
Tel (0115) 938 5551

Long Eaton
(Derbyshire)
Alan Buttler Cycles
44 College Street
Tel (0115) 973 2300

Push'N'Pedal
49 Tamworth Road
Tel (0115) 972 6335

Tracey Maid
Regent Mills, Regent
Street
Tel (0115) 973 0719

Mansfield Woodhouse
A & C Sports
1 Morven Avenue
Tel (01623) 23389

On Yer Bike
181 Yorke Street
Tel (01623) 421033

Newark on Trent
A1 Cycle Repairers
57-59 Castle Gate
Tel (01636) 707277

Castle Cycles
16 Boar Lane
Tel (01636) 79893

The Factory Cycle Shop
50a Lombard Street
Tel (01636) 611642

Marriott's
16a Appleton Gate
Tel (01636) 704842

Staples Cycles
8 Lombard Street
Tel (01636) 702759

Nottingham

Arnold
Arnold Cycles
35 Nottingham Road
Tel (0115) 920 9311

Aspley
D & D Savage
441 Beechdale Road
Tel (0115) 929 1828

Bulwell
Charlie's Cycles
200 Highbury Road
Tel (0115) 976 3118

Evans Cycles
53 Main Street
Tel (0115) 927 1026

Carlton
Rex Robinson Cycles
27 Burton Road
Tel (0115) 961 9069

City centre
Bunney's Bikes
97 Carrington Street
Tel (0115) 947 2713

Freewheel
34-36 Goose Gate,
Hockley
Tel (0115) 952 0200

Super Cycles
219-223 Mansfield Road
Tel (0115) 941 9239

Clifton
Clifton Cycles
111 Rivergreen
Tel (0115) 940 5847

Lenton
Lenton Cycles
12 Abbey Street, Old
Lenton
Tel (0115) 978 4756

Mapperley
Langdale Lightweights
455-457 Westdale Lane
Tel (0115) 960 5933
Fax (0115) 953 7100

Netherfield
Graham Read's
105 Victoria Road
Tel (0115) 961 4555

Sherwood
Geoff's Cycles Centre
488 Mansfield Road
Tel (0115) 960 3461

199

Retford
Discount Cycles,
Carolgate
Tel (01777) 703128

Halfords
8 Market Square
Tel (01777) 860177

Ruddington
Ruddington Cycles
10 High Street
Tel (0115) 921 1393

Southwell
Go Bike
85a King Street
Tel (01636) 815541

Olympic Cycles
213 Valley Road
Tel (0115) 985 8001
Fax (0115) 985 8002

West Bridgford
Radcliffe Road Cycles
152b Radcliffe Road
Tel (0115) 982 2459

sShokwave
120 Melton Road
Tel (0115) 981 6191

Jack Taylor Cycles
40 Gordon Road
Tel (0115) 981 1060

Pleasley
Blazing Saddles
516 Chesterfield Road
North
Tel (01623) 812350

Sutton-in-Ashfield
Coronation Street Cycles
58 Coronation Street
Tel (01623) 553765

Shepperson Bros
Market Place
Tel (01623) 557345

We recommed buying bikes from a proper bike-shop, not by mail order

TICs

Tourist Information
Centres can supply full
information on places
to visit and where to
stay (including
campsites and self-
catering) in their area.
Most will book

accommodation for you
for a small charge
under the 'Book a Bed
Ahead' (BABA)
scheme.

Newark on Trent
The Gilstrap Centre,
Castlegate
Tel (01636) 78962

Nottingham
1-4 Smithy Row
Tel (0115) 947 0661

Ollerton
Sherwood Heath,
Ollerton Roundabout
Tel (01623) 824545

Retford
Arncott House Annexe
40 Grove Street
Tel (01777) 860780

Sherwood Forest Visitor Centre
Edwinstowe
Tel (01623) 824490

West Bridgford
County Hall,
Loughborough Road
Tel (0115) 977 3558

Worksop
Worksop Library
Memorial Avenue
Tel (01909) 501148

Basic Maintenance and Repair; ed Ed
Pavella (Rodale Press, 1990); ISBN 0 87857 902 8

The Bicycle Book;
Geoff Apps (Salamander, 1993); ISBN 0 86101 652 1

Bicycle Maintenance and Repair; ed Sara J
Henry (Rodale Press, 1994); ISBN 0 87596 207 6

The Bicycle Repair Book; Rob van der
Plas (Bicycle Books, 1992); ISBN 0 933201 11 7

The Bike Book; Fred
Milson (Haynes, 1995); ISBN 1 85960 117 9

A Dictionary of English Place-Names;
A D Mills (Oxford University Press, 1991); ISBN 0 19 869156 4

Nottinghamshire; Jeff and Margaret Hopewell (Shire County Guide Series, Shire Publications, 1993); ISBN 0 7478 0194 0

Nottinghamshire Curiosities; Geoffrey
Oldfield (Curiosities of England Series; Dovecote Press, 1992); ISBN 0 946159 98 X

The Nottinghamshire Village Book; (Villages
of Britain Series, Countryside Books/ NFWI, 1994); ISBN 1 85306 057 7

Pedal Power!; Tim and
Roger Hughes (Blandford Press, 1995); ISBN 0 7137 2434 X

Pedal Pusher's Guide to Nottingham;
compiled by Lawrence Geary (Pedals); no ISBN

Richards' Bicycle Repair Manual;
Richard Ballantine and Richard Grant (Dorling Kindersley, 1994); ISBN 0 7513 0087 X

Richard's New Bicycle Book; Richard
Ballantine (Pan, 1990); ISBN 0 330 31315 0

Roadside Bicycle Repair; Rob van der
Plas (Bicycle Books, 1995); ISBN 0 933201 67 2

Sloane's Bicycle Repair; Eugene A
Sloane (Simon & Schuster, 1993); ISBN 0 671 76943 X

Tales of Old Nottinghamshire;
Polly Howatt (Country Tales Series, Countryside Books, 1991); ISBN 1 85306 160 3

201

What is Pedals?

Pedals was founded in 1979 to encourage more people to use bikes and to campaign for safer and more attractive conditions for cyclists in the Nottingham area. Pedals has helped to get Nottingham one of England's largest networks of urban cycle routes and is pressing for many more facilities, especially in the City Centre and the north side of Nottingham. Pedals also campaigns for much more attention to be given to cyclists' needs in *all* highway planning and traffic management, including making traffic-calming more cycle-friendly.

Pedals has helped to get hundreds of cycle stands installed locally and is campaigning for further secure cycle parking, including cycle lockers. Pedals campaigns for better surfaces on roads and cycle paths and for prompter attention to defects including vandalised signs and broken glass.

Pedals started the Great Nottinghamshire Bike Ride in 1982, now run by Nottinghamshire County Council. The GNBR is the largest mass cycle ride in the country, outside the south-east. Pedals in 1983 started the Summer Guided Cycle Rides Programme, and continues to play a major part in these events, now run by the County Council.

Pedals produces a newsletter three times a year to keep you informed of developments and issues for cyclists, as well as to tell members about our monthly meetings and other forthcoming events. Pedals has produced two editions of the *Pedal Pushers' Guide to Nottingham*, the first handbook of maps and practical advice for local cyclists.

Pedals members get a 10% discount on cash sales with selected local dealers (see *Pedals Pushers' Guide* for details).

Join Pedals: The power behind Nottingham's cyclists!

● For more information telephone Nottingham (0115) 981 6206 or write to Pedals, 162 Musters Road, West Bridgford, Nottingham NG2 7AA.

A hundred years of the CTC's Notts DA

The Nottinghamshire District Association of the Cyclists' Touring Club proudly celebrates its centenary in 1997. To understand the history of the CTC locally, it is necessary first to learn a little about the CTC as a national organisation.

Some people may be surprised to learn that the Bicycle Touring Club was founded as long ago as 1878, for the bicycles of that time, High Ordinaries ('Penny-farthings') were certainly not paragons of comfort and safety. Nonetheless, riders enjoyed their activity and wished to band together to exchange information and to press for a legal right to use the highways. By 1883, tricycles and even quadricycles were numerous enough that to accommodate them the name of the BTC was changed to 'The Cyclists' Touring Club' – the name it has had ever since.

By the early 1890s the modern bicycle had evolved and Nottingham was a centre of cycling-related activity with the Raleigh Cycle Company in the city and Thomas Humber's large factory at Beeston.

In August 1894 about forty CTC members rode from Nottingham, Mansfield, Worksop, Tuxford and Retford to a meeting at the Ram Hotel, Newark. County membership at that time was around two hundred. More meetings were planned and by 1896 club rides – all on Saturday afternoons and evenings – were being held in Nottinghamshire under the title of 'Notts. District Section'.

On 15 May 1897 the Revd W H Kynaston of Annesley organised a ride to the Saracen's Head at Southwell, where a meeting was held to inaugurate formally the Nottingham (later to be adjusted to Nottinghamshire) District Association of the Cyclists' Touring Club.

The bicycle brought with it liberation, education and pleasure: bicycles were cheaper and more convenient than horses that had to be fed, stabled and exercised. Here at last was mass personal mobility and the Notts DA flourished. Bicycles and tricycles were taking people on extended tours of the British Isles and overseas.

By 1909, cyclists from Derby were also riding with the Notts DA and the name was changed to 'Nottingham-shire and Derbyshire District Association' – long names were obviously not a problem then! – and this was not to be reversed until 1924 when Derbyshire formed its own DA. In the same year a meeting was held at the Broad Oak Inn at Strelley and the Broad Oak Road Club was formed for local CTC members who wished to race. The DA had survived the lean membership of the first world war years (when nationwide CTC membership fell to 8546) and was now developing in challenging directions. The Broad Oak RC had an illustrious history for over three decades but slowly expired with the advancing popularity of the car.

Membership of the Notts DA has also fluctuated alongside an undulating graph of cycling popularity. Since the 1970s there has been an increasing awareness of environmental and health problems and the role the bicycle can play in improving matters. DA numbers are now between six and seven hundred.

Throughout its existence the DA has worked to safeguard the interests of cyclists both in the town and the countryside. It has striven to provide an interesting leisure cycling programme and currently has seven Nottingham-based sections covering different tastes and abilities, plus others in Mansfield, Retford and Newark.

Cycling can be enjoyed by people of all ages whatever their abilities – it's healthy, useful and educational – and does no harm to fellow beings. As the Notts DA marks its centenary, why not join us to start the next hundred years?

Doreen Leheup

● For information on CTC activities in Nottinghamshire phone: (0115) 933 4971.

To find out more about the CTC nationally, write to CTC, 69 Meadrow, Godalming, Surrey GU7 3HS, phone (01483) 417217, fax (01483) 426994, E-mail cycling@ctc.org.uk or visit the CTC's website at http://www.ctc.org.uk. The CTC has rather over 40 000 members and membership confers a number of benefits: *free* third-party insurance; a *free* cycle-touring magazine every two months; legal aid from the CTC's legal experts; special cycle insurance deals; access to the CTC's special-ised touring information, which covers most countries in the world; access to the CTC's technical department for advice on cycle equipment and technical problems; *discounts* on holidays; and *free* membership of your local CTC group.

NOTTINGHAM GREEN PARTNERSHIP

The Nottingham Green Partnership was launched by Nottingham City Council in 1991. Business, voluntary groups and the two universities in Nottingham have combined

'To establish, through co-operative effort, a comprehensive and practical approach to solving environmental problems in Nottingham.'

The Partnership is pleased to support the production of this guide as a valuable source of information for new and potential cyclists, promoting cycling in the City and beyond.

● For further information about the Nottingham Green Partnership, please contact Steve Waller, Nottingham City Council, The Guildhall, Burton Street, Nottingham; tel (0115) 948 3500.

The Greenwood Community Forest is a multi-purpose forest being created in 161 square miles of Nottinghamshire countryside – one-fifth of the county. The many partners involved in its creation aim to develop a better environment for local people to use, cherish and enjoy, reflecting the needs and desires of local people who live in and around the area.

It will be a rich mosaic of wooded landscapes and land uses including farmland, villages and leisure enterprises, nature areas and public open space. It will create well-wooded land-scapes for wildlife, work and education, with new opportunities for a range of recreational facilities, all on the doorsteps of thousands of people.

It is an initiative of the Countryside Commission and Forestry Commission, who are working in partnership with Nottinghamshire County Council, Ashfield District Council, ˙ Broxtowe Borough Council, Gedling Borough Council. Mansfield District Council, Newark and Sherwood District Council and Nottingham City Council.

Helping to create the **GREENWOOD** COMMUNITY FOREST

● For more information on the Greenwood Community Forest, phone (01623) 758231.

205

Top to bottom: Lenton, Nottingham; Southwell; the old graveyard at Flawford; near Ruddington; Wollaton Park, Nottingham; Tuxford lock-up

206